The Black Flag

Brian Jackson

The Black Flag

*A look back at the strange case of
Nicola Sacco and Bartolomeo Vanzetti*

Routledge & Kegan Paul
Boston, London and Henley

First published in 1981
by Routledge & Kegan Paul Ltd
9 Park Street, Boston, Mass. 02108, USA,
39 Store Street, London WC1E 7DD and
Broadway House, Newtown Road,
Henley-on-Thames, Oxon RG9 1EN
Set in 11/13pt Palatino by
Rowland Phototypesetting Ltd, Bury St Edmunds, Suffolk
and printed in the United States of America

ISBN 0-7100-0897-X

'Man carries in his heart the principle of a morality superior to himself. This principle does not come from outside. It is secreted within him. It is immanent.'

Pierre-Joseph Proudhon
('Master of us all,' said Michael Bakunin,
surveying the leaders of anarchy)

'Berardelli, with three bullets in him, was on his knees and coughing blood, in the gutter. A gunman stood over him, and, under a hundred eyes, shot him twice more.'

Common to every other day to me. I peddled fish.'

Bartolomeo Vanzetti

'There's no story in it – just a couple of wops in a jam.'

News reporter quoted by Eugene Lyons,
defence lawyer

For

Dominic, Christian, Rebecca, Lucy, Ellen, Seth

Contents

Prelude

I do not know why I began to write this book. I had never before heard of Nicola Sacco and Bartolomeo Vanzetti. Or if I had, it was a very faint trace in the patterns of faraway memory. Were they a pair of comics on the old silent films? Or was it a once-famous and now-forgotten boxing match? Or maybe the name of a chain store or some bought-out company ('. . . made only by Sacco and Vanzetti')?

No. My interest then and now was in martyrs. *Why* was it that some man or woman, by the moment and manner of their dying, pulled the future towards them, twisted the skeins of the world in improbable and unexpected ways? After all people died every day and night in their multitudes: naturally, cruelly, inevitably, accidentally, wilfully. Why were some deaths so potent, so vivid in our moral, intellectual or political landscapes? Was martyrdom thrust upon them or did they seek it out? Or were they caught at some cultural crossroad – unfortunates who found themselves at the wrong place at the right time, and, unknown to themselves, their suffering became part of human glory?

At that time we spent our family holidays in the misty summers of the west of Ireland: Galway, the Aran Isles, Tralee and the ring of Kerry, the rough ride to Tory Island, the fiddles and fuschia of the Dingle Peninsula, the abandoned Blaskets, Achill Island and the vast peatland of the County Mayo. It was a world of martyrs and of saints, and I was trying to understand what those two powerful ideas had meant in the past, and still meant now. Further north, in Derry, like everyone else I walked around the spots on the pavement – always marked by a fresh wreath of flowers – where some Irish boy had been killed in a struggle that few of us confidently understood.

The idea of significant dying was as alive now as it ever had been. I read and thought about disparate events – Wat Tyler killed by the Lord Mayor of London, the crowd that was massacred at Sharpeville or Peterloo, Jan Palach turning himself into a human torch in Prague. It was difficult to pull the patterns together, and analyse the many different weaves.

One summer we were staying in a cottage not far from Clifden in Galway, where the Connemara Pony Show (a fine title for a unique but humble rural fair) is annually held. Connemara is dense with delights, and there are many better things to do there than read books. But somewhere in my reading I had picked up these Italian names. It was really more like one name: Sacco–Vanzetti. I thought I would look down this byway too, expecting another *cul-de-sac*. So I took out every book on the shelf at the University Library at Cambridge, and stuffed them into our old Austin A40. I hoped to read in those rare moments when the rain, the Guinness, the blarney and the cries of the children all stopped at once. Dry old books most of them – though I dutifully record them in the bibliography here – mostly by New England lawyers, and mostly about finer points of law in the most litigious and legislative of states that man has ever seen, Massachusetts. Later I was to fall utterly in love with Boston, yet even then I couldn't help laughing that though you could never find a cobbler or a plumber in New England, you only had to whisper the word and lawyers of every academic hue flocked around you.

I read the verbatim transcript of the Sacco and Vanzetti case, and all the many books that were published in the years after their execution. A strange kaleidoscope of figures moved across the stage, or for a moment emerged from the crowd. Some were prohibition hoodlums, like my distant relative, 'Legs' Diamond. Others were shadows from the European past, like Albert Dreyfus, who had been sent to Devil's Island, and the discovery of whose innocence was the greatest individual scandal of its time. Others were dictators of the present, like Benito Mussolini, or the officials in charge of America's immigration and counter-intelligence services. But most of all the eye focused on three tense groups in Boston itself. First of all the Boston Brahmins. Their part will unfold in this story, but they were the educated and wealthy voice of the old English ascendency in New England. In part this is their sad adieu to modern America. Their distinction is beyond dispute: strands here lead us not only to the king figure of Robert Lowell, president of Harvard, but to Henry James or to T. S. Eliot and to that upsurge of creative writing which the plight of Sacco and Vanzetti so suddenly provoked or inspired in American literature.

The contrasting group were the migrant workers – short of money, thinking keenly about politics, arguing intensely in the coffee houses and the fugitive journals about anarchism, Trotsky, social credit or Marx, taking the promise of the New World at its face value. It was a marriage of innocence and humble politics, such as sometimes changed the world.

And there was a third party. Mediating between the two, in the courts and universities, were people like Fred Moore, who almost made a profession out of defending the rights of that half of the population which lay to the left on any political spectrum; and Felix Frankfurter who, as the first Jewish lawyer of distinction to emerge from Harvard, was trying to reinterpret the spirit of the law of the Commonwealth and of the Republic from within.

All three are major parts of America. And yet was the case worth all this? I realized that though I, and few of my age, knew little or anything at all about it, it was once nevertheless very familiar in its outline. There is a canyon of knowledge between one generation and the next. We all experience this. Events of a century ago are quite familiar to us: we learned all about them at school. Today is familiar too, after all, we're living it. But there is always a blind spot in history lurking just behind us.

That is where Nicola Sacco and Bartolomeo Vanzetti were for me. In the very centre of that blind spot.

So I read and thought and acted about them with a pristine curiosity. Were they guilty or not? I had no doubts whatsoever in the beginning. They were clearly innocent. Victims of one of those waves of political hysteria that cyclically attacks the United States. Legal *tesserae* bred complexity which then spawned more complexity; and the only casualty was common sense.

And yet as I investigated the case, I found my mind changing – often against my own will. Why did they carry those guns, and where were they going? How could it happen *twice*: once a mistake, but the second time . . .?

And is anarchism a peaceful approach? Can it escape violence, or only cover it up? Even deeper, might you not commit a murder and then deny it, not only to the court but to yourself? Might you not forge a new identity in that furnace, and emerge a phoenix of our time?

I do not know. I wondered about their innocence. The political circumstances are clear. I wondered about their guilt: why the guns on the tramcar? I thought about one being guilty and one being innocent, and tried to imagine such private knowledge carried to its ultimate in Death Row. I thought about innocence and about guilt. Single or double. And more difficult than that – guilt which self-deceives and is purged. If you read the pages that follow, you will pick up these ripples of uncertainty.

Books like this are not texts, but experiences. I begin by stating the bare story as fairly as I can. Its enigmas remain, and each reader must unpuzzle them for himself. I then snatch the chance of returning to Boston half a century later. There is just time to speak to people who once knew and still care. There is also the new opportunity that the downfall of President Nixon brought – the Freedom of Information Act. I am able to ask questions or look at files that were denied since that execution day in Death Row. Last, we can come back to our beginning. What was their anarchy and why did it once so threaten the most powerful nation in the world? And why – I stand in the snow-filled woods of New England only a degree less puzzled than in the mists of Connemara – was the terror of the crime and the horror of their death nevertheless a bequest to human value?

Acknowledgments

In preparing this book I have been immensely helped by many friends in both the United States and in Great Britain. I depended a good deal on the generous co-operation of the librarians at the Widener Library at Harvard, at Boston University, at the City of Boston Library, and in Britain I made extensive use of the libraries at Cambridge University and at Bristol University.

In Boston and in Cambridge, Massachusetts, I was helped by many veterans of this case, but I would particularly like to record my debt to Spencer Sacco, and through him to Rosa Sacco; to Hon. Michael Dukakis, then Governor of Massachusetts; to Alexander J. Cella of Suffolk University; to Hugo Bedau, Austen Professor of Philosophy at Tufts University; to Robert Healey of the *Boston Globe* and to Steven J. Cohen. Whilst researching at Harvard and Boston I was the guest of Richard and Valerie Kahan of Concord and their delightful family who showed me why New England hospitality is so renowned.

In Cambridge, England, I am indebted to Dr Sydney Smith of St Catharine's College, Peter Laslett of Trinity College and Jonathan Steinberg of Trinity Hall. My colleagues at Cambridge, San Last, Julia McGawley and Barrie Knight all gave me practical encouragement; and at Oxford I drew on the considerable knowledge of A. H. Halsey of Nuffield College.

In London, I benefited from the editorial expertise and intellectual perspectives of Marian Boyars, Liz Calder, Margaret Carter, Norman Franklin, Frank Pakenham and Dieter Pevsner.

My original opportunity to look at the new American material was made possible by Ron Hall of the *Sunday Times*, and subsequently I was shrewdly guided by Jacqueline Korn of David Higham Associates, W. L. Webb, literary editor of the *Guardian*, and Richard Mills of the Gulbenkian Foundation.

My deepest debt is to Sonia Jackson.

Brian Jackson
Bristol University

Part one

A winter's tale

Chapter One

Christmas
Eve 1919

On Christmas Eve 1919 the police chief at Bridgewater, Massachusetts was Michael Stewart. The warmth of his station was
besieged by the frosty snap and drifting snow of a New England
winter. Then the new Bell telephone rang. The pay truck of the
White Shoe Company with Christmas wages aboard had just
been held up. It found its path to the factory blocked by a dark
touring car, possibly a Buick or Hudson. Two men stayed at the
wheel of the car, two scrambled out of the back doors. One ran
towards the pay truck, bent his knees, raised a shotgun and
started firing. The second stayed closer to the car and began
shooting from the hip with a revolver.

The security guards in the pay truck were taken completely by
surprise. They drew guns and blazed back out of the rear
window. The driver forgot about the wheel and the truck
smashed to a stop round a telegraph pole. For two minutes both
sides shot rapidly and wildly. Then suddenly the bandits lost
heart, tumbled back into their car which was already accelerating
and made their getaway down the road to Cochesett. Amazingly
nothing in this violent spray of bullets and pellets had hit
anyone.

Chief Stewart rapidly decided that the hold-up was most likely
the work of Russian anarchists or foreign-born radicals out to
raise funds for revolution. The few startled witnesses said the
gunman looked 'dark' and 'not American'. With these leads,
Chief Stewart set out to look for dark-skinned foreign workers,

probably with radical opinions, who owned a Buick or a Hudson and lived in or around Cochesett.

But his energies were partly diverted through a new move by Mitchell Palmer, the Attorney General. As the bleak winter of 1919 settled on the United States, he decided it was up to him to give a war-weary nation a lead, and protect it from the anarchists, socialists, communists and radicals.

'Each and every adherent of this movement is a potential murderer or a potential thief, and deserves no consideration,' he said. 'The Red Movement is not a righteous or honest protest against alleged defects in our present political and economic organization of society. It is a distinctly criminal and dishonest movement in the desire to obtain possession of other people's property by violence and sabotage. All their new words, "Bolshevism", "Syndicalism", "Sabotage", etc. are only new names for old theories of vice and criminality.'

Around him American boys were freshly home from the war in Europe. The country surrendered itself to patriotic dinners, ceremonies around the flag, and thanksgiving marches to church. But the mood was marred. Idle newspapers, void of war news, worked up a crime wave. Lootings, safe-breakings, hold-ups, gangsters in cars dominated the headlines. Though later analysis suggested that there had been no unusual increase in that ever-violent society, private citizens reacted with fear, and with demands for tougher police protection, severer legal punishments. Editors and churchmen announced the causes of this non-existent increase in crime. It was due to drugs, or to alcohol. It was a sour legacy of war. Above all it was the Reds.

The fear that your home would be broken into at night by armed gangsters shaded imperceptibly into the rising hysteria about a Red Plot. 'Bolshevik Plan for Conquest of America' shouted the *Boston Herald*. Later it rallied citizens with 'Boston Armed at all Points against Reds', and warned New York in fresh headlines that 'Reds Pervade Empire State'. A traditional American witch hunt was afoot, and nowhere more strongly than in the old witch-burning counties of New England. To the United States Attorney General there was little distinction to be made between the smell of radicalism in the air and the crime wave in the morning papers. He gave a crusading lead, and many politicians, city officials, churchmen and police thought it right and opportune to strike the same note.

The Department of Justice itself decided on a nationwide harassment of Reds, with particular emphasis on New England. A massive raid on suspects' homes was made on January 2, 1920 and 2,500 arrests were made. The police style was fierce, arbitrary and public, and clearly enjoyed strong public support. At last someone was doing something. In Boston the Department of Justice marched their prisoners, handcuffed, through the streets. Bail was fixed at $10,000 – an impossible sum for the kind of low-paid workmen arrested – and all normal constitutional rights ignored. Warrants were delivered – in bundles of telegrams – after the arrests.

The Attorney General warned the country that there were 60,000 dangerous radicals in the United States. As the wave of raids built up, 6,000 warrants were issued and 4,000 arrests made. Wretched little prison camps were set up, and thousands of dependants found themselves without money, protection, or any idea of what blow would fall the next day.

The Attorney General's drive was highly popular with the press which wanted to see troop carriers sailing to Europe packed with deported radicals. 'Shipping Lenin's Friends to Him' ran the jubilant headlines of the *Literary Digest* as the steamship *Buford* sailed with the first load. The police action was only stopped when the acquiescent Secretary of Labor fell ill, and was replaced by his deputy Louis F. Post – a man with a quite different sense of justice. He was immediately backed by many in the legal profession who protested about this violent extension of police action into a kind of 'official lawlessness'. The opposition of the new Secretary of Labor resulted in 3,000 of the warrants being cancelled, and in the number of deportees dropping to 1,000 – far below the fat number that the papers had hurrahed.

All this kept Chief Stewart busy, but nevertheless he made progress with his hold-up enquiry. He discovered an Italian workman in Cochesett called Mike Boda who owned a Buick or Overland. Moreover Boda shared a shack with another Italian called Coacci, on whom the police had served a deportation order.

And then on April 15, 1920 came the cold-blooded murders at South Braintree. At 9.15 that morning the money to pay the workers at Slater and Morrill's shoe factory arrived at the station, where it was received and checked by Shelly Neal, the American Express agent. The amount was $15,776 and 51 cents. Neal was accustomed to check on anyone hanging round his office, and noticed a large black seven-seater, with the engine running. He also noted a slight, rather emaciated man hanging around on the pavement nearby.

Twelve minutes later, having checked the consignment and separated some other items from it, he decided to take it across the road to the Slater and Morrill offices. There were two cars parked outside. As he passed between them, he heard the driver of one call across 'All right', and both cars moved off – in opposite directions. At the offices, the paymistress divided the money into individual paypackets and stacked these in two metal boxes. Each box was quite bulky: 2 feet 6 inches by 1 foot 6 inches by 1 foot. By 3 o'clock the money was ready to be taken the short distance down Pearl Street to the factory block where the wages were given to the workers. It was carried by Frederick A. Parmenter, who was acting paymaster that week and had the job of actually handing the wage packets out. He tucked one box under his left arm. With him was a guard, Alessandro Berardelli, armed with a .38 revolver. He took the second box and packed it under his right arm.

They walked down Pearl Street, crossed the level crossing, stopped for a chat and then – Berardelli leading the way – strode down the hill towards the factory. Half way there they passed a group of fifteen Italian labourers digging out the foundations for a new restaurant. Opposite, leaning against the iron fence, between two telegraph posts, were two smallish men with dark clothes, caps, probably Italians too.

As Berardelli and Parmenter passed, the two bystanders stiffened. One stepped out, and grabbed at Berardelli, who swung round to him. So did Parmenter. The second bystander started firing. He put three bullets into Berardelli and one into Parmenter. Parmenter dropped his box, and staggered across the street towards the workmen. One of the gunmen followed him, and put another bullet into his back. He collapsed against the waggon and horses, backed up by the excavation.

Berardelli, with three bullets in him, was on his knees cough-ing blood, in the gutter. A gunman stood over him, and under a hundred eyes, shot him twice more.

A seven-seater Buick crawled down the street, the gunmen grabbed the boxes and scrambled in. A third bandit came out of hiding behind a brick pile and tumbled in too. The car gathered speed. At the level crossing the gatekeeper was already lowering the gates for a coming train. One of the bandits yelled at him, thrust a revolver through the window, and he let them through. The car accelerated, a gun poking out of its back and someone inside throwing out strips of rubber with tin tacks on, to puncture the tyres of pursuing cars. It doubled back into town, successfully throwing off pursuers – including the Chief Michael Stewart – and disappeared south into wild and thickly wooded country.

The next day, April 16, the papers were filled with this latest outrage, and speculation ran riot. The same day Chief Stewart called at Coacci's house, demanding to know why he had not appeared, as expected, at an appeal hearing against the deportation order. He found Coacci packing his trunk and clearly anxious to get out of the country.

The next day the local press suggested that the gang leader was probably a draft dodger – someone who had gone into hiding or fled to Mexico to avoid service in the American forces in Europe. It said the police already had clues. In fact they hadn't but that day they found a Buick abandoned in the Manley woods near West Bridgewater. They concluded it was the 'murder car'. Tracks of another vehicle led away from it.

Chief Stewart decided it all hung together – the Bridgewater hold-up and the South Braintree murders were the work of the same gang; that gang was linked with Boda and Coacci; and Boda's Buick was probably the second vehicle in the Manley woods.

That same day Boda took his Buick to Johnson's garage in Cochesett for repairs. The police visited the Johnsons and arranged that when anyone called for the car they should be phoned immediately. They mentioned the possibility of reward.

Chief Stewart decided to press harder, and three days later interviewed Boda. No one knows what took place at this meeting. Possibly the police chief didn't reveal what crime he was interested in.

On the night of May 5 the phone call came. Mike Boda and a friend, Orciani, had arrived in a motorcycle and sidecar. With them on foot were two other Italians, Nicola Sacco and Bartolomeo Vanzetti. They had called for the car, but when the garage owner pointed out that it had not got a 1920 licence, and that it was unwise to run it without one, they had gone off. Sacco and Vanzetti walked towards Sunset Avenue to catch the trolley back for Brockton.

When the trolley reached Campello, police officer Connolly boarded it and picked out the two Italians at once. He demanded to know where they were coming from:

'Bridgewater.'

'What was you doing at Bridgewater?'

'We went down to see a friend of mine.'

'Who is your friend?'

'A man by the – they call him Poppy.'

'Well, I want you. You are under arrest.'

Connolly was nervous in case either Sacco or Vanzetti drew a gun, and covered them pistol in hand: 'Keep your hands on your lap or you will be sorry.'

Vanzetti's memory of the phrase is quite different: 'You don't move, you dirty thing.'

Police officer Vaughn boarded the car, and Connolly told him to 'fish' Vanzetti. He found Vanzetti was carrying a .38 Harrington and Richardson revolver, and a number of loose shotgun shells.

A policecar drew alongside, and Sacco and Vanzetti were put in the back seat with Vaughn covering them. Connolly slewed round to face them from the front seat. He reported that Sacco moved his hand to his pocket: 'Mister, if you put your hand in there again, you are going to get into trouble.'

According to Connolly, Sacco replied: 'I don't want no trouble.'

According to Sacco, his reply was: 'You need not be afraid of me.'

At the police station, Sacco too was searched. Tucked down inside his trousers was a .32 Colt automatic, fully loaded. In his hip pocket was a load of ammunition. In another pocket was the draft for a notice in Vanzetti's handwriting:

Fellow Workers, you have fought all the wars. You have worked for all the capitalists. You have wandered over all countries. Have you harvested the fruits of your labors, the price of your victories? Does the past comfort you? Does the present smile on you? Does the future promise you anything? Have you found a piece of land where you can live like a human being and die like a human being? On these questions, on this argument, and on this theme the struggle for existence, Bartolomeo Vanzetti will speak. Hour – day – hall. Admission free. Freedom of discussion to all. Take the ladies with you.

Chapter Two

Nicola Sacco and Bartolomeo Vanzetti

Nicola Sacco was twenty-nine, dark, smiling, small in stature. His father was the prosperous owner of a stretch of olive groves and vineyards on the south Adriatic coast. He left home, following the tracks of an elder brother who had settled in Massachusetts. In the United States he sought work in the shoe factories of New England. He married an Italian girl, Rosina, and in 1913 his son Dante was born. In his spare time he drank coffee in the Italian cafés of Boston, mixing with academics, journalists on the Italian-language papers, and voluble prophets of a myriad shades of visionary republicanism. He was a quiet listener, but gradually his views shifted from the Garibaldi republicanism of his home to utopian socialism and then – much influenced by his personal affection for Galleani, the leading thinker in his café society – he became a philosophic anarchist.

From 1913 he began to play a clear part in assisting strikes at neighbouring factories. He took a quiet pride in picketing longer hours and more reliably than anyone else. He and Rosina put on amateur plays and raised funds for the strikers' families. He kept a 'war garden', and usually gave his employer the excess vegetables to distribute among the poor.

Then in 1917 came the Draft Law. To avoid military service he fled to Mexico, grew homesick and returned to New England calling himself Mosmacotelli. He worked making candy in Cambridge, and for a few days at the factory in South Braintree outside which the murders were to take place.

With the Armistice he became Nicola Sacco again and took a job at the 3-K Shoe Factory in Stoughton. He was highly-paid as an edger, earning up to $70 a week. A savings account in his wife's name built up to $1,500. Sometimes he doubled as night watchman, and for this bought himself a .32 Colt automatic. Despite some prodding from the factory owner, he never took out a licence.

Early in March Sacco received a letter from Torremaggiore to tell him that his mother, after a long illness, had died. It was years since he had seen his family. They had never met Rosina nor seen Dante. His mind filled with Italy, and he decided that they should all sail for Naples. He told his employer, and promised not to leave before he 'broke in' another workman to take over his edging. He asked for a day off soon, to visit the consulate in Boston and obtain his passport. George Kelley, his employer, mentioned that he had heard the police were looking into Sacco's radicalism.

On April 12 a bundle of letters came from Italy. 'What you must do is embark the moment you receive this letter,' wrote his father. There were welcoming notes to Rosina from Marietto and Felicetto: 'Come quick for we are desirous to make your acquaintance.' And Marietto inserted a special letter: 'Dear Brother, Don't forget what I am telling you. When you come please bring me a black velvet coat of American style because such fine clothing does not exist here. Pay any price for when you come back I will pay for it.'

After work on April 14 he had a word with George Kelley. The new man was fine, and next day if possible he'd like to go to Boston with his passport photo. Maybe he'd be back soon after lunch.

On the day of the killings he caught the 8.56 train to Boston. He recollected that leaving South Station in Boston he walked over to the North End, and in Prince Street bought *La Notizia*. After looking at the straw hats and new suits in the windows, 'I say probably I go get my dinner first, so I have a little time and I go there, so I went over to Boni's restaurant.' At Boni's he found Professor Gaudagni, and over lunch they chatted about the Italian trip. Then off to the consulate, which was less crowded than usual. Then trouble. Guiseppe Andrower, the passport official, wouldn't accept his photograph. It was much too large for the *foglio di via.* Sacco offered to cut it down to size with a pair of scissors. Against regulations, argued Andrower, and insisted on a fresh photograph, passport size. There was nothing much Sacco could do. He retired instead to Giordani's coffee house, and forgot his own problems when he was introduced there to Antonio Dentamore, a former editor of *La Notizia*, who was like Sacco, a philosophical anarchist. Then home.

He got the correct passport photo taken in Stoughton. There was so much to be done – clear up at work, sell up their home and pack for Italy. And Rosina was pregnant again. When Vanzetti called to make the trip to Johnson's garage there was not much time left. The boat sailed on Saturday.

Bartolomeo Vanzetti was thirty-two. Dark and short like Sacco, he looked a good deal older – possibly because of his long moustache. In six years he only once allowed Vernazano the barber to trim three hairs on it. The occasion so impressed the barber that he could in an instant sketch the exact position of each trimmed whisker.

Vanzetti's father was a successful farmer, growing corn, potatoes, red and yellow peppers and asparagus in the foothills of Piedmont. His son left school at thirteen and worked as a pastry cook in Turin. When his mother died, he decided to sail for New York. He was reading, thinking and eternally talking. His father's suggestions that he give him a little capital and set him up in business fell on sealed ears: 'My conscience do not permit me to be a business man and I will gain my bread by work.' He never tried to earn more than simple needs required, nor ever attempted to make his way in any job. Talk, ideas, social questions were the quick of his living. In New York he worked as a kitchen hand at Mouquin's restaurant. He then moved to the brickyards and quarries of Connecticut. Back to New York now as a pastry cook, then to Springfield working on the railway: 'the Italian live and work like a beast,' he noted. Next to the iron mills of Worcester, then over to Plymouth as a gardener, a labourer on the breakwater, a brickie's mate, an ice cutter. In 1916 he was working at the cordage factory in Plymouth at the time of a hard and bitter strike. Pay was $9 a week for the men, $6 for the women. Vanzetti was now a firm follower of Galleani, and as an anarchist strike leader he opposed both the management and the big unions. The strikers got their wages raised by $1 a week, but the company refused to re-employ Vanzetti. The union did not protest. From then on he had no settled employment, but earned his living by digging clams on the sea shore and peddling fish and eels from a handcart in the Italian quarter.

Like Sacco he fled to Mexico when the Draft Law was passed, coming back after the Armistice. The mass arrests of radicals worried him a good deal; many friends of Sacco and Vanzetti were taken off by the police. Coacci had been served with a deportation order, and one of the leading figures in their circle, Salsedo, had not only been arrested but was held *incommunicado* by federal agents in a building in Park Row. Friends tried raising a little money to get legal help for Salsedo, and Vanzetti was asked to go to New York on April 25 to find out exactly what Salsedo's situation was. His contacts in New York had been tipped off that a new wave of arrests was planned for May 1. Vanzetti was advised to return home, warn others, and hide their stocks of radical literature. On May 3 Salsedo fell to his death from the room on the fourteenth floor where he was held. The papers regarded it as suicide, and on May 4 the *Boston Herald* said that Salsedo had been helping the police round up the 'Galleani group of bombers', planners of a great 'death conspiracy' whose existence was one reason for the mass arrests. Sacco and Vanzetti decided that Salsedo had been murdered by the police.

Back home they determined to get rid of their anarchist literature and other hot property, the guns and bullets. To collect and cache the literature required a car. The only person who had one was Mike Boda, and his was being repaired at Johnson's garage. On May 5, Boda agreed to meet them there, and see if the car was ready. They brought their guns and shells along too (some of which didn't fit their automatics) planning to sell the weapons if they could, the shells too maybe, but anyway fire off any left-over ammunition in the nearby woods. Half an hour later they were under arrest, and the questioning of this story – which is theirs – began.

It was 11 p.m. when Chief Stewart began to put his questions: 'Are you a socialist? I.W.W.? A communist? A radical? A Black Hand?' Sacco denied being an anarchist or anything else, contenting himself with, 'Some things I like different.' Vanzetti was vaguer still when asked if he was an anarchist: 'Well, I don't know what you call him. I am a little different.' Both gave untrue accounts of how long they had possessed their guns, and whom they had bought them from. Neither the South Braintree murders nor the Bridgewater hold-up were mentioned. Sacco concluded that their arrest was something connected with their politics or their draft dodging: 'Because I was not registered, and I was working for the movement for the working class, the labouring class.'

They were locked in the cells for the night. Vanzetti protested they had no blankets, only a bare board to sleep on. He claims the duty officer replied: 'Never mind you catch warm by and by, and tomorrow morning we put you in a line in the hall between the chairs and we shoot you.' The policeman slowly loaded his revolver and pointed it through the bars. But spat instead.

Next day, Frederick Katzmann, the District Attorney, arrived. He pressed them about the 15th, the day of the killings. 'Common to every other day to me. I peddled fish,' said Vanzetti. Sacco said he thought he was at work. Both elaborated their false stories about guns and bullets. A stream of witnesses visited them, and Sacco was told to stoop and, as it were, aim a gun. 'I don't refuse because I don't know I have the right to refuse.' Mrs Johnson, who had made the telephone call at the garage after speaking to them, was brought in. Sacco denied having ever seen her. They were questioned about Boda and Coacci. They protested that they had never heard of such people.

The police arrested Coacci. Chief Stewart remembered his trunk, which was on board ship. He decided he'd 'skipped with the swag', and requested the Italian police to send the trunk back. But there was nothing in the trunk but old clothes, and Coacci had been at work all day on April 15. He was released and deported. Three days later Mike Boda took a boat to Italy and never returned.

Stewart and Katzmann pooled impressions. The DA decided to prosecute. Sacco was at work the day of the Bridgewater hold-up. Vanzetti said he was peddling fish. Sacco was away from work on the day of the killings. Vanzetti said he was peddling fish.

The Commonwealth of Massachusetts charged Bartolomeo Vanzetti with 'assault with intent to murder' at Bridgewater. It then charged Nicola Sacco and Bartolomeo Vanzetti with armed robbery at South Braintree, and the murders of Allesandro Berardelli and Frederick Parmenter.

The District Attorney, Frederick Katzmann, arranged that Vanzetti would stand trial for the Bridgewater hold-up as a prelude to the joint trial for the South Braintree killings. The hold-up trial began on June 22, 1920 at Plymouth before Judge Webster Thayer.

Judge Thayer was sixty-three, a man of considerable reputation in Massachusetts, but unknown outside it. Two months before he had hit the *Boston Herald* headlines when presiding over the trial of Sergei Zabraff, who was charged with breaking the criminal laws against anarchy. The jury found that Zabraff had been exercising his constitutional right of stating his social views, and acquitted him. The judge strongly criticized their decision, much to the approval of the local press.

Vanzetti was defended by J. P. Vahey, a prominent Plymouth lawyer and established local politician. Vahey began by advising Vanzetti not to take the stand in his own defence, nor to introduce evidence of his life and character. Either step, argued Vahey, would stress Vanzetti's radical views, and prejudice the jury.

'It seems that if a Radical', notes Vanzetti, 'when accused of a crime, does not testify, that is enough to convict him; and if he does testify, his radicalism will convict him anyway, and also he is blamed for opening up the subject of radicalism. What is a Radical to do under these circumstances?'

His sole defence would be his alibi – sixteen fellow Italians who had seen him peddling fish at the time of the hold-up. He himself would simply sit in the dock and listen. No one would mention politics.

The prosecution produced five witnesses who all identified Vanzetti as one of the hold-up men. First came two men on the pay truck, Ben Bowles and Alfred Cox. Bowles was the guard who got so excited during the shooting that he grabbed at the wheel and pulled the truck into a telegraph pole. He recognized Vanzetti largely by his 'trimmed moustache, very dark and bushy'. He was positive the man he shot at was Vanzetti. His colleague, Albert Cox, was not quite as sure. 'Vanzetti answers the man's description; he looks like the man,' he said. A passerby, who saw the gunman rush past him and then, a few feet in front, crouch and fire, thought he looked like a Pole, but brought to Brockton police station by Chief Stewart, he recognized Vanzetti. Mrs

Georgina Brooks had been taking her five-year-old boy for a walk. She had passed the bandits' car before the hold-up, and got a distant view of the shooting. She identified Vanzetti: again the moustache was the giveaway. Finally Maynard Shaw, a fourteen-year-old newspaper boy, caught a rapid glimpse of the gangster. 'I could tell he was a foreigner. I could tell by the way he ran.' This was the heart of the prosecution attack.

It was supported by two other points. When Vanzetti was arrested on the tramcar, he had in his pockets both Winchester and Peters 12 gauge shotgun shells. A Winchester shell had been picked up by a Dr Murphy at the scene of the hold-up, and a Peters shell was found in the abandoned Buick in the Manley Woods. No proof was offered, or asked for, on this Peters shell. The second point was more evanescent. It was the original link of the Buick car and Mike Boda, and amounted to the fact that a number of people had observed an Italian driving a car, probably a Buick.

Vanzetti's defence was his alibi. Sixteen working-class Italians, all using an interpreter, supported his case. It was a custom among the Italians to eat eels on Christmas Eve, and Vanzetti claimed the day had been a busy one. Mrs Fortini, his landlady, explained how he had prepared eels till midnight on the 23rd. Carlo Balboni reported buying eels from Vanzetti very early on the 24th as he set off to work. Di Carli, a shoemaker, remembered buying eels soon after he opened shop at 7 a.m. Enrico Bastoni recalled that Vanzetti asked to borrow his horse at 8 a.m., but he needed it himself to deliver the Christmas bread. Rosa Balboni, who was in the bakers' shop at the time, bought her eels from him in the afternoon. Terese Malaquci, Emma Borsari and Adeladi Bongianni described the delivery of their eels. Marjaretta Fiochi said she had ordered her eels on the Sunday, but had asked Vanzetti not to deliver them till the 24th because 'if I kept them in salt longer it would be more delicious to eat'. And Vincent Longhi, a weaver on his way to work, recalled a short talk with Vanzetti – about the eels he was to deliver.

To deliver eels on this busy day, Vanzetti called on the help of thirteen-year-old Beltrando Brini, who recounted the day's deliveries. Under powerful cross-examination, he admitted he had learned his evidence off by heart, repeated it to his parents – who also witnessed for Vanzetti – and even to other witnesses.

Some witnesses admitted being friends of Vanzetti, others claimed not to know him except as a passing eel-seller. Di Carli the shoemaker was asked if he had heard Vanzetti's speeches, or ever discussed government, the poor and the rich, with Vanzetti. Through the interpreter, he said no.

The jury took five and a half hours to reach their verdict. It was guilty.

'*Coraggio,*' said Vanzetti turning, after an instant, to his friends. Judge Thayer took control, thanking the jury: 'You may go to your homes with the feeling that you did respond as the soldier responded to his service when he went across the seas to the call of the Commonwealth.' The punishment for armed hold-up was usually eight to ten years in prison. The judge decided that something severer was required. He sentenced Vanzetti to fifteen years in Charlestown State Penitentiary.

Chapter Three

A crime punishable by death

The early summer of 1921 brought back more war memories. The new anniversaries were celebrated with sadness and pride. On May 29 there was a great renaming of public streets and squares in Boston to honour the dead. On May 30 came the poignant ceremonies of Memorial Day. On May 31 the trial of Sacco and Vanzetti for the South Braintree killings began.

The trial judge was Webster Thayer. Five hundred people were called before the court as likely jurors. Many found excuses for not serving. Judge Thayer spoke to them:

'It is not sufficient excuse that the service is painful, con-
fining and distressing. It is not sufficient excuse that a juror
has business engagements and other duties more profitable
and pleasant that he would rather perform, for you must
remember that the American soldier had other duties he
would have rather performed than those that resulted in his
giving up his life upon the battlefields of France, but he with
undaunted courage and patriotic devotion that brought
honor and glory to humanity and the world rendered the
service and made the supreme sacrifice. He answered the
call of the Commonwealth.

'So, gentlemen, I call upon you to render this service here
that you have been summoned to perform with the same
spirit of patriotism, courage and devotion to duty as was
exhibited by our soldier boys across the seas, and let no

juror decline this call of the Commonwealth excepting in such cases that he can swear in fact and in truth, before man and Almighty God, that his conscience will not permit him to find a defendant guilty of a crime punishable by death.'

Nevertheless, by July 3 – over a month later – the original jury list had only yielded seven wholly qualified jurors. On the evening of Thanksgiving Day, the Judge sent the Sheriff out to collect more jurors. He raided a nearby Masonic Lodge, and the twelve were complete. None were Italians.

There was talk in the press that the case had hidden connections with the Salsedo affair. Newsmen descended on the court. Judge Thayer issued strict instructions that the public was to be searched for guns. More press comment. Armed policemen were everywhere. The Italian government, worried lest the defendants' views should play an unfair part in the trial, sent the Marquis di Ferrante as observer. The Greater Boston Federation of Churches, uncertain about the whole affair, also placed an observer in court. Sacco and Vanzetti were represented by new lawyers, John Vahey having now joined Katzmann in the public prosecutor's office.

Frederick Katzmann, the prosecutor, attacked Sacco and Vanzetti on three main lines – he claimed they could be identified by eye-witnesses, that the murder bullets could be shown as coming from their guns, and that their whole pattern of behaviour revealed their guilt.

Four people identified Vanzetti as being in the neighbourhood of the shootings, and seven people recognized Sacco. Ten of these eleven witnesses had not seen the actual shooting.

On the day of the crime, John Faulkner, a pattern-maker, had taken the 9.20 a.m. train from Plymouth which stopped at Braintree. He remembered a nervous foreigner 'with a black moustache and cheek bones', who had leaned over and asked if this was East Braintree. Later he saw Vanzetti's photo in the papers. He went to the police station where he was shown five men, one of them Italian. He identified the Italian as Vanzetti.

Harry Dolbeare, a piano repairer, was one of the men summoned for service on the jury and then excused. While sitting in the courtroom he recognized Vanzetti, both as a man whose photo he had seen in the press, and as one of 'a carload of foreigners' he had noticed in South Braintree at 10 a.m. on the day. He could not remember the others in the car, except as an impression, but of Vanzetti he had no doubt, 'not a particle'.

Michael Levangie was the man who was closing the level crossing gates when the escaping car roared up, and someone inside pointing 'a shiny revolver' between the blinds ordered him to let them through. Afterwards he told some people that he had actually seen no one through the car blinds, but to others he said he had seen a light-haired man. After seeing Vanzetti in the police station, he identified him as the man.

A crossing keeper further on, Austin Reed, had also been putting his gates down when the car stopped forty feet away, and one of its passengers roared: 'What to hell are you holding us up for?' It raced across, and a few minutes later returned, doubling back on its tracks. Reed saw Vanzetti's photo in the paper, and went to Brockton police station where he was shown 'the Italian'. He identified him.

Seven witnesses identified Sacco. Lola Andrews and Mrs Campbell were out looking for work in the South Braintree shoe factories on April 15. Near the Rice and Hutchins factory they saw a parked car with one man at the wheel, and another underneath it. Mrs Andrews said she spoke to the man under the car, and he climbed up and gave them directions. Incredulous, Sacco stood up in the defendant's cage: 'I am the man? Do you mean me? Take a good look!" Later at the police station she was shown Sacco in a room, and identified him. Her companion, Mrs Campbell, claimed that there was indeed a car, but neither of them spoke to any men. As to Sacco and Vanzetti: 'I do not think I ever saw them men in the world.' The defence pressed the cross-examination hard. Lola Andrews fainted on the witness stand.

William Tracy, a real estate man, recalled that around 11.30 a.m. on April 15 he saw two men leaning against a shop window on Pearl Street. He couldn't recall their dress, except that they wore hats and overcoats. Later that day a friend phoned him and told him about the shootings. After the arrests, Sacco's photo was printed in the *Post*, and he went along to Dedham jail. There, like Mrs Andrews, he was taken to a balcony and shown Sacco sitting in a sunken room. In court, he testified 'that to the best of my opinion he was the man, but I wouldn't positively say so.'

William Heron, a railroad detective, was at South Braintree station with a lost child at 12.27 p.m. on April 15. He noticed two nervous Italians in the waiting room. Later he went to Quincy Court House to see Sacco brought in. He arrived, handcuffed to Officer Scott, and Heron exclaimed aloud, 'Gee, that is the fellow I saw down at South Braintree the day of the shooting.' The police chief, who heard his remarks, invited him to identify Sacco.

Mary Spillane, a bookkeeper at the Slater and Morrill factory, had actually heard the shots and looked out of the window. She glimpsed a car going past, with a man leaning out of it. She described his hand and face in detail. She too saw a press picture of Sacco, and rapidly identified him at the police station. Her testimony wavered. At a preliminary hearing, she said, 'I don't think my opportunity afforded me the right to say he is the man.' But now in court she was positive. The defence made great play of the fact that they had previously shown her a photo of an Italian gangster, then serving time in Sing Sing, whom she identified, with equal rapidity, as being both the escaping gunman and Nicola Sacco.

Her friend, Frances Devlin, had also jumped up from her desk and looked through the window. She too was shown Sacco at the police station. At the preliminary hearing she said 'I don't say positively' when asked if Sacco was the man. This time, looking at Sacco in the defendant's cage, her doubts disappeared. He was the man.

Carlos Goodridge, a salesman, had come out of the pool room just after the shootings. A car came towards him at 10 or 20 m.p.h. 'Just as I stepped out halfway on the sidewalk, there was a fellow poked a gun over towards me, and I was probably within twenty feet of it, or twenty-five.' He scuttled back into the pool room. He had told the story, in different forms, to his friends. Some said he claimed to recognize one of the men, others that all he saw was a pointing revolver, and ran. When Sacco was brought for his preliminary hearing at Quincy Court House, Goodridge was himself about to face Frederick Katzmann in the same court on a charge of larceny. He had a long record of small thefts and bail-skipping. At Quincy, he told the District Attorney that he recognized Sacco, and would appear as a witness for the prosecution. The larceny charge was not pressed.

But there was also Lewis Pelser, a shoe worker at the factory. He had opened a window by three or four inches, and only seven feet away: 'I seen this fellow shoot this fellow. It was the last shot.' The murderer 'flashed a gun over towards the factory . . . two bullets right over the window where I was standing.' He took the number of the escaping car – 49783. But when interviewed by the defence before the trial, he had said that he ducked under the table when the shooting began, like all the other workers, and saw nothing. Several workmates supported this version. However, the prosecution too had interviewed him before the trial, and the assistant District Attorney took him to identify Sacco when he at once exclaimed, 'By George! If Sacco isn't the man, he's a dead ringer for him.'

There were thirty-two other witnesses. Most glimpsed the car flashing by, or, like the Italian construction workers, had first taken the shots for fire crackers and gone towards them; or realized it was gunfire, and run for cover. Their image of the gunmen often varied widely or was stereotyped ('One fellow looked like a regular wop'). Six of these witnesses refused to identify, the remaining twenty-six said Sacco and Vanzetti were not the men. 'Well, for God's sake, I said they don't resemble those men,' exclaimed Emilio Falcone, one of the labourers. 'Why do you ask me again?'

Katzmann's second attack centred on the bullets. Four shells were picked up near the scene by an eye-witness. One was a Winchester. Six bullets were taken out of the bodies of the dead men. As he cut each one out, Dr Magrath scratched a Roman numeral on its base with his needle. The third one he removed was a Winchester. It was this bullet which finally killed Berardelli.

All six were shown to Captain Proctor of the State Police. He concluded that five had been fired through a Savage automatic pistol. But the fatal bullet came from a .32 Colt.

It was already established that when Officer Connolly arrested Sacco on the tram he had on him a fully loaded .32 Colt and twenty-three loose shells, of which six were Winchesters. But Captain Proctor told Katzmann that he was uncertain whether the bullet that killed Berardelli came from *that* particular Colt. There was the added difficulty that the eye-witnesses had described one man as shooting Berardelli, yet the two types of bullets probably meant that two guns were used on him.

Katzmann was asked by the defence before the trial what argument he would advance. He told them that he would not argue the specific link between bullet and gun, but base his case on general probability. Then, nearly halfway through the trial, the defence asked permission to fire test bullets into piles of sawdust through Sacco's Colt, hoping to close the question. Katzmann reacted by saying that 'in the light of the result of the experiments' he would take a stronger line, and now argue a specific link between this bullet and this gun.

The defence produced the two ballistics experts who had conducted the test firings. They stated that five of the bullets might have been fired either by a Savage or a Walther. As to the fatal bullet, that had come from a Steyr 765 mm pistol – closely similar to a .32 Colt. All six might or might not be from the same gun.

Katzmann also produced two ballistics experts. Charles van Amburgh argued that five came from a Savage, and one from a .32 Colt. He 'was inclined to believe' that it came from Sacco's Colt. But Captain Proctor was more undecided, and outside court told Katzmann so. He pointed out that if he was asked outright in court whether he had found evidence that the fatal bullet came from Sacco's pistol, he would be compelled to say 'No'. Katzmann therefore drafted a different question, and before judge and jury, the exchange went:

'Have you an opinion as to whether bullet number 2 was fired from the Colt automatic which is in evidence?'

'I have.'

'And what is your opinion?'

'My opinion is that it is consistent with being fired by that pistol.'

Katzmann backed up these two prime attempts at identification with a couple of secondary lines. He argued that a dark, working-man's cap found near the scene of the shootings belonged to Sacco, and that the revolver discovered in Vanzetti's pocket had first been lifted from the dead body of Berardelli by Sacco, and then given to Vanzetti.

The dark, working-man's cap was picked up by Fred Loring, one of the factory workers, several hours after the killings. By then hundreds of people had crowded round the spot, and the defence argued that the cap had probably been lost by one of them. It was handed over to Gallivan, Chief of Police at Braintree. He made a hole in the lining, seeking for any marks of identification. Finding nothing, he put it under his car seat and there it remained for ten days. At the trial it reappeared as Exhibit 29.

Sacco normally hung his cap on a nail at work. Katzmann questioned George Kelley, his employer, who had many times seen the hat hanging there: 'The only thing I could say about that cap, from hanging up on a nail in the distance, it was similar in colour. As far as details are concerned, I could not say it was.'

Judge Thayer intervened and pressed his own questions to clarify the matter:

'Mr Kelley, according to your best judgment is the cap I show you alike in appearance to the cap worn by Sacco?'
    'In color only.'
    'That is not responsive to the question. I wish you would answer it, if you can.'
    'I can't answer it when I don't know right down in my heart that that is the cap.'
    'I don't want you to. I want you should answer according to what is in your heart.'
    'General appearance, that is all I can say. I never saw that cap so close in my life as I do now.'
    'In its general appearance, is it the same?'
    'Yes, sir.'

No one else identified the cap. The prosecution then pointed to the tear in the lining and stated that this was the mark of the nail on which Sacco regularly hung it. Neither prosecution nor defence asked the chief of police about the tear, nor did he say anything until the trial was over.

Katzmann then produced two more caps. One of these had been taken from Sacco's home by the police. The other had no connection with the case. He pressed Sacco to identify them as his or not. He identified them correctly, but with hesitations and withdrawals.

'Is that your cap?'
'I think it is. It looks like, but it is probably dirt – probably dirt after.'

It was enough for the prosecution to seize on, and claim to the jury – though challenged by the defence – that Sacco had 'falsified to you before your very faces'.

Finally, the fit. Sacco put on his own hat, then the one found near the crime. The report of the *Herald* described how 'it stuck on the top of his head and he turned with a satisfied air to let the jury see'. The prosecution claimed he was not really trying ('Try and pull it down in back and see if it can't go in'), and that both caps fitted well. Katzmann invited any juror with a head size of 7⅛ to try the caps himself.

Then came the other object linking Sacco and Vanzetti with the scene of the shooting – the revolver in Vanzetti's pocket. Berardelli had owned a .38 Harrington and Richardson revolver. A few weeks before his death he had taken it to Ivor Johnson's repair shop to have a new hammer fitted. After the gunmen drove off, the revolver was missing. No one could prove beyond doubt that Berardelli had collected his revolver from the repair shop, or that he had it that day, or that the gunmen took it. But it seemed likely that this was so.

When Vanzetti was arrested, he had lied about the revolver – how long he had had it, and where he got it from ('I was scared'). The defence produced Luigi Falzini, who stated that he had sold the gun to Vanzetti for five dollars. He himself had bought it from Orciani – whom the police had originally suspected as one of the gunmen. Orciani had bought it for four dollars from another workman, Rexford Slater.

None of its owners had recorded its serial number, and under pressure all could be made to hesitate about whether this was their former revolver – or only one similar to it. The gun was of a cheap and common type, and none of its owners knew anything about guns.

Employees at the Ivor Johnson workshop could not positively identify it either. They too had not noted the serial number, had misrecorded the calibre of Berardelli's gun in their books, and were kept so busy – each man repairing twenty to thirty revolvers a day – that it was hard to recall any one gun in such detail.

But after scrutinizing it, George Fitzmeyer, their repair clerk, said he thought it had indeed had a new hammer fitted because, considering the gun's age, it was so little worn. Defence experts thought it still had its original hammer, which was so little worn because, though the gun had been much bought and sold, it had seldom been fired.

Katzmann drew attention to the fact that the gun was fully loaded. Vanzetti had no spare cartridges for this make – consistent with his having taken over Berardelli's already loaded gun. The defence argued that if a gunman picked up a revolver from the dying Berardelli, he would be highly unlikely to give it to an accomplice, and crazy to be riding round with it three weeks later.

This was the full strength and deployment of the evidence identifying Sacco and Vanzetti as the gunmen. To thrust it home, the prosecution had one further major argument – before and after their arrest Sacco and Vanzetti had behaved exactly as one might expect of two captured murderers.

First, their visit to Johnson's garage: their need of a car was urgent, yet they gave it up and scattered when Johnson advised them that it was not licensed for 1920. The true explanation, argued the prosecution, was that they saw Mrs Johnson go to a neighbour's house, noted the telephone wires, and guessed what was afoot.

Second, when arrested on the streetcar both were heavily armed. This implied not only that they had something to fear – but that whatever it was, was very considerable.

Third, their weapons and ammunition fitted with at least part of the shootings.

Fourth, they attempted to resist arrest and were prepared to shoot the police, had they been given the chance.

Fifth, on arrest they gave false accounts of who they were visiting and why, and lied about the source of their weapons.

To explain all this, the defence was compelled to bring in the issue of radicalism. For the first time this came openly into the case, and revealed a whole new territory for Katzmann to explore and the jury to observe. The defence explanation was that there had been no suspicious incident at the Johnson's garage – the drama lay entirely in Mrs Johnson's head; Sacco and Vanzetti were there seeking a car in order to hide their radical literature before the expected police raids. Their guns had been acquired for self-protection in their work – Sacco as a nightwatchman, Vanzetti as a street pedlar – and these too were to be disposed of before the expected police raids on radicals. Finally they denied resisting arrest – 'You are a liar!' shouted Vanzetti as Connolly made the critical statement. All their falsehoods at the police station were simply to protect fellow radicals.

To meet this five-pronged attack, the defence built up the alibis of Sacco and Vanzetti. Sacco's account of his day seeking a passport in Boston was supported by the Italian consulate official, by the fellow radicals he had lunch and coffee with, and by the Italian acquaintances he met at the station or on the streets. He also recognized a spectator in the court – James Hayes – as a man sitting in the same carriage on the return journey. Hayes did not recall Sacco, but agreed he was on that train, in that carriage, and sitting in the place that Sacco described.

It was now over a year since the killings, and the prosecution did not deny the visit to Boston, or the encounters Sacco described. Instead Katzmann reminded the jury that immediately after his arrest, Sacco had claimed he was at work on April 15 – and this Boston alibi had only been built up later. Katzmann argued that the Boston visit may have been true enough, but had taken place on some other day. How could the witnesses be so sure of the date, he wondered, and pressed minutely their reasons for linking their memory with that specific day. As to the Italian consular official:

> 'Mind you, he has 150 or 200 applications for passports a day, or they had in the consul's office, and that the 15th was a very slack day and that he remembered that Sacco was in on that day because when he came in with the family photograph of large size, taking it into the secretary to the consul, they looked at it and laughed. Andrower says, and expects twelve men in the county of Norfolk to believe it, "I remember the day because I happened to look at a calendar pad on the desk of the secretary." Gentlemen, if I were to be hanged because I could not tell the day I have looked at a diary or a calendar since this trial first opened, I would be hanged forty times a day.'

Vanzetti's alibi was similar to his previous one at the Bridge-water hold-up trial. He had peddled fish all morning, and spent the afternoon chatting on the shore to Italian acquaintances. Many of his witnesses had difficulty in recalling the details of the day, and the prosecution attempted to unsettle their certainty that April 15 was the day they were describing. Katzmann pointed out that everything described could easily have happened on any other day, that the witnesses were largely Italian friends of the defendant, that on their own admission they had discussed the dating amongst themselves, and that one – Mrs Brini – had also given him an alibi 'in another case'.

Chapter Four

Cross-
examination

Frederick Katzmann now seized his opportunity to reveal to the jury the political as well as the criminal challenge which Sacco and Vanzetti presented. He asserted his legal right to test their credibility. Perhaps of all the passages in this long and complex trial, time shows this to have been the most deadly of cross-examinations: Katzmann ruthlessly insistent, Sacco at first bewildered, then at bay, and finally making his speech.

Rather than re-writing the episode, I would like to turn to the official transcript and (leaving out some by-passages, repetition and technical interruptions) present it as, according to the court shorthand writer, it actually happened. Nicola Sacco is in the dock. Fred H. Moore is defending him, as Jeremiah McAnarney is defending Vanzetti, Frederick Katzmann is the prosecutor, and Judge Webster Thayer presides.

Katzmann	Did you say yesterday you love a free country?
Sacco	Yes, sir.
Katzmann	Did you love this country in the month of May 1917?
Sacco	I did not say – I don't want to say I did not love this country.
Katzmann	Do you understand the question?
Sacco	Yes.
Katzmann	Then will you please answer it?
Sacco	I can't answer in one word.

Katzmann   You can't tell this jury whether you loved the country or not?

Moore   I object to that.

Sacco   I could explain that, yes, if I loved . . .

Katzmann   What?

Sacco   I could explain that, yes, if I loved, if you give me a chance.

Katzmann   I ask you first to answer that question. Did you love this United States of America in May 1917?

Sacco   I can't answer in one word.

Katzmann   Don't you know whether you did or not?

Moore   I object, your Honor.

Judge Thayer   What say?

Moore   I object to the repetition of this question without giving the young man an opportunity to explain his attitude.

Judge Thayer   That is not the usual method that prevails. Where the question can be categorically answered by yes or no, it should be answered. The explanation comes later. Then you can make any inquiry to the effect of giving the witness an opportunity of making whatever explanation at that time he sees fit to make, but under cross-examination counsel is entitled to get an answer either yes or no, when the question can be so answered. You may proceed, please.

Katzmann   Did you love this country in the last week of May 1917?

Sacco   That is pretty hard for me to say in one word, Mr Katzmann.

Katzmann   There are two words you can use, Mr Sacco, yes or no. Which one is it?

Sacco   Yes.

Katzmann   And in order to show your love for this United States of America when she was about to call upon you to become a soldier you ran away to Mexico?

McAnarney   Wait.

Judge Thayer   Did you?

Katzmann   Did you run away to Mexico?

Judge Thayer   He has not said he ran away to Mexico? Did you go?

Katzmann   Did you go to Mexico to avoid being a soldier for this country that you loved?

Sacco   Yes.

Katzmann   You went under an assumed name?

Sacco   No.

Katzmann   Didn't you take the name of Mosmacotelli?

Sacco   Yes.

Katzmann   That is not your name, is it?

Sacco   No.

Katzmann   How long did you remain under the name of Mosmacotelli?

Sacco   Until I got a job over to Mr Kelley's.

Katzmann   When was that?

Sacco   The armistice.

Katzmann   After the war was practically over?

Sacco   Yes, sir.

Katzmann   Then for the first time, after May 1917, did you become known as Sacco again?

Sacco   Yes, sir.

Katzmann   Was it for the reason that you desired to avoid service that when you came back in four months you went to Cambridge instead of Milford?

Sacco   For the reason for not to get in the army.

Katzmann   So as to avoid getting in the army.

Sacco   Another reason why, I did not want no chance to get arrested and one year in prison . . .

Katzmann   Did you love your country when you came back from Mexico?

Sacco   I don't think I could change my opinion in three months.

Katzmann   You still loved America, did you?

Sacco   I should say yes.

Katzmann   And is that your idea of showing your love for this country?

(Witness hesitates)

Katzmann   Is that your idea of showing your love for America?

Sacco   Yes.

Katzmann   And would it be your idea of showing your

love for your wife that when she needed you, you ran
away from her?

Sacco   I did not run away from her.
Moore   I object.
Sacco   I was going to come after if I need her.
Judge Thayer   He may answer. Simply on the question of
credibility, that is all.
Katzmann   Would it be your idea of love for your wife
that you were to run away from her when she needed
you?
McAnarney   Pardon me. I ask for an exception on that.
Judge Thayer   Excluded. One may not run away. He has not
admitted he ran away.
Katzmann   Then I will ask you, didn't you run away from
Milford so as to avoid being a soldier for the United
States?
Sacco   I did not run away.
Katzmann   You mean you walked away?
Sacco   Yes.
Katzmann   You don't understand me when I say 'run
away', do you?
Sacco   That is vulgar.
Katzmann   That is vulgar?
Sacco   You can say a little intelligent, Mr Katzmann.
Katzmann   Don't you think going away from your country
is a vulgar thing to do when she needs you?
Sacco   I don't believe in war.
Katzmann   You don't believe in war?
Sacco   No, sir.
Katzmann   Do you think it is a cowardly thing to do what
you did?
Sacco   No, sir.
Katzmann   Do you think it is a brave thing to do what
you did?
Sacco   Yes, sir.
Katzmann   Do you think it would be a brave thing to go
away from your own wife?
Sacco   No.
Katzmann   When she needed you?
Sacco   No.

Katzmann	What wages did you first earn in this country?
Sacco	Wage?
Katzmann	Wages, money, pay?
Sacco	I used to get before I leave?
Katzmann	When you first came to this country?
Sacco	$1.15.
Katzmann	Per day?
Sacco	Yes.
Katzmann	What were you getting at the 3-K factory when you got through?
Sacco	Sometimes sixty, fifty, seventy, eighty, forty, thirty, twenty-five, thirty-five. Depends on how much work was.
Katzmann	That was within eight years after you first came to this country, isn't it?
Sacco	After seven years – no after twelve years.
Katzmann	1908. I beg your pardon. That is my mistake, Mr Sacco. I did not mean that. That is within thirteen years?
Sacco	Yes, sir.
Katzmann	From the time you came to this country?
Sacco	Yes.
Katzmann	From $1.15 a day to $5 a day or better?
Sacco	Yes.
Katzmann	And your child was born in this country, wasn't it?
Sacco	Yes.
Katzmann	And your marriage took place in this country?
Sacco	Yes.
Katzmann	Is Italy a free country? Is it a republic?
Sacco	Republic, yes.
Katzmann	You love free countries, don't you?
Sacco	I should say yes.
Katzmann	Why didn't you stay down in Mexico?
Sacco	Well, first thing, I could not get my trade over there. I had to do any other job.
Katzmann	Don't they work with a pick and shovel in Mexico?
Sacco	Yes.
Katzmann	Haven't you worked with a pick and shovel in this country?

Sacco	I did.
Katzmann	Why didn't you stay there, down there in that free country, and work with a pick and shovel?
Sacco	I don't think I did sacrifice to learn a job to go to pick and shovel in Mexico.
Katzmann	Is it because – is your love for the United States of America commensurate with the amount of money you can get in this country per week?
Sacco	Better conditions, yes.
Katzmann	Better country to make money, isn't it?
Sacco	Yes.
Katzmann	Mr Sacco, that is the extent of your love for this country, isn't it, measured in dollars and cents?
McAnarney	If your Honor please, I object to this particular question.
Judge Thayer	You opened up this whole subject.
McAnarney	To the substance and form.
Katzmann	I will change the form, if your Honor please.
Judge Thayer	Better change that.
Katzmann	Is your love for this country measured by the amount of money you can earn here?
McAnarney	To that question I object.
Judge Thayer	Now you may answer.
Sacco	I never loved money.
Katzmann	What is the reason you came back from Mexico if you did not love money, then?
Sacco	The first reason is all against my nature, is all different food over there, different nature, anyway.
Katzmann	That is the first reason. It is against your nature. The food isn't right.
Sacco	Food and many other things.
Katzmann	You stood it for four months, didn't you?
Sacco	Three months.
Katzmann	Three months?
Sacco	Yes.
Katzmann	You came back all right physically, didn't you?
Sacco	I should say yes.
Katzmann	And you had Italian food there, didn't you?
Sacco	Yes, made by ourselves.

Katzmann   You could have had it all the time if you sent for it, couldn't you?

Sacco   Not all the time. I don't know.

Katzmann   Why couldn't you send to Boston to get Italian food sent to Monterey, Mexico?

Sacco   If I was a D. Rockefeller I will.

Katzmann   Then, I take it, you came back to the United States first to get something to eat. Is that right? Something that you liked?

Sacco   No, not just for eat.

Katzmann   Didn't you say that was the first reason?

Sacco   The first reason . . . .

Katzmann   Didn't you say that was the first reason?

Sacco   Yes.

Katzmann   All right. That wasn't a reason of the heart, was it?

Sacco   The heart?

Katzmann   Yes.

Sacco   No.

Katzmann   That was a reason of the stomach, wasn't it?

Sacco   Not just for the stomach, but any other reason.

Katzmann   I am talking first about the first reason. So, the first reason your love of America is founded upon is pleasing your stomach. Is that right?

Sacco   I will not say yes.

Katzmann   Haven't you said so?

Sacco   Not for the stomach. I don't think it is a satisfaction just for the stomach.

Katzmann   What is your second reason?

Sacco   The second reason is strange for me, the language.

Katzmann   Strange language?

Sacco   Yes.

Katzmann   Were you in an Italian colony there?

Sacco   If I got them? I can't get that, Mr Katzmann.

Katzmann   Pardon me. Were you in a group of Italians there?

Sacco   Yes.

Katzmann   When you came to America in 1908, did you understand English?

Sacco	No.
Katzmann	A strange language here, wasn't it?
Sacco	Yes.
Katzmann	What is the third reason, if there is one?
Sacco	A third reason, I was far away from my wife and boy.
Katzmann	Couldn't you have sent for your wife and your boy?
Sacco	I wouldn't send for my wife and boy over there, because it was the idea to come back here.
Katzmann	I know that. You are back here. My question is, couldn't you have sent for Mrs Sacco and your boy?
Sacco	Extreme conditions it would be bad. I could not go back in this United States, why I would get my wife and my boy.
Katzmann	Your answer means, does it not, you could have had Mrs Sacco and the boy come down there to live with you?
Sacco	Yes.
Katzmann	You preferred to come back to this country?
Sacco	Yes.
Katzmann	But you preferred to remain under the name of Mosmacotelli until the armistice was signed, didn't you?
Sacco	Yes.
Katzmann	Now, is there any other besides those three reasons why you loved the United States of America?
Sacco	Well, I couldn't say. Over here there is more accommodation for the working class, I suppose, than any other people, a chance to be more industrious, and more industry. Can have a chance to get anything he wants.
Katzmann	You mean to earn more money, don't you?
Sacco	No, no money, never loved money.
Katzmann	Never loved money?
Sacco	No, money never satisfaction to me.
Katzmann	What was the industrial condition that pleased you so much here if it wasn't a chance to earn bigger money?
Sacco	A man, Mr Katzmann, has no satisfaction all through the money, for the belly.
Katzmann	For the what?

Sacco   For the stomach, I mean.

Katzmann   We got away from the stomach. Now, I am talking about money.

Sacco   There is lots of things.

Katzmann   Well, let us have them all. I want to know why you loved America so that after you got to the haven of Mexico when the United States was at war you came back here.

Sacco   Yes.

Katzmann   I want all the reasons why you came back.

Sacco   I think I did tell you already.

Katzmann   Are those all?

Sacco   Yes. Industry makes a lot of things different.

Katzmann   Then there is food, that is one?

Sacco   Yes.

Katzmann   Foreign language is two?

Sacco   Yes.

Katzmann   Your wife and child is three?

Sacco   Yes.

Katzmann   And better industrial conditions?

Sacco   Yes.

Katzmann   Is that all?

Sacco   That is all . . . .

Katzmann   Did you find love of country among those four reasons?

Sacco   Yes, sir.

Katzmann   Which one is love of country?

Sacco   All together.

Katzmann   All together?

Sacco   Yes, sir.

Katzmann   Food, wife, language, industry?

Sacco   Yes.

Katzmann   That is love of country, is it?

Sacco   Yes.

Katzmann   Is standing by a country when she needs a soldier evidence of love of country?

McAnarney   That I object to, if your Honor please. And I might state now I want my objection to go to this whole line of interrogation.

Judge Thayer   I think you opened it up.

McAnarney   No, if your Honor please, I have not.

Judge Thayer   It seems to me you have. Are you going to claim much of all the collection of literature and the books was really in the interest of the United States as well as these people and therefore it has opened up the credibility of the defendant when he claims that all that work was done really for the interest of the United States in getting this literature out of the way?

McAnarney   That claim is not presented in anything tantamount to the language just used by the Court, and in view of the record as it stands at this time I object to this line of inquiry.

Judge Thayer   Is that not your claim, that the defendant, as a reason that he has given for going to the Johnson house, that they wanted the automobile to prevent people from being deported and to get this literature all out of the way? Does he not claim that was done in the interest of the United States, to prevent violation of the law by the distribution of this literature? I understood that was the . . . .

McAnarney   Are you asking that as a question to me?

Judge Thayer   Yes.

McAnarney   Absolutely we have taken no such position as that, and the evidence at this time does not warrant the assumption of that question.

Judge Thayer   Then you are not going to make that claim?

McAnarney   I am going to make whatever claim is legitimate.

Judge Thayer   I want to know what that is. You are going to claim in argument . . . .

McAnarney   I am going to claim this man and Vanzetti were of that class called socialists. I am going to claim that riot was running a year ago last April, that men were being deported, that twelve to fifteen hundred were seized in Massachusetts.

Judge Thayer   Do you mean to say you are going to offer evidence on that?

McAnarney   I am going to claim . . . .

Judge Thayer   I am asking the claim. You must know when I ask the claim I mean a claim that is founded on fact, evidence introduced in the case, and not upon anything else.

McAnarney   We have not concluded the evidence if your Honor please.

Judge Thayer   Do you say you are going to introduce evidence to that effect?

McAnarney   We have witnesses which we may introduce here. I do not know whether we will introduce them or not.

Judge Thayer   When you address me, I wish you would direct yourself to either evidence introduced or evidence you propose to introduce.

McAnarney   Your Honor now sees . . . .

Judge Thayer   So I can pass judgment then upon that, and I cannot pass judgment as to the competency of something that may not be introduced and never come before me for consideration.

McAnarney   Your Honor now sees the competency of my remarks, when I said to your Honor that I objected to the question in the present state of the evidence?

Judge Thayer   Are you going to claim that what the defend-ant did was in the interest of the United States?

McAnarney   Your Honor please, I now object to your Honor's statement as prejudicial to the rights of the defendants and ask that this statement be withdrawn from the jury.

Judge Thayer   There is no prejudicial remark made that I know of, and none were intended, I simply asked you, sir, whether you propose to offer evidence as to what you said to me.

McAnarney   If your Honor please, the remarks made with reference to the country and whether the acts that he was doing were for the benefit of the country. I can see no other inference to be drawn from those except prejudicial to the defendants.

Judge Thayer   Do you intend to make that claim?

McAnarney   What claim, please?

Judge Thayer   The one that I am suggesting.

McAnarney   When this evidence is closed, if your Honor please, I shall argue what is legitimate in the case.

Judge Thayer   All I ask is this one question, and it will simplify matters very much. Is it your claim that in the collection of the literature and the books and papers that that was done in the interest of the United States?

McAnarney   No, I make no such broad claim as that.

Judge Thayer   Then I will hear you, Mr Katzmann, on the competency of this testimony.

Katzmann   I am sorry I did not hear what Mr McAnarney said.

Judge Thayer   Mr McAnarney says it is not his claim, as I got it, he does not propose to make the claim that the collection and distribution of this literature was any matter to be done by either or both of the defendants in the interest of the United States.

Katzmann   Then, if your Honor please, I offer the line of cross-examination I have started upon as tending to attack the credibility of this man as a witness.

Judge Thayer   As to what part of his testimony?

Katzmann   As to any part of his testimony to affect his credibility as a witness *in toto*.

Judge Thayer   You can't attack a witness's credibility *in toto* excepting concerning some subject matter about which he has testified.

Katzmann   Well, he stated in his direct examination yesterday that he loved a free country, and I offer it to attack that statement made in his examination by his own counsel.

Judge Thayer   That is what I supposed, and that is what I supposed that remark meant when it was introduced in this cross-examination, but counsel now say they don't make that claim.

Katzmann   They say they don't make the claim that gathering up the literature on May 5 at West Bridgewater was for the purpose of helping the country, but that is a different matter, not related to May 5.

Judge Thayer (to the jury)   Of course, gentlemen, you understand, and you should understand by this time, that the Court is simply to pass upon the competency of testimony that is offered. The Court has no opinion of any facts. You heard me say so. The Court has no opinion in reference to this matter. I made simply the inquiry with a view of ascertaining what the claim of counsel might be, what might be argued, and inasmuch as counsel said they made no such claim, then I have reserved the right to pass upon the competency after inquiry has been made with reference to said testimony of the witness. I think you should know, and I repeat it, anyhow, there is no disposition, nothing has been said to do the slightest thing in any manner whatsoever to prejudice the rights of either of these defendants, and anything that has been said you will not consider it if anybody can draw such an inference. You will give it not the slightest consideration in the world. It deserves none, and you will give it none. The only question I was passing upon was the competency of testimony and nothing else. Questions are not evidence. Statements of counsel are not evidence. Statements by the Court are not evidence. You will be governed by absolutely nothing but testimony that is admitted and heard by you from the witnesses upon the stand. You may proceed.

Katzmann   What did you mean when you said yesterday you loved a free country?

Sacco   First thing I came in this country . . . .

Katzmann   No, pardon me. What did you mean when you said yesterday you loved a free country?

Sacco   Give me a chance to explain.

Katzmann   I am asking you to explain now.

Sacco   When I was in Italy, a boy, I was a republican, so I always thinking republican has more chance to manage, education, develop, to build someday his family, to raise and education, if you could. But that was my opinion; so when I came to this country I saw there was not what I was thinking before, but there was all the difference, because I been working in Italy, not so hard as I been work in this country. I could live free there just as well. Work in the same condition, but not so hard, about seven or eight hours a day, better food. I mean genuine. Of course, over here is good food, because it is bigger country, to any those who got money to spend, not for the working and laboring class, and in Italy it more opportunity to laborer to eat vegetable, more fresh, and I came

in this country. When I been started work here very hard
and been work thirteen years, hard worker, I could not
been afford much a family the way I did have the idea
before. I could not put any money in the bank. I could no
push my boy to go to school and other things. I teach over
here men who is with me. The free idea gives any man a
chance to profess his own idea, not the supreme idea, not
to give any person, not to be like Spain in position, yes,
about twenty centuries ago, but to give a chance to print
and education, literature, free speech, that I see it was all
wrong. I could see the best men, intelligent, education,
they been arrested and sent to prison and died in prison
for years and years without getting them out, and Debs,
one of the great men in his country, he is in prison, still
away in prison, because he is a socialist. He wanted the
laboring class to have better conditions and better living,
more education, give a push his son if he could have a
chance some day, but they put him in prison. Why?
Because the capitalist class, they know, they are against
that, because the capitalist class, they don't want our child
to go to high school or to college or Harvard College.
There would not be no chance, there would be no – they
don't want the working class educationed; they want the
working class to be a low all the times, be underfoot, and
not to be up with the head. So, sometimes, you see the
Rockefellers, Morgans, they give fifty – mean they give
five hundred thousand dollars to Harvard College, they
give a million dollars for another school. Everybody say
'Well, D. Rockefeller is a great man, the best in the
country.' I want to ask him who is going to Harvard
College? What benefit the working class they will get by
those million dollars they give by Rockefellers, D. Rockefellers. They won't get, the poor class, they won't have no
chance to go to Harvard College because men who is
getting $21 a week or $30 a week, I don't care if he gets
$80 a week, if he gets a family of five children he can't live
and send his child and go to Harvard College if he wants
to eat anything nature will give him. If he wants to eat like
a cow, and that is the best thing, but I want men to live
like men. I like men to get everything that nature will give

best, because they belong – we are not the friend of any other place, but we belong to nations. So that is why my idea has been changed. So that is why I love people who labor and work and see better conditions every day develop, makes no more war. We no want fight by the gun, and we don't want to destroy young men. The mother been suffering for building the young man. Some day need a little more bread, so when the time the mother get some bread or profit out of that boy, the Rockefellers, Morgans, and some of the peoples, high class, they send to war. Why? What is war? The war is not shoots like Abraham Lincoln's and Abe Jefferson, to fight for the free country, for the better education, to give chance to any other peoples, not the white people but the black and the others, because they believe and know they are mens like the rest, but they are war for the great millionaire. No war for the civilization of men. They are war for business, million dollars come on the side. What right we have to kill each other? I been work for the Irish, I have been working with the German fellow, with the French, many other peoples. I love them people just as I could love my wife, and my people for that did receive me. Why should I go kill them men? What he done to me? He never done anything, so I don't believe in no war. I want to destroy those guns. All I can say, the Government put the literature, give us educations. I remember in Italy, a long time ago, the Government they could not control very much these two – devilment went on, and robbery, so one of the government in the cabinet he says, 'If you want to destroy those devilments, if you want to take off all those criminals, you ought to give a chance to socialist literature, education of people, emancipation. That is why I destroy governments, boys.' That is why my idea I love socialists. That is why I like people who want education and living, building, who is good, just as much as they could. That is all.

Katzmann   And that is why you love the United States of America?

Sacco   Yes.

Katzmann   She is back more than twenty centuries like Spain, is she?

Sacco	At the time of the war they do it.
Katzmann	Are we in time of war now?
Sacco	No.
Katzmann	Were we in time of war when you came back from Mexico?
Sacco	Yes.
Katzmann	Do you love work as much as you love the United States?
Sacco	The reaction of the United States I did not like.
Katzmann	When you came over to this country, you had certain ideas, didn't you, of what was here?
Sacco	No.
Katzmann	Didn't you say when you came over you were thinking about education, building for your family, and raising a family?
Sacco	Yes, but I was a republican in my country.
Katzmann	Didn't you say that you had those ideas of this country when you came here.
Sacco	Yes.
Katzmann	And didn't you say when you came you saw a difference?
Sacco	Yes.
Katzmann	And the things were better in Italy than they were here?
Sacco	No, not that.
Katzmann	In substance, haven't you said that in this long answer you gave?
Sacco	No. Buy fruit more fresh for the working class, but no education and other things. It is just the same.
Katzmann	Didn't you say you did not have to work so hard in Italy?
Sacco	Yes.
Katzmann	That you could live just as well in Italy?
Sacco	Yes.
Katzmann	And that there was better food?
Sacco	Yes.
Katzmann	And fresher vegetables in Italy?
Sacco	Yes.
Katzmann	Why didn't you go back?
Sacco	Well, I say already . . . .

Katzmann   Say it again. Why didn't you go back when you were disappointed in those things?

Sacco   I say men established in this country, it is pretty hard to go back, change mind to go back.

Katzmann   You say on April 15, 1920, you were in Boston getting a passport to go back with your wife and children?

Sacco   Yes. That is not the reason I go back to the old country, for the fruit, but to see my father. For twelve years I never saw him, my brother, my sister or my folks.

Katzmann   It is just as easy, isn't it, to go back to see your father as to go back for fruit. You go back in either case?

Sacco   I do the greatest sacrifice in the life to go there.

Katzmann   To go back to a country where you get those things and could not get them here – is that a sacrifice?

Sacco   The great sacrifice is to see my folks.

Katzmann   The great sacrifice. All right. Do you believe in obedience to constituted governmental authority?

McAnarney   I object, if your Honor please . . . .

Katzmann   Did you say in substance you could not send your boy to Harvard?

Sacco   Yes.

Katzmann   Unless you had money. Did you say that?

Sacco   Of course.

Katzmann   Do you think that is true?

Sacco   I think it is.

Katzmann   Don't you know Harvard University educates more boys of poor people free than any other university in the United States of America?

McAnarney   I object.

Judge Thayer   You may answer . . . .

Katzmann   Do you know that to be the fact?

Sacco   How many there are?

Katzmann   What?

Sacco   How many?

Katzmann   How many? Don't you know that each year there are scores of them that Harvard educates free?

McAnarney   I object.

Judge Thayer   He may answer yes or no, whether he knows or not.

McAnarney   Save an exception.

Katzmann   The question is, do you know?

Sacco   I can't answer that question, no.

Katzmann   So without the light of knowledge on that subject, you are condemning even Harvard University, are you, as being a place for rich men?

Katzmann   Did you intend to condemn Harvard College?

Sacco   No, sir.

Katzmann   Were you ready to say none but the rich could go there without knowing about offering scholarships?

Sacco   Yes.

Katzmann   Does your boy go to the public schools?

Sacco   Yes.

Katzmann   Are there any schools in the town you came from in Italy that compare with the school your boy goes to?

McAnarney   I object.

Judge Thayer   Isn't this quite a good way now from that? Of course, I see, or think I see, what you have in mind eventually, but it seems to me the boy going to schools is quite a considerable distance.

Katzmann   Does your boy go to the public school?

Sacco   Yes.

Katzmann   Without payment of money?

Sacco   Yes.

Katzmann   Have you free nursing where you come from in Stoughton?

Sacco   What do you mean?

Katzmann   A district nurse?

Sacco   For the boys?

Katzmann   For anybody in your family who is ill?

Sacco   I could not say. Yes, I never have them in my house.

Katzmann   Do you know how many children the city of Boston is educating in the public schools? . . .

McAnarney   I object.

Katzmann (continued)   . . . free?

McAnarney   I object.

Judge Thayer   Ask him if he knows.

Katzmann   I did.

Judge Thayer   Answer yes or no.

Katzmann	Do you know?
Sacco	I can't answer yes or no.
Katzmann	Do you know it is close to one hundred thousand children?
McAnarney	I object.
Sacco	I know millions of people don't go there.
McAnarney	Wait. When there is objection, don't answer. I object to that question.
Judge Thayer	He says he doesn't know.
McAnarney	I object to that answer. I object to the question and the answer.
Judge Thayer	The question may stand, and the answer also.

On July 14, 1921, fifteen months after the killings, Judge Thayer took his place on the bench. Behind him were bouquets of flowers, including one from the Sheriff. He summarized the case, and gave the jury their charge:

'I therefore now commit into your sacred keeping the decision of these cases. You will therefore take them with you into yonder jury room, the silent sanctuary where may the great Dispenser of Justice, wisdom and sound judgment preside over all your deliberations. Reflect long and well so that when you return your verdict shall stand forth before the world as your judgment of truth and justice. Gentlemen, be just and fear not. Let all the end thou aimest at be thy country's, thy God's and truth's.'

The court broke for lunch, and at the beginning of the afternoon session, the jury withdrew, taking the exhibits with them. Part way through the afternoon, they asked for a magnifying glass. At 7.30 p.m. they filed back into court.

Clerk Worthington	Gentlemen of the jury, have you agreed upon your verdict?
Foreman	We have.
Clerk Worthington	Nicola Sacco.
Sacco	Present.

(Defendant Sacco stands up.)

Clerk Worthington	Hold up your right hand. Mr Foreman, look upon the prisoner. Prisoner, look upon the Foreman.

What say you, Mr Foreman, is the prisoner at the bar guilty or not guilty?

Foreman   Guilty.

Clerk Worthington   Guilty of murder?

Foreman   Murder.

Clerk Worthington   In the first degree?

Foreman   In the first degree.

Clerk Worthington   Upon each indictment?

Foreman   Yes, sir.

Clerk Worthington   Bartolomeo Vanzetti. Hold up your right hand. Look upon the Foreman. Mr Foreman, look upon the prisoner. What say you, Mr Foreman, is Bartolomeo guilty or not guilty of murder?

Foreman   Guilty.

Clerk Worthington   In the first degree upon each indictment?

Foreman   In the first degree.

Clerk Worthington   Harken to your verdicts as the Court has recorded them. You, gentlemen, upon your oath, say that Nicola Sacco and Bartolomeo Vanzetti is each guilty of murder in the first degree upon each indictment. So say you, Mr Foreman? So, gentlemen, you all say?

Jury   We do, we do, we do.

Judge Thayer   I can add nothing to what I said this morning, gentlemen, except again to express to you the gratitude of the Commonweath for the service that you have rendered. You may now go to your homes, from which you have been absent for nearly seven weeks. The court will now adjourn.

Sacco   They kill an innocent men. They kill two innocent men . . . .

Chapter Five

Eels and the electric chair

'Common to every other day to me, I peddled fish,' said Vanzetti.
Now, with Sacco, he faced Death Row. The verdict, claimed the
defence, defied the evidence, and yet the jury (as at the Plymouth
trial) had no doubts. Nevertheless, the defence was not beaten.
They filed a motion for a new trial, citing a dozen discrepancies.
Under the law of the Commonwealth, this motion could only be
decided by the trial judge – Webster Thayer. For five months he
considered the matter in his chambers.

Meanwhile Nicola Sacco was largely confined to his cell, kept
strictly apart from other prisoners. Under state law a convicted
but unsentenced prisoner was not allowed to work in the prison
shop or mix with the others. Vanzetti was more fortunate:
convicted and sentenced for the Bridgewater hold-up, he was
allowed to work in the paint shop, making out licence plates for
cars registered in the state.

Even before the murder trial began, there had been doubts
outside the court. In an article in the *New Republic* on December
20, 1920 (the Dedham trial did not begin until the following May)
John Nicholas Bethell had written about the eel-seller and the
electric chair:

> Vanzetti is in a Massachusetts penitentiary, destined to stay
> there for fifteen years, unless something happens. That
> something may be a reversal of the conviction which put him
> aside – or it may be another conviction which will send him
> through a little green door into a wired chamber of death.

And now it *was* a second conviction.

A Sacco–Vanzetti Defense Committee was founded. At first its funds – 5,000 dollars in the first three months – came in hundreds of small donations from the Italian community. Then the liberal community in New England – especially women – began to join, and plays, concerts, shows and picnics were organized to raise more money. The Defense Committee produced articles, a bulletin and pamphlets (*Are They Doomed?*), and gradually the organized labour movement stirred and lent support. By the time Judge Thayer considered the motion for a new trial, some 60 or 70 trade unions were helping fund the Defense Committee, and the Sacco–Vanzetti case was a flashpoint in the class war.

Within the prisons, Sacco retired into himself. His daughter Ines was born. He grew moody with the well-wishing New England women. He expected nothing. Vanzetti, busy in the paint shop, was (said the Governor) 'a model prisoner'. He hurried back to his cell to write his letters, and soon built up a considerable circle of correspondents. His message was clear-cut, and rhetorically set within a great Italian tradition:

> I do not need to become a bandit. I like the teaching of Tolstoi, Saint Francesco and Dante. I like the example of Cincinatti and Garibaldi. The epicuream joi do not like me [sic]. A little roof, a field, a few books and food is all I want.

He began to take lessons in English from New England ladies. Sacco struggled with English too, and used one of his permitted letters to write to Vanzetti:

> Yes, Bartolo, I do study all the time with very care to get near always nearest to definite and perfection this beautiful English language, but woe is me! It is very hard for me to reach the definitely perfection and final pronounciation of Shakespeare language.

On Christmas Eve they were told that Judge Thayer had refused the motion.

In his written refusal, Judge Thayer pointed out that in addition to the verbal evidence, the jury had had the advantage of seeing the exhibits and studying the defendants. On the question of the bullets he noted that 'the jury had the fullest opportunity of comparing with the naked eye and magnifying glasses in the court and jury rooms, the various identifying marks on the fatal bullets.' And as with the disputed question of Sacco's cap, 'it is not for me to decide what the jurors did or did not see with their own eyes.' He analysed Sacco and Vanzetti's behaviour when arrested on the streetcar – 'why should he be afraid of being deported to Italy,' he asked, since 'he had in his pocket at the time of his arrest a passport for Italy upon which he of his own choice expected to sail two days following.' And 'why fear these two public officers when they had nothing to do with the enforcement of the deportation or espionage laws.' And why, he insisted, should one assume that the jury 'violated the sanctity of their oaths, threw to the four winds of bias and prejudice their honor, judgment, reason, and conscience, and thereby abused the solemn trust reposed in them by the law as well as by the Court. And all for what? To take away the lives of two human beings created by their own God.'

Finally, he pointed out that if there was any error in the trial ('nobody will welcome the correction more than I') then the Supreme Judicial Court will put all to right 'in due time'.

Vanzetti was bitter, and saw the timing of the refusal as another vindictive thrust – to 'lay down your decision on the eve of Christmas – just on the eve of Christmas, eve of Christmas. We do not believe in Christmas, neither in the historical way, nor in the church way. But you know, some of our folks still believe in that, and because we do not believe in that, it don't mean we are not human.'

At this point Katzmann was promoted, and no longer played a direct part in the case, though he was appointed assistant Attorney General so that he could give help and advice to the prosecution. Sacco and Vanzetti began to change their lawyers. Their counsel, Fred Moore, came from California with a reputation for defending radicals. The Massachusetts establishment had closed its ranks against him – more because of his abrasive style and Californian background than because of his legal speciality in radical cases. Then the Sacco–Vanzetti Defense Committee quarrelled with him. He formed a breakaway committee and Sacco in particular – bitter and depressed – was sucked into all the *minutiae* of their disputes. He several times told Moore to leave the case: 'So tell me please, why you waiting now for? Do you wait till I hang myself? That's what you wish?' But it was rather more than a year after Judge Thayer's refusal that Moore finally dropped out, and handed over entirely to William G. Thompson. The Sacco–Vanzetti Defense Committee paid Moore fees of $34,000 and expenses of $88,000. It gave Thompson a once-and-for-all fee of $25,000.

Meanwhile the defence filed its first supplementary – the Ripley motion. They claimed that Ripley, the foreman of the jury had brought some .38 shells into the jury room, tried them in Vanzetti's revolver, and discussed this unauthorized exhibit with other jurors. One juror recalled that they had discussed these shells, another remembered Ripley producing them but no discussion. The other ten recalled nothing. Then, while the defence was preparing its papers ready for an interview with Ripley, he suddenly died.

At a late stage, the defence tagged on to this motion a remark he was supposed to have made to his friend Daly. Several months after Ripley died, Daly told the defence that they had both walked to the court together for the original selection of the jury. They talked about the case, and Daly said he thought Sacco and Vanzetti were probably innocent. He claimed that Ripley replied, 'Damn them, they ought to hang them anyway.'

Judge Thayer pondered the new motion. Six months later, while he was still considering it, a second supplementary motion – the Gould motion – was placed on his desk.

The Defense Committee had the funds not only to meet the fees and costs of Moore and Thompson but also to mount quite elaborate investigations. One of these uncovered Roy Gould, a pedlar who had been in Pearl Street, near the railway crossing, when the gunmen made their escape. He claimed that one fired at him, and the bullet went through his overcoat. He was taken to see Sacco and Vanzetti by the defence, and said neither resembled the gunmen. The defence added to this motion a retraction from Lewis Pelser who had claimed that he opened a window an inch or two and saw the shooting. Now he said he was drunk and out of work when he first told his eye-witness story to Katzmann. However, a few days later, after an interview with Katzmann, Pelser retracted his retraction.

Another six weeks and the defence put in their third supplementary – the Goodridge motion. Goodridge was the eyewitness who claimed he came out of a pool room when the gunmen's car came by. He alleged Sacco was not only in the car, but took aim at him. At the trial Goodridge's disreputable record had been brought to the jury's attention. Fred Moore now pursued the point harder. He tracked Goodridge down, threatened him, and even got the police in August to arrest him for two days though no charge could be produced. But Goodridge would not be shaken, and the motion rested largely on details of his petty criminal record, the fact that his name wasn't Goodridge anyway but Erastus Corney Whitney, and an affidavit by his former wife who claimed he had always been violently anti-Italian ('all Italians coming over on the ships to America ought to be sunk in the harbors').

Seven weeks later the defence put in a fourth supplementary – the Andrews motion. Moore had visited Mrs Andrews, the witness who originally claimed to have seen Sacco under a car and asked him the way. He had pressed her hard on the witness stand, and his cross-examination only ended when she fainted. He now investigated her past life, and openly threatened a public revelation unless she formally retracted her evidence. He found her nineteen-year-old son and persuaded him to press his mother too. She retracted.

Katzmann heard of this and invited Mrs Andrews to a talk in the comfort of his office. She told him how she came to retract:

> 'They dipped the pen in the ink and tried to pass it into my hand. I refused again, and said "No, I can't sign it". All the time I was crying and asking them not to force me to sign it. My son then said "Mother, I want you to sign that paper, for it means a whole lot to me." I do not seem to remember much what happened after that, only that some one of the three men – I do not remember which one did it – put the pen in my hand and told me to sign it.'

Before she left Katzmann's office, she retracted the retraction.

1922 dragged into 1923. No decision came from Judge Thayer, and in April 1923 the defence filed their fifth supplementary – the Hamilton motion. Albert Hamilton was a criminologist with a keen interest in ballistics. Soon after the trial closed, he wrote to Judge Thayer saying he possessed techniques which could conclusively settle which bullets came from which guns. The Judge ignored the letter. But Hamilton carried on talking in the same vein. On a train journey he spilled out his assertions to a reporter. The reporter told Fred Moore, and Moore arranged for him to examine both shells and guns. He used a high-power microscope which could measure up to one hundred thousand parts of an inch. He photographed this enlargement, studied the exhibits and concluded that there was no connection between the bullets used at the shooting, and Sacco's revolver. He also claimed that Vanzetti's revolver still had its original hammer, and so could not possibly have been taken from the body of Berardelli. Some of his conclusions were supported in the motion by Professor Gill of the Massachusetts Institute of Technology.

Thereupon the prosecution produced other ballistic experts who, on much the same evidence, came to the opposite conclusion – the bullets did come from Sacco's revolver. The point about Vanzetti's revolver was passed over, and this prosecution evidence was forwarded to Judge Thayer.

The summer of 1923 passed and still no decision. In November the defence filed their sixth supplementary – the Proctor motion. Captain Proctor had always felt unhappy about his pre-arranged exchange with Katzmann before judge and jury, in which he had said that the fatal bullet was 'consistent with' having come from Sacco's gun. He now signed an affidavit for the defence, repeating what he had often said in private, that by 'consistent with' he merely meant that it *could* have come from Sacco's pistol, not that he had any evidence that it did so: it *could* have come from another Colt altogether. While this motion too rested upon the judge's desk, Captain Proctor died. It was not possible to delve further.

Meanwhile Vanzetti was still painting number plates, then hurrying off to use the last hours of light writing in his cell. He drafted and redrafted articles, manifestos, testimonies and appeals for the Defense Committee. But Nicola Sacco, under the technical regulations, remained an unsentenced prisoner – allowed out of his cell for an hour a day, and forbidden to mix or work with other prisoners. He grew increasingly depressed, and then went on hunger strike. After 31 days he ended it when the prison authorities decided on forcible feeding. Instead they transferred him to Bridgewater State Hospital for the Criminally Insane. He remained there six months before being brought back to his cell at Dedham jail.

On October 1, 1924 Judge Thayer issued his decision. He turned down all six motions.

A mad world my masters

Vanzetti began to have hallucinations. He had violent stomach pains too and was examined for ulcers. None were found. He was taken out of the work shop and put in the prison hospital. He got no better, and the prison authorities transferred him also to the Bridgewater State Hospital for the Criminally Insane. He spent five months there:

> I have already experienced that in the name of 'Psycho-therapy' may be committed the same, if not more cruelty, injustice and partiality, as in the name of the law . . . . the 'curing' upon the 'punishing' may become, by environment and men's vices, a bloody insult to misfortune and truth.

His contacts with psychologists and doctors were all the same:

> They believe my principles to be aberration and insanity; they believe my friends (I mean the comrades and Italians) arch-criminals; they believe (and told me so) that the Americans in our behalf are fools and cheaters. But, what is worse, they asked me if I believed in God, in the golden rule; if the murderers shall not be punished. If they do not nail me, I will answer.

He was allowed books, and began to translate Proudhon's *The Peace and the War*. He built up, and worked carefully over, a tiny library – Dante's *Divine Comedy*, Marcus Aurelius' *Meditations*, Emerson's *Essays*, and Thoreau's *Friendship*.

Suddenly he was transferred back to Charleston prison and work in the paint shop. Despite protests his books and tiny collection of mementoes given by supporters did not follow him. It was never clear what happened to them, but to Vanzetti it was all part of a slow execution: '¼ of our execution is already a fact – an irreparable fact.'

The defence had now exhausted all possible supplementary motions, and concentrated instead on preparing its papers for an appeal to the Supreme Court of Massachusetts.

Over in Dedham jail, Sacco discovered that Carbone, the prisoner in the next cell, was a Federal Agent, placed next to him to pick up any leads about Red plots and bombings. There were plans for another Federal Agent to take lodgings with Rosina Sacco.

In the cell on the other side of Carbone was Celestino Madeiros, a young epileptic from the Azores, convicted of murder and bank robbery. He observed the comings and goings at Sacco's cell, particularly the visits of Mrs Sacco. Then he began to send roundabout messages. One told Sacco to get friends to visit 'Thomas' in Oak Street, Randolph. Then, through a prison trusty he passed on a yellow slip of paper, with a rudimentary map of Randolph. The house where 'Thomas' lived was marked with a cross. Sacco decided this was some new Federal scheme, and tore up the plan. Madeiros persisted. While emptying slops, or exercising under Sacco's windows he hissed, 'Nick, I know who did the South Braintree job.' Sacco at first ignored the messages, but as they continued he reported them to Mr Crocker, the night officer. Crocker ignored the report. On November 16, Madeiros tried to smuggle a note out of prison addressed to the Editor of the *Boston American*:

Dear Editor
I hereby confess to being in the shoe company crime at
South Braintree on April 15, 1920, and that Sacco and
Vanzetti was not there.
                                        Celestino F. Madeiros.

The note was intercepted by Deputy Sheriff Curtis, who ignored it.

Madeiros then wrote a near-identical note, and slipped it to Miller, the trusty. Miller hid the note between the pages of a magazine, and then passed it to Sacco. A few minutes later he came by Sacco's cell again 'and he was standing leaning against the wall trembling, with the paper in his hands sent to him by Madeiros, and tears in his eyes. He asked me, "What is this?"'

Sacco sent the note to his new defence counsel, William Thompson, and next day Thompson interviewed Madeiros in Sacco's presence.

Madeiros began his story: 'On April 15, 1920 I was picked up at about 4 a.m. at my boarding house, 181 North Maine Street, Providence, by four Italians . . . .'

He told how he had met the Italians in a pool room. They were 'professionals' and needed an extra man to give armed cover from the back of the car while they did 'a job'. He described the crime, but not in much detail since he had been lodged in the rear seats, was taken by surprise and pretty scared at the killings. He said he only knew the professionals by names like 'Mike' and 'Bill'. They had double-crossed him over the share-out, and he got nothing from it all. He would add little to all this.

Thompson made an odd decision. He called in Herbert Ehrmann, a lawyer specializing in business cases, and asked him to investigate the Madeiros story. Ehrmann decided that the confession was 'too good to be true', probably motivated by a desire to be in the spotlight – or maybe Madeiros hoped in some bizarre way that by confessing to this murder, as well as the one he was already sentenced for, he might escape the electric chair.

But he decided to drive out and track the story. He began at the Bluebird Inn in Providence where Madeiros had been a 'bouncer'. The proprietor's wife laughed in his face: 'Fred couldn't have been on it. I believe he was in Mexico at the time.' She described his Mexican spree: 'It lasted for nearly two years. His friend was a circus girl.'

'Did he tell you how much money he had when he started?'

'Yes – he said he took twenty-eight hundred dollars with him.'

A quick calculation showed that $2,800 was slightly more than one-sixth of the Braintree payroll. More questions revealed that her memory for dates was shaky, and the Mexican spree probably came *after* the Braintree killings.

While Ehrmann was at work, Madeiros's lawyers were also busy appealing to the Supreme Court against his conviction on a number of technical points. On March 31 the Supreme Court granted Madeiros a new trial. On May 12 it rejected the appeal by Sacco and Vanzetti. On May 20 Madeiros was found guilty once more.

On May 26 the defence filed their seventh supplementary – the Madeiros motion. Ehrmann had uncovered a remarkable chain of coincidences. He discovered that in New England in 1920 there was a notorious mob known as the Morelli gang – led by Joe Morelli, and including his brothers Fred and Frank. At the time of the shooting they were out on bail, waiting trial for a rail robbery – largely of shoe shipments from South Braintree. They badly needed funds for their defence next month. A few days before the killings, local police had grown suspicious of the Morellis – especially Mike Morelli who was driving a Buick which appeared to carry different number plates at different times. The Buick was never seen after the murder day. A few days after the killings, Sergeant Jacobs of the New Bedford police walked over to the Morelli gang at Joe Fiore's restaurant at the corner of Purchase Street. There was a tense moment when one of the Italians went for his gun, and Jacobs was frightened. Frank Morelli broke the tension – 'What's the matter, Jake? What do you want with me? Why are you picking on me all the time?' – and Jacobs was glad to get out, badly scared. 'I can never forget that man's face.'

Piecing together tantalizing fragments of evidence, Ehrmann decided he had identified the gang and could name all six – five in the car, and one on guard in the Randolph woods ready to switch vehicles in the getaway. In the back seat of the car he placed Madeiros, who saw little of what happened. Mike Morelli, the owner of the Buick, was probably posted in the wood. Frank and Joe Morelli were in the car. Steve the Pole was the driver, whom several witnesses had noticed, and an unguarded remark of Joe Morelli's led him to Tony Mancini – possibly the man who drove bullets into the dying Berardelli under fifty frightened pairs of eyes. Mancini was serving a life sentence at Auburn penitentiary for the cold-blooded shooting of a fellow gangster in a crowded street outside New York City Police Headquarters. Records noted that the gun he used was a foreign make called Star. Ehrmann recalled that the defence ballistics expert had said that five of the bullets could have come from an Austrian gun, a Steyr. Possibly this was a mis-entry, but a check on the original weapon would settle it.

Ehrmann felt he had almost brought the complete crime into focus. The Morelli gang had the motive for the crime, it was in their territory and parts of it similar to previous raids they had carried out, they were convicted criminals and gunmen, and shortly after the crime they had plenty of money. It was nearly a perfect fit – especially when several of the eye-witnesses mistook photos of Joe Morelli for photos of Nicola Sacco.

But the missing pieces would not fall into place. The New York police had lost Mancini's gun. More predictably, Joe Morelli, now serving time at Leavenworth penitentiary, denied every-thing – he had hopes of parole, and was soon successful. Mancini yielded nothing: 'Sacco and Vanzetti – they're radicals, not stick-up men,' he said. 'I'm sorry I can't do something in this case – I would if I could. But there isn't anything I know. I hope they won't electrocute Sacco and Vanzetti. Killing them won't bring the dead to life.' Steve the Pole was traced to Canada, but a few months earlier his bullet-riddled body had been dumped on his sister's doorstep. The Morelli brothers stuck together, and Madeiros flatly refused, in interrogation after interrogation, to say more – maintaining that he had done enough.

Ehrmann approached the opposing lawyers – they had all been in the same class at Harvard and moved in the same social and legal circles. He suggested that the Morelli hypothesis was at least as likely as the Sacco–Vanzetti one, and that – to avoid further conflict – defence and prosecution should jointly inter-view everyone connected with the Morelli gang, and work from there.

His proposal was politely rejected. The prosecution prepared counter-evidence, picking holes in the Morelli hypothesis, obtaining signed denials from Joe Morelli and Tony Mancini, and concentrating on weaknesses in the Madeiros confession such as his failure to account convincingly enough for the getaway route and the time it took.

Both sides placed their evidence before Judge Thayer. After nearly four months' consideration he gave his assessment. He rejected the Madeiros confession in its entirety. 'Madeiros is, without doubt, a crook, a thief, a robber, a liar, a rum-runner, a "bouncer" in a house of ill-fame, a smuggler, and a man who has been convicted and sentenced to death.' In Judge Thayer's view the story was too insubstantial, and originally arose because Madeiros had read the published accounts of the Sacco–Vanzetti Defense Committee. 'Was Madeiros given to understand that he would receive the same aid if he had the power of this organiz-ation behind him?'

But there was another side to the defence submission, over-shadowed by the drama of Madeiros's confession and Ehrmann's detection of the Morelli gang. In 1922 Fred Moore, with his much more political approach to the case, had started a line of enquiry into how far agents of the Department of Justice had helped Katzmann mount his case. It was known that the Department had files on the case, its agents were present in court, had been infiltrated into jail and even on to the Sacco–Vanzetti Defense Committee. But there was nothing for the defence to clutch at until Thompson obtained sworn statements from two ex-agents, Lawrence Letherman and Fred Weyand. Both confirmed that the Department were watching Sacco and Vanzetti, were anxious to deport them 'because they did not believe in organized government or in private property', but that they 'could not be deported as anarchists unless it could be shown that they were believers in anarchy, which is always a difficult thing to show. It usually can only be shown by self-incrimination.' The agents had therefore armed Katzmann with details of their radical background, hoping that he would use it in cross-examination ostensibly to convince the jury that they were gunmen hiding under cover of radicalism. Either the jury would accept this, or Sacco and Vanzetti in their own defence would persuade them that they were dangerous radicals – and even if the prosecution failed, the transcript of this section would be enough to pin a deportation order on them. Whichever way they took, Sacco and Vanzetti were caught – either hustled on the boat to Europe, or sunk away in prison, or despatched to the electric chair. Not that any of the Federal Agents, believed them guilty of the South Braintree murders. 'It was the general opinion of the Boston agents of the Department of Justice having knowledge of the affair that the South Braintree crime was committed by a gang of professional highwaymen.'

The Attorney General refused to open up the files to the defence. William Thompson argued the case passionately on old liberal grounds before Judge Thayer:

'This case started with a background of persecutions, intolerance, and unwillingness to give men a chance to believe in their minds what they wanted to, an impatience with men who did not believe in the Great American prosperity and American ideals and standards, and in notions of common law and the protection of private property, which you and I, sir, know lie at the very foundation of civilization.

'But if men are to be treated in this way for being mistaken, for being violently mistaken, for even being willing to use force – if you are going to treat them this way instead of having a few dozen Reds in one place or another, a mere bubble on the surface of this great stream of nationality, you will have Reds multiplied by thousands . . . .'

Judge Thayer listened impassively. He made a few jokes. He considered this part of the submission too. He rejected it.

'Since the trial before the Jury of these cases, a new type of disease would seem to have developed. It might be called "lego-psychic neurosis" or "hysteria" which means: "a belief in the existence of something which in fact and truth has no such existence".

'This disease would seem to have reached a very dangerous condition from the argument of counsel, upon the present Motion, when he charges Mr Sargent, Attorney-General of the United States and his subordinates, and subordinates of former Attorney-General of the United States, Mr Palmer and Mr Katzmann and the District Attorney of Norfolk County, with being in a conspiracy to send these two defendants to the electric chair, not because they are murderers but because they are radicals.'

Until this last decision, the press had by and large backed up the courts. Only one Massachusetts newspaper, the *Springfield Republican*, took a different line, arguing that 'a dog ought not to be shot on the weight of evidence brought out in the Dedham trial'. But three days after the decision, the *Boston Herald* changed its mind and published an editorial:

We submit:
We do not know whether these men are guilty or not. We have no sympathy with the half-baked views which they profess. But as months have merged into years and the great debate over this case has continued, our doubts have solidified slowly into convictions, and reluctantly we have found ourselves compelled to reverse our original judgment.

We hope the supreme judicial court will grant a new trial on the basis of new evidence not yet examined in open court.

Until now, the voice for Sacco and Vanzetti had been the Defense Committee – an alliance of liberal and wealthy New England women with a group of Italian workmen who were all philosophic anarchists, all subscribers to Proudhon's cry for 'Liberty of conscience, freedom of the press, freedom of labour, of commerce and of teaching, the free disposal of the products of labour and industry – liberty, infinite, absolute, everywhere and forever.'

Now the ripples moved outwards. The liberal women infected their menfolk. The editorial from the *Boston Herald* did not free Sacco or Vanzetti, but it was awarded the Pulitzer Prize. It was followed by letters to the press from Harvard professors, of established lineage, suggesting that 'the government had not proved its case and probably Sacco and Vanzetti had not committed the murder charged'.

Meanwhile the Communist Party began to show belated but efficient interest. At first the Communist press was highly critical of the Defense Committee, infected by the 'slow poison of middle class treachery'. The accused did not need blue-blooded Boston lawyers, but the 'mass movement of labor that could surround Sacco and Vanzetti with a wall of iron'. The Communist Party began to organize that wall – resolutions, demonstrations, outbreaks of violence in a dozen different countries: 'Sacco and Vanzetti were being legally assassinated because of their political and economic views and activities.'

The house of Samuel Johnson in West Bridgewater was blown up by a bomb. Everyone believed this was a mistake – the bomb was meant for his brother, Simon, who had collected a reward for his critical evidence of Sacco and Vanzetti's behaviour when they called to see about Mike Boda's car on that spring night now lost six years back in time.

But as the world began to attend to the case, and yet another Christmas came round, the prisoners' New Year message to their supporters was piercingly unhopeful: 'We are convinced that our murderers are determined to burn us within this, 1927, and that it is most probable that they will succeed.'

Sacco withdrew more deeply into himself, and was for wasting no more energies on legal processes. But Vanzetti was even more active, corresponding with his New England ladies, reading Emerson ('so exquisitely anarchist'), and with unforced vitality discovering paradisal memories of Italy:

> And the singing birds there: black merles of the golden beak, and ever more golden throat; the golden orioles, and the chaffinches; the unmatchable nightingales, the nightingales over-all. Yet, I think that the wonder of the garden's wonders is the banks of its paths. Hundreds of grass leaves of wild flowers witness there the almighty genius of the universal architect – reflecting the sky, the sun, the moon, the stars, all of its lights and colors. The forget-me-nots are nations there, and nations are the wild daisies. The blue, scented violets thrive well, the capel Venere are luxurious, the prim-times are at the vanguard. And the blue-blossoms erect themselves soberly dark blue toward the light blue sky, like breasts, turgid mother's breasts. And the white and red clover and all the other scented, sky bestowed and beloved wild flowers of which I do not know the names.
>
> You ought to see the king wasps, big velvety, lucid ravishing forcefully on these flowers' calices, and the virtuous honey-bees – the wasp, the white, the yellow, the forget-me-nots, the hedge's butterflies and the variated armies of several genuses of grass eaters, the red concon- cinas, the meadows gri-gri. Each of your step would arise from the ground a rainbow cloud of these creatures, with a multiphoned vibration of wings. Well, I have told you something about my native place.

The defence appealed to the Supreme Court challenging Judge Thayer's denial of the Madeiros case. The appeal could, in law, only be based on technical points of procedure – not on a review of the whole case. On April 5 the Supreme Court came out in support of Judge Thayer. Every legal escape hatch was closed.

There was a general feeling in Massachusetts that it was time to make an end. A prominent citizen remarked he would now 'rejoice in the electrocutions whether the accused are innocent or guilty'. There had been letters from, amongst others, the British Labour Party, signed by James Maxton, Ellen Wilkinson and George Lansbury. But as G. B. Shaw told Upton Sinclair:

'Americans must decide for themselves.' He felt that 'the moment a foreigner interferes, to yield to him would be an unbearable humiliation: perish a thousand Saccos first.'

At 10 a.m. on April 29, 1927 the Superior Criminal Court, under Judge Thayer, met to pass sentence:

Mr Wilbar   It appears by the record of this Court, if
    your Honor please, that on indictment No. 5545,
    Commonwealth vs Nicola Sacco and Bartolomeo Vanzetti
    that these defendants stand convicted of murder in the
    first degree. The records are clear at the present time, and
    I therefore move the Court for the imposition of sen-
    tence . . . .
Clerk Worthington   Nicola Sacco, have you anything to say
    why sentence of death should not be passed upon you?
Statement by Nicola Sacco
    Yes, sir, I am not an orator. It is not very familiar with me
the English language, and as I know, as my friend has told
me, my comrade Vanzetti will speak more long, so I thought
to give him the chance.

    I never know, never heard, even read in history anything
so cruel as this Court. After seven years prosecuting they
still consider us guilty. And these gentle people here are
arrayed with us in this court today.

    I know the sentence will be between two class, the
oppressed class and the rich class, and there will be always
collision between one and the other. We fraternize the
people with the books, with the literature. You persecute the
people, tyrannize over them, and kill them. We try the
education of people always. You try to put a path between
us and some other nationality that hates each other. That is
why I am here today on this bench, for having been the
oppressed class. Well, you are the oppressor.

    You know it, Judge – you know all my life, you know why
I have been here, and after seven years that you have been
persecuting me and my poor wife, and you will today
sentence us to death. I would like to tell all my life, but what
is the use? You know all about what I say before, and my
friend – that is, my comrade – will be talking, because he is
more familiar with the language, and I will give him a

chance. My comrade, the man kind, the kind man to all the children, you sentence him two times, in the Bridgewater case and the Dedham case, connected with me, and you know he is innocent. You forget all the population that has been with us for seven years, to sympathize and give us all their energy and all their kindness. You do not care for them. Among that peoples and the comrades and the working class there is a big legion of intellectual people which have been with us for seven years, but to not commit the iniquitous sentence, but still the Court goes ahead. And I think I thank you all, you peoples, my comrades who have been with me for seven years, with the Sacco–Vanzetti case, and I will give my friend a chance.

I forgot one thing which my comrade remember me. As I said before, Judge Thayer know all my life, and he know that I am never been guilty, never, – not yesterday or today nor forever.

Clerk Worthington   Bartolomeo Vanzetti, have you anything to say why sentence of death should not be passed upon you?

Statement by Bartolomeo Vanzetti

Yes. What I say is that I am innocent, not only of the Braintree crime, but also of the Bridgewater crime. That I am not only innocent of these two crimes, but in all my life I have never stole and I have never killed and I have never spilled blood. That is what I want to say. And it is not all. Not only am I innocent of these two crimes, not only in all my life I have never stole, never killed, never spilled blood, but I have struggled all my life, since I began to reason, to eliminate crime from the earth.

Everybody that knows these two arms knows very well that I did not need to go in between the street and kill a man to take the money. I can live with my two arms and live well. But besides that, I can live even without work with my arm for other people. I have had plenty of chance to live independently and to live what the world conceives to be a higher life than not to gain our bread with the sweat of our brow.

My father in Italy is in a good condition. I could have come back in Italy and he would have welcomed me every

time with open arms. Even if I come back there without not
a cent in my pocket, my father could have give me a
possession, not to work but to make business, or to oversee
upon the land that he owns. He was wrote me many letters
in that sense, and other well to do relatives have wrote me
many letters in that sense that I can produce . . . .

Well, I want to reach a little point farther, and it is this –
that not only have I not been trying to steal in Bridgewater,
not only have I not been in Braintree to steal and kill and
have never steal or kill or spilt blood in all my life, not only
have I struggled hard against crimes, but I have refused
myself the commodity or glory of life, the pride of life of a
good position, because in my consideration it is not right to
exploit man. I have refused to go in business because I
understand that business is a speculation on profit upon
certain people that must depend upon the business man,
and I do not consider that that is right and therefore I refuse
to do that.

Now I should say that I am not only innocent of all these
things, not only have I never committed a real crime in my
life – though some sins but not crimes – not only have I
struggled all my life to eliminate crimes, the crimes that the
official law and the official moral condemns, but also the
crime that the official moral and the official law sanctions
and sanctifies – the exploitation and the oppression of the
man by the man, and if there is a reason why I am here as a
guilty man, if there is a reason why you in a few minutes
can doom me, it is this reason and none else.

You see it is seven years that we are in jail. What we have
suffered during these seven years no human tongue can say,
and yet you see me before you, not trembling, you see me
looking you in your eyes straight, not blushing, nor changing
colour, not ashamed or in fear.

Eugene Debs say that not even a dog – something like that
– not even a dog that kill the chickens would have been
found guilty by American jury with the evidence that the
Commonwealth have produced against us. I say that not
even a leprous dog would have his appeal refused two times
by the Supreme Court of Massachusetts – not even a leprous
dog.

They have given a new trial to Madeiros for the reason that the Judge had either forgot or omitted to tell the jury that they should consider the man innocent until found guilty in the court, or something of that sort. That man has confessed, and the court give him another trial. We have proved that there could not have been another Judge on the face of the earth more prejudiced and more cruel than you have been against us. We have proven that. Still they refuse the new trial. We know, and you know in your heart, that you have been against us from the very beginning, before you see us. Before you see us you already know that we were radicals, that we were underdogs, that we were the enemy of the institution that you can believe in good faith in their goodness – I don't want to condemn that – and that it was easy on the time of the first trial to get a verdict of guiltiness.

We know that you have spoke yourself and have spoke your hostility against us, and your despisement against us with friends of yours on the train, at the University Club of Boston, on the Golf Club of Worcester, Massachusetts. I am sure that if the people who know all what you say against us would have the civil courage to take the stand, maybe your Honor – I am sorry to say this because you are an old man, and I have an old father – but maybe you would be beside us in good justice at this time.

This is what I say: I would not wish to a dog or to a snake, to the most low and misfortunate creature of the earth – I would not wish to any of them what I have had to suffer for things that I am not guilty of. I am suffering because I am a radical and indeed I am a radical; I have suffered because I was an Italian, and indeed I am an Italian; I have suffered more for my family and for my beloved than for myself; but I am so convinced to be right that if you could execute me two times, and if I could be reborn two other times, I would live again to do what I have done already.

I have finished. Thank you.

Judge Webster Thayer Under the law of Massachusetts the jury says whether a defendant is guilty or innocent. The Court has absolutely nothing to do with that question. The law of Massachusetts provides that a Judge cannot deal in any way with the facts. As far as he can go under our law is to state the evidence.

During the trial many exceptions were taken. Those exceptions were taken to the Supreme Judicial Court. That Court, after examining the entire record, after examining all the exceptions – that Court in its final words said 'The , verdicts of the jury should stand; exceptions overruled.' That being true, there is only one thing that this Court can do. It is not a matter of discretion. It is a matter of statutory requirement, and that being true there is only one duty that now devolves upon this Court, and that is to pronounce the sentences.

First, the court pronounces sentence upon Nicola Sacco. It is considered and ordered by the Court that you, Nicola Sacco, suffer the punishment of death by the passage of a current of electricity through your body within the week beginning on Sunday, the tenth day of July, in the year of Our Lord, one thousand, nine hundred and twenty-seven. This is the sentence of the law.

It is considered and ordered by the Court that you, Bartolomeo Vanzetti . . . .

Vanzetti   Wait a minute, please, your Honor. May I ·
    speak for a minute with my lawyer, Mr Thompson?
Thompson   I do not know what he wants to say.
Judge Thayer   I think I should pronounce the sentence.
    Bartolomeo Vanzetti, suffer the punishment of death . . .
Sacco   You know I am innocent. That is the same
    words I pronounced seven years ago. You condemn two
    innocent men.
Judge Thayer   . . . by the passage of a current of electricity
    through your body within the week beginning on Sunday,
    the tenth day of July, in the year of Our Lord, one
    thousand nine hundred and twenty-seven. This is the
    sentence of the law.
    We will now take a recess.

The next day *Pravda* reported that Sacco and Vanzetti were held in 'a specially constructed padded room having a mirrored ceiling on which appeared at intervals a spot which gradually took the form of a terrifying open-jawed creature. Meanwhile, a human voice shouted: "Tell the names of your accomplices!"'

But Vanzetti was in his cell worrying that he had not addressed the court in praise of Sacco. 'I would have given half my blood to be allowed to speak again.' The next day he handed to friends the note he had composed.

> I have talked a great deal of myself but I even forgot to name Sacco. Sacco too is a worker from his boyhood, a skilled worker lover of work, with a good job and pay, a bank account, a good and lovely wife, two beautiful children and a neat little home at the verge of a wood, near a brook. Sacco is a heart, a faith, a character, a man; a man lover of nature, and of mankind. A man who gave all, who sacrifice all to the cause of Liberty and to his love for mankind; money, rest, mundain ambitions, his own wife, his children, himself and his own life. Sacco has never dreamt to steal, never to assassinate. He and I have never brought a morsel of bread to our mouths, from our childhood to today – which has not been gained by the sweat of our brows. Never. His people also are in good position and of good reputation.
> Oh yes, I may be more witfull, as some have put it, I am a better babbler than he is, but many, many times in hearing his heartful voice ringing a faith sublime, in considering his supreme sacrifice, remembering his heroism I felt small at the presence of his greatness and found myself compelled to fight back from my eyes the tears, and quanch my heart trobling to my throat to not weep before him – this man called thief and assasin and doomed. But Sacco's name will live in the hearts of the people and in their gratitude when Katmann's and yours bones will be dispersed by time, when your name, his name, your laws, institutions, and your false god are but a *deem rememoring of a cursed past in which man was wolf to the man.*

Chapter Six

In Death Row

Outside prison, the world was quivering with the names of Sacco and Vanzetti. At first their support had come overwhelmingly from Italian migrants. Then came the groups of wealthy, liberal New England women who circled around Vanzetti. In 1926 their menfolk began to break ranks and declare their sympathies. The Communist Party belatedly tried to take over the Defense Committee, failed, and then attacked it for 'trying to represent the martyrdom of Sacco and Vanzetti as an "unfortunate" error which can be rectified by the "right" people proceeding in the "right" way.' It organized worldwide fund raising of which $6,000 eventually reached the Committee, though critics claimed many 'millions' were actually collected by Red Aid. Possibly these millions, if they existed, went on promoting the demonstrations now held in a dozen different countries, putting the American government under increasing pressure.

But at home the American unions, though passing sympathetic resolutions, were not astir. A planned demonstration by 100,000 workers brought out less than 200. And the press gave bigger headlines to Lindbergh's plan to fly the Atlantic, to the coming fight between Jack Dempsey and Gene Tunney, and the murder of a suburban husband by his wife and her corset-salesman lover.

There were protests from Albert Einstein, Thomas Mann, John Galsworthy and Fritz Kreisler. In a strange flashback, Albert Dreyfus emerged from oblivion and offered to plead. But in the poor white districts of Boston, the Reverend Billy Sunday sent his message from the pulpit: 'Give 'em the juice. Burn them, if they're guilty. That's the way to handle it. I'm tired of hearing these foreigners, these radicals, coming over here and telling us what we should do.'

Nevertheless, the Governor, Alvan T. Fuller, had to act. Pressure was building up on United States ambassadors through-out the world. Petitions were piling up at his own office. The legal profession had broken out into pamphlet warfare on the case, and the Bishop of Massachusetts was pressing him 'to call to your aid several citizens of well known character, experience, ability, and sense of justice to make a study of the trial and advise you'.

Governor Fuller was decisive, energetic, firm in his beliefs. He published a piece in *Success* magazine called 'Why I Believe in Capital Punishment'. Next month he refused three Irishmen's plea for clemency, and left for Europe on 'a second honeymoon trip'.

Sacco and Vanzetti read the article: 'And we understood.'

On January 5, I learned that the three men will be killed immediately after midnight. Because the participants and witnesses of the execution use to eat after it, at the warden's house, three hams had been cooked in our kitchen, and they were carried to the warden's house on January 5. So we knew. I wished and tried to keep awake that night to attend to the execution from my cell. But, I fell asleep against my will, and at my awakening I was told of the triple murder. Three pair of eyes for one pair, three lives for one life. Massachusetts, Fuller that preaches to the children, the golden rule and the Sermon on the Mount, practiced a pre-Mosaic custom.

Nevertheless friends pressed them to petition the Governor for clemency. Sacco refused to sign. 'These seven years have told their take on him,' noted Vanzetti. Yet 'in a way, Nick is right, there are all the reasons for mistrust, pessimism, and scorn for further appeals after so many vain ones.'

Governor Fuller read Vanzetti's petition and threw himself into re-reading the evidence and interviewing people. Working fourteen hours a day on the case, he twice interviewed Vanzetti, and spent considerable energy on the Italians who were his alibi – especially the boy, Beltrando Brini, who claimed to have been eel-selling with Vanzetti on Christmas Eve 1919 when the Bridge-water hold-up took place. Vanzetti sent him a long, hopeful summary of his defence.

On June 1 the Governor stilled pressure by setting up an Advisory Committee to make a rapid review of the case. He appointed President Lowell of Harvard, President Stratton of the Massachusetts Institute of technology, and Judge Grant. There was some unease by the Defense Committee at whether the eyes and judgment of the American establishment would be very different from those of Judge Thayer or Governor Fuller; and some play was made of the fact that it was President Lowell who had fixed the quota plan for Polish Jews at Harvard.

Nevertheless a slightly new case was put to the Committee by the defence. First, they tackled the question of Sacco's cap, allegedly found near the shooting, and partly identified as his by a small tear in the lining where he hung it every day on a nail at work.

The police chief at Brockton now admitted that the cap had not been handed in until the Saturday following the killings. He had put it under his car seat and forgotten it for a fortnight. When he did remember it, he had picked it up and made the tear himself – to see if there were any identifying marks in the lining. He had not been asked to give evidence at the trial.

Second, they argued that Judge Thayer had revealed his prejudice against radicals by several unguarded remarks out-side the courtroom. Professor James Richardson, who held the chair of law at Dartmouth College, claimed that he joined Judge Thayer's party at a football match at Hanover in November 1924. 'He has known me a long time. He immediately went into the subject of the Sacco–Vanzetti case.' 'Judge Thayer said, as near as I can remember "Did you see what I did with those anarchistic bastards the other day? I guess that will hold them for a while."'

'I wanted to go away from the scene as fast as I could,' said Richardson, 'and did so as fast as I could without absolutely turning my back on the judge.' Professor Richardson had now forwarded this memory to Governor Fuller, and there had been a move by his colleagues to dismiss him from Dartmouth.

Frank Sibley, the senior reporter covering the trial, reported that the judge spoke contemptuously of Fred Moore, the defending counsel, as 'a long-haired anarchist from California'; and generally made his presence felt among the pressmen, warning them of unfavourable reports. 'I avoided walks or talks with him.'

George Crocker, formerly the City Treasurer of Boston, recalled Judge Thayer pinning him down at breakfast in the University Club, and going on about 'the duty of protecting the court against anarchism lay upon him' and 'we must stand together to protect ourselves against anarchists, reds.' 'In fact I spoke to the head waiter or steward at the Club: "For heaven's sake, don't put me with that man."'

Robert Benchley, the dramatic editor of *Life,* appeared before the Committee and told of driving out to pick up his friend Loring Coes at Worcester Golf Club in 1921. Coes came bouncing down the steps. 'He was very enthusiastic. He was talking with Web Thayer. He said "Web has been telling me about these people down in Boston, the Reds".' 'He said Web Thayer was quite proud of his stand in this matter and the stand he was going to take in upholding the best traditions of the bar and that he would get these guys sooner or later.'

Mr Coes refused to confirm this, and had broken off with Robert Benchley: 'He thought I had violated the country club code of etiquette.'

The defence also pointed to the unusual number of guards around the courthouse and the fact that one of the jurymen pointedly saluted the American flag behind the judge every morning, and cited similar details to claim that the atmosphere, if not the transcript, betrayed that it was the radicalism of the accused that was on trial.

The Committee interviewed Judge Thayer in private, and the eleven remaining jurymen. This session too was *in camera* and unrecorded. But twenty-three years later the *Standard-Times* of New Bedford, Massachusetts, traced the seven surviving members of the jury. All thought it was a fair trial, that it was a murder trial not a political one, that Sacco and Vanzetti were guilty, and that Judge Thayer (whatever his private opinions) conducted it with scrupulous fairness. They had spoken similarly to the Advisory Committee.

Juryman John Ganley said: 'I was impressed by one aspect of the trial especially. That was that Judge Thayer was absolutely fearless and absolutely on the level. He was trying to do his job thoroughly and not leaning either way.'

Juryman King, a shoeworker like Nicola Sacco, said: 'Anybody who says Sacco and Vanzetti were convicted because they were radicals and not on the evidence is all wet. Propaganda about their being radicals and framed on the charges did not reach me before the trial. I was just a man in the street, minding my own business.'

Juryman Frank Marden expressed their main feeling: 'The outstanding fairness of Judge Thayer. He was fair to the other side too, fair all round. I never have had a bit of reason to think the trial was anything but fair. I don't think we jurors thought of the defendants in any way except as two persons accused of murder.'

Whilst the Committee deliberated, Vanzetti read *The Rise of American Civilization* until lights out at 9 p.m.: 'then I sit on the end of my bed, place a pillow against the wall, a blanket on my shoulder, and in the corner of my room beside the window, I enjoy that history in the light of one lamp, managing to avoid the window's bars shadows.'

Sacco wrote to Ines, his six-year-old daughter, whom he had never seen and whom he decided never to see whilst in prison:

My dear Ines:
I would like that you should understand what I am going to say to you, and I wish I could write you so plain, for I long so much to have you hear all the heart-beat eagerness of your father, for I love you so much as you are the dearest little beloved one.

It is quite hard indeed to make you understand in your young age, but I am going to try from the bottom of my heart to make you understand how dear you are to your father's soul. If I cannot succeed in doing that, I know that you will save this letter and read it over in future years to come and you will see and feel the same heart-beat affection as your father feels in writing it to you.

I will bring with me your little and so dearest letter and carry it right under my heart to the last day of my life. When I die, it will be buried with your father who loves you so much, as I do also your brother Dante and holy dear mother.

You don't know, Ines, how dear and great your letter was to your father. It is the most golden present that you could have given to me or that I could have wished for in these sad days.

It was the greatest treasure and sweetness in my struggling life that I could have lived with you and your brother Dante and your mother in a neat little farm, and learn all your sincere words and tender affection. Then in the summertime to be sitting with you in the home nest under the oak tree shade – beginning to teach you of life and how to read and write, to see you running, laughing, crying and singing through the verdent fields picking the wild flowers here and there from one tree to another, and from the clear vivid stream to your mother's embrace.

The same I have wished to see for other poor girls, and their brothers, happy with their mother and father as I dreamed for us – but it was not so and the nightmare of the lower classes saddened very badly your father's soul.

For the things of beauty and of good in this life, mother nature gave to us all, for the conquest and the joy of liberty. The men of this dying old society, they brutally have pulled me away from the embrace of your brother and your poor mother. But, in spite of all, the free spirit of your father's faith still survives, and I have lived for it and for the dream that some day I would have come back to life, to the embrace of your dear mother, among our friends and comrades again, but woe is me!

I know that you are good and surely you love your mother, Dante and all the beloved ones – and I am sure that you love me also a little, for I love you much and then so much. You do not know Ines, how often I think of you every day. You are in my heart, in my vision, in every angle of this sad walled cell, in the sky and everywhere my gaze rests.

Meantime, give my best paternal greetings to all the friends and comrades, and doubly so to our beloved ones. Love and kisses to your brother and mother.
With the most affectionate kiss and ineffable caress from him who loves you so much that he constantly thinks of you.
Best warm greetings from Bartolo to you all.
Your Father

On August 3 Governor Fuller issued a statement saying there was no case for a new trial, and that Sacco and Vanzetti should die on August 10. In cool, measured prose, reassuring middle opinion, he gave his verdict:

> This task of review has been a laborious one and I am proud to be associated in this public service with clear-eyed witnesses, unafraid to tell the truth, and with jurors who discharged their obligations in accordance with their convictions and oaths.
>
> As a result of my investigation, I find no sufficient justification for executive intervention.
>
> I believe, with the jury, that these men, Sacco and Vanzetti, were guilty, and that they had a fair trial. I furthermore believe that there was no justifiable reason for giving them a new trial.

There were riots outside American embassies all round the world. In the massive protests, Mussolini and Stalin found themselves, for the first and last time, on the same side – though both on closer enquiry might have found that they detested all for which Sacco and Vanzetti stood.

Governor Fuller immediately published the Advisory Committee's advice. It supported his decision to the hilt. Its only minor qualification to the previous judgment was that the Judge's conversations in the Golf or University Clubs were 'a grave breach of official decorum' but had absolutely no effect on 'his conduct of the trial or the opinions of the jury'.

On August 10 Sacco and Vanzetti had their heads shaved where the electrodes would be clamped. They dressed in new clothing, specially prepared so as to conduct electricity efficiently, and slit at the bottom for more electrodes. Rosina Sacco was told where to collect the corpse. So was Vanzetti's sister Luigia who had come from Italy to comfort him.

Thirty-six minutes before the switch was thrown, Governor Fuller postponed the execution for twelve days.

Desperately the defence lawyers were trying to get a writ of *habeas corpus* from Federal judges alleging that the appeals law of Massachusetts violated the constitution of the United States. Lawyers flew to judges whose wives or daughters were known to be sympathetic. Justice Oliver Wendell Holmes of the Supreme

Court ruled that he had no power to issue a writ. So did Judge Anderson. So, on August 19, did Judge Morton.

On August 20 defence lawyers tried for a writ of *a certiorori* from Justice Holmes, a request for the Supreme Court to look again at the decision of a state court. 'It is a power rarely exercised,' he wrote, 'and I should not be doing my duty if I exercised it unless I thought that there was a reasonable chance that the Court would entertain the application and ultimately reverse the judgment.' He refused the application. The lawyers tackled Justice Stone. On August 22 he wrote *no*.

Charlestown State Prison, August 23 1927

Sacco and Vanzetti had abandoned a despairing fifteen-day hunger strike when the prison authorities prepared for forcible feeding. 'So, last Saturday evening', noted Vanzetti, 'I drank half a cup of sugarless tea.'

Sacco wrote to his son:

Since the day I saw you last I had always the idea to write you this letter, but the length of my hunger strike and the thought I might not be able to explain myself, made me put it off all this time.

The other day, I ended my hunger strike and just as soon as I did that I thought of you to write to you, but I find that I did not have enough strength and I cannot finish it at one time. However, I want to get it down in any way before they take us again to the death-house.

I never thought that our inseparable life could be separated, but the thought of seven dolorous years makes it seem it did come, but then it has not changed really the unrest and the heart-beat of affection. That has remained as it was. More. I say that our ineffable affection reciprocal, is today more than any other time, of course. That is not only a great deal but it is grand because you can see the real brotherly love, not only in joy but also and more in the struggle of suffering. Remember this, Dante. We have demonstrated this, and modesty apart, we are proud of it.

Well, my dear boy, after your mother had talked to me so

much and I had dreamed of you day and night, how joyful it
was to see you at last. To have talked with you like we used
to in the days – in those days. Much I told you on that visit
and more I wanted to say, but I saw that you will remain the
same affectionate boy, faithful to your mother who loves you
so much, and I did not want to hurt your sensibilities any
longer, because I am sure that you will continue to be the
same boy and remember what I have told you. I knew that
and what here I am going to tell you will touch your
sensibilities, but don't cry Dante, because many tears have
been wasted, as your mother's have been wasted for seven
years, and never did any good. So, Son, instead of crying,
be strong so as to be able to comfort your mother, and when
you want to distract your mother from the discouraging
soulness, I will tell you what I used to do. To take her for a
long walk in the quiet country, gathering wild flowers here
and there, resting under the shade of trees, between the
harmony of the vivid stream and the gentle tranquility of
the mother nature, and I am sure that she will enjoy this
very much, as you surely would be happy for it. But
remember always, Dante, in the play of happiness, don't
you use all for yourself only, but down yourself just one
step, at your side and help the weak ones that cry for help,
help the persecuted, and the victim, because that are your
better friends; they are the comrades that fight and fall as
your father and Bartolo fought and fell yesterday for the
conquest of the joy of freedom for all and the poor workers.
In this struggle you will find more love and will be loved.

I am sure that from what your mother told me about what
you said during these last terrible days when I was lying in
the iniquitous death-house – that description gave me
happiness because it showed you will be the beloved boy I
had always dreamed.

Therefore whatever should happen tomorrow, nobody
knows, but if they should kill us, you must not forget to look
at your friends and comrades with the smiling gaze of
gratitude as you look at your beloved ones, because they
love you as they love every one of the fallen persecuted
comrades. I tell you, your father is all the life to you, your
father that love you and saw them, and knows their noble

faith (that is mine) their supreme sacrifice that they are still doing for our freedom, for I have fought with them, and they are the ones that still hold the last of our hope that today they can still save us from electrocution, it is the struggle and fight between the rich and the poor for safety and freedom, Son, which you will understand in the future of your years to come, of this unrest and struggle of life's death.

Much I thought of you when I was lying in the death-house – the singing the kind tender voices of the children from the playground, where there was all the life and the joy of liberty – just one step from the wall which contains the buried agony of three buried souls. It would remind me so often of you and your sister Ines, and I wish I could see you every moment. But I feel better that you did not come to the death-house so that you could not see the horrible picture of three lying in agony waiting to be electrocuted, because I do not know what effect it would have on your young age. But then, in another way if you were not so sensitive it would be very useful to you tomorrow when you could use this horrible memory to hold up to the world the shame of the country in this cruel persecution and unjust death. Yes, Dante, they can crucify our bodies today as they are doing, but they cannot destroy our ideas, that will remain for the youth of the future to come.

Dante, when I said three human lives buried, I meant to say that with us there is another young man by the name of Celestino Madeiros that is to be electrocuted at the same time with us. He has been twice in that horrible death-house, that should be destroyed with the hammers of real progress – that horrible house that will shame forever the future of the citizens of Massachusetts. They should destroy that house and put up a factory or school, to teach many of the hundreds of the poor orphan boys of the world.

Dante, I say once more to love and be nearest to your mother and the beloved ones in these sad days, and I am sure that with your brave heart and kind goodness they will feel less discomfort. And you will also not forget to love me a little for I do – O Sonny! thinking so much and so often of you.

Best fraternal greetings to all the beloved ones, love and kisses to your little Ines and mother. Most hearty affectionate embrace.

Your Father and Companion

PS Bartolo send you the most effectionate greetings. I hope that your mother will help you to understand this letter because I could have written much better and more simple, if I was feeling good. But I am so weak.

On August 22 Charlestown State Prison was guarded by machine guns. Five hundred armed patrolmen defended it.

Rosina Sacco called, again and again, making the farewell visit. William Thompson, the last big defence lawyer, came. In the privacy of the death cell he asked Vanzetti if he really was guilty. 'With great emphasis and obvious sincerity he said "no".'

Yet his doubt lingered: 'There was a chance, however remote, that I might be mistaken; and that I thought he ought for my sake, in this closing hour of his life when nothing could save him, to give me his most solemn reassurance.'

A doubt niggled in the mind of the establishment lawyer who had sweated so hard for them, as it had done with his predecessor, Fred Moore. 'I then told Vanzetti that I hoped he would issue a public statement advising his friends against retaliating by violence and reprisal.'

'I said that, as he well knew, I could not subscribe to his views or to his philosophy of life; but that I could not but respect any man who consistently lived up to altruistic principles, and was willing to give his life for them.'

After a resentful exchange, Thompson urged Vanzetti 'to reflect on the career of One infinitely superior to myself and to him', and argued forgiveness.

I then made a reference to the possibility of personal immortality, and said that, although I thought I understood the difficulties of a belief in immortality, yet I felt sure that if there was a personal immortality he might hope to share it.

This remark he received in silence.

He then returned to his discussion of the evil of the present organization of society, saying that the essence of the wrong was the opportunity it afforded persons who were powerful because of ability or strategic economic position to oppress the simple-minded and idealistic among their fellow men, and that he feared that nothing but violent resistance could ever overcome the selfishness which was the basis of the present organization of society and make the few willing to perpetuate a system which enabled them to exploit the many.

Thompson turned to the next cell:

To Sacco, who lay upon a cot bed in the adjoining cell and could easily have heard and undoubtedly did hear my conversation with Vanzetti. My conversation with Sacco was very brief. He rose from his cot, referred feelingly though in a general way to some points of disagreement between us in the past, said he hoped that our differences of opinion had not affected our personal relations, thanked me for what I had done for him, showed no sign of fear, shook hands with me firmly, and bade me good-bye. His manner also was one of absolute sincerity. It was magnanimous in him not to refer more specifically to our previous differences of opinion, because at the root of it all lay his conviction, often expressed to me, that all efforts on his behalf, either in court or with public authorities, would be useless, because no capitalistic society could afford to accord him justice. I had taken the contrary view; but at this last meeting he did not suggest that the result seemed to justify his view and not mine.

Police broke up the protest marches outside the prison. Cameramen flashed their calcium bulbs and caught the silhouettes of mounted guards, tall prison walls and demonstrators. American embassies throughout the world faced angry crowds.

In the prison, Madeiros over-ate, Vanzetti wrote to his father, Sacco paced his cell. And the permitted press observed the proceedings from behind a glass panel.

'Sacco marched to the death chair at 12.11 and was pronounced lifeless at 12.19.

'Vanzetti entered the execution room at 12.20 and was declared dead at 12.26.'

A long shadow

Such was the strange case of Nicola Sacco and Bartolomeo Vanzetti. Its tremors shuddered around the world like an emotional earthquake. It ended in execution. I have presented the facts as dispassionately as I can, and the reader is free to make his own judgment. Were they guilty, were they innocent? Or was one guilty and dragging the other down to shared death?

We have those facts in a way that Chief Stewart could hardly have imagined when he picked up the Bell telephone on Christmas Eve 1919. And yet something more is needed before we close the file. In the second half of the book I write in the first person and invite the reader to be not so much a factual as an intellectual and historical detective. I use the Freedom of Information Act and introduce some fresh evidence. It is not decisive. Nor claimed to be so. But as you rake over the embers of this trauma-ridden case, you pick up the odd circumstantial clue; and above all a sense of the fierce heats of that furnace which smoulders away in the guilts and ideals of the United States.

Then I try to see the case in its historical setting – at the epicentre of one of those anti-Red convulsions that have several times swept the United States. But curiously Sacco and Vanzetti were not Reds at all. They lived under the black flag of anarchy and were shaped by that culture created by Proudhon, Prince Kropotkin, Michael Bakunin. They are not, as they may first seem, two lonely Italian workmen ('Wops in a jam'). They belong to a dense and active political and philosophical world that – if

82

only for a brief spell – seemed to have some chance of reshaping the human future. I ask the reader's patience as we condense this almost forgotten strand of thought and example. It merits a book in its own right. But it is presented here, for the attention of our historical detective, to suggest that there was something at the centre of the case which the courts of Massachusetts with their label thinking never quite grasped; and that was that Sacco and Vanzetti made a universal sense.

Lastly I venture into one of the strangest worlds of all, and end with our beginning. Why is it that almost all human death is of transient significance – and yet the death of some is so highly charged with value that they live on as martyrs, pulling the future towards them?

It is fifty years later and I return to Boston looking for a last attainable clarity on the case that once shook the world.

Part two

Half a century later

Chapter Seven

In State House

The Governor

The gold-leafed dome of State House glistened in the winter
sunshine. Below stretched Boston Common where the workers
played crap during the great Police Strike of 1919. Crisp fresh
snow covered all. The children's railway was drifted nine foot
deep. The great black police horses – at two o'clock in the
afternoon – were cossetted back into their warm trailers. Man,
woman and child wore wet overboots or rubber galoshes; and all
complained, like a city scripted in monologue, about the weather.
Perhaps it was an annual surprise, much as it had been for Chief
Michael Stewart ensconced in the Bridgewater Police Station on
Christmas Eve, 1919. But the years had ticked by, and now – half
a century later – I came to look for new light, or for time's
perspectives.

   This visual perspective of Boston had hardly changed at all
since Governor Fuller had stared down at the crowds gathering
for Sacco and Vanzetti's funeral. Beacon Hill, with its huge
merchant houses and pretty ironwork, was as majestic as ever.
Here had lived that Anglo-Saxon establishment which had split
so bitterly over the execution. Beyond, the land slopes away –
this side to the huddled skyscrapers of the financial district, that
side to the indigo sweep of the wide Charles River with Harvard,
the Massachusetts Institute of Technology and Charlestown
Prison on the far bank. From the upper windows of State House
you glimpse far patches of this still segmented city: Roxbury
where the blacks live; South Boston, the great Irish centre; and,

along the margins of the river basin, the 'little Italy' of North End.

I had come to Boston fifty years after the execution. My purpose was to see what new evidence and what fresh patternings time had given to this world-shattering case. My first call was on the new Governor, Michael Dukakis, for on Tuesday August 23, 1977, in the crowded Senate Chamber at State House, Massachusetts, he issued a Proclamation stating that whether or not Sacco and Vanzetti were jointly or severally innocent or guilty, there was little doubt that by today's standards they had not received a fair trial. The Proclamation was publicly accepted by Spencer Sacco, Nicola's unseen grandchild who then travelled to Italy to give a copy to Bartolomeo Vanzetti's surviving sister.

The Proclamation reads:

The Commonwealth of Massachusetts
By His Excellency
Michael S. Dukakis
Governor

A PROCLAMATION
1977

WHEREAS: A half century ago next month, Nicola Sacco and Bartolomeo Vanzetti were executed by the Commonwealth of Massachusetts after being indicted, tried, and found guilty of murdering Alessandro Berardelli and Frederick A. Parmenter; and

WHEREAS: Nicola Sacco and Bartolomeo Vanzetti were Italian immigrants who lived and worked in Massachusetts while openly professing their beliefs in the doctrines of anarchism; and

WHEREAS: The atmosphere of their trial and appeals was permeated by prejudice against foreigners and hostility toward unorthodox political views; and

WHEREAS: The conduct of many of the officials involved in the case shed serious doubt on their willingness and ability to conduct the prosecution and trial of Sacco and Vanzetti fairly and impartially; and

WHEREAS: The limited scope of appellate review then in effect did not allow a new trial to be ordered based on the prejudicial effect of the proceedings as a whole; and

WHEREAS: This situation was later rectified as a direct result of their case by the adoption of Chapter 341 of the Acts of 1939, which permitted the Massachusetts Supreme Judicial Court to order a new trial not merely because the verdict was contrary to the law, but also if it was against the weight of the evidence, contradicted by newly discovered evidence, or 'for any other reason that justice may require'; and

WHEREAS: The people of Massachusetts today take pride in the strength of their governmental institutions, particularly in the high quality of their legal system; and

WHEREAS: They recognize that all human institutions are imperfect, that the possibility of injustice is ever-present, and that the acknowledgment of fault, combined with a resolve to do better, are signs of strength in a free society; and

WHEREAS: The trial and execution of Sacco and Vanzetti should serve to remind all civilized people of the constant need to guard against our susceptibility to prejudice, our intolerance of unorthodox ideas, and our failure to defend the rights of persons who are looked upon as strangers in our midst; and

WHEREAS: Simple decency and compassion, as well as respect for truth and an enduring commitment to our nation's highest ideals, require that the fate of Nicola Sacco and Bartolomeo Vanzetti be pondered by all who cherish tolerance, justice and human understanding; and

WHEREAS: Tuesday, August 23, 1977, will mark the fiftieth anniversary of the execution of Nicola Sacco and Bartolomeo Vanzetti by the Commonwealth of Massachusetts;

NOW, THEREFORE, I, Michael S. Dukakis, Governor of the

Commonwealth of Massachusetts, by virtue of
the authority conferred upon me as Supreme
Executive Magistrate by the Constitution of the
Commonwealth of Massachusetts, and by all
other authority vested in me, do hereby
proclaim Tuesday, August 23, 1977, 'NICOLA
SACCO AND BARTOLOMEO VANZETTI
MEMORIAL DAY'; and declare, further, that
any stigma and disgrace should be forever
removed from the names of Nicola Sacco and
Bartolomeo Vanzetti from the names of their
families and descendants, and so, from the
name of the Commonwealth of Massachusetts;
and I hereby call upon all the people of
Massachusetts to pause in their daily endeavors
to reflect upon these tragic events, and draw
from their historic lessons the resolve to
prevent the forces of intolerance, fear and
hatred from ever again uniting to overcome the
rationality, wisdom, and fairness to which our
legal system aspires.

Given at the Executive Chamber in Boston,
this nineteenth day of July in the year of our
Lord, one thousand nine hundred and
seventy-seven and of the independence of
the United States of America the two
hundred and first.

By His Excellency the Governor   MICHAEL S. DUKAKIS

PAUL GUZZI
Secretary of the Commonwealth

How had it come about? Was this mere but timely electioneer-
ing to capture the American-Italian vote (and certainly an election
loomed)? Was it grander political theatre lifting the Governor to
statesmanlike heights? Or was it a suppressed sense of injustice
invading that Commonwealth and those courts which had so
long in the American civic imagination been entwined with
Boston, 'the cradle of liberty', quintessential city of the Revolution, of the written Constitution, and the celebration in law of
individual freedoms?

I enquired into the background of the Proclamation. Earlier that year the Governor had been reminded by a New York journalist that this would bring the fiftieth anniversary of the execution. What was the Commonwealth of Massachusetts planning to do? Already there were plans afoot in New York and Washington, and proposals being put to the White House and the President. Governor Dukakis asked his legal counsel for a formal report on 'whether there are substantial grounds for believing – at least in light of the criminal justice standards of today – that Sacco and Vanzetti were unfairly convicted and executed, and, second, if so, what action can now appropriately be taken.'

The report of the Governor's chief legal counsel, Daniel A. Taylor was submitted on July 13, 1977. It is reprinted for the first time in the first part of the 'Background Sources' to this book. It makes seven major points.

1   Prejudice in the judge

It was said at the time, and has been said since, that the defense itself made political beliefs central to the trial. In the sense that the defendants' explanations for their behavior, including the various falsehoods told at the time of arrest, was that they were afraid that they and their friends were to be persecuted for being anarchists. that is true. Whether that justified the extraordinary, indeed brutal, cross-examination of the defendants, especially of Sacco, is another matter. Many of the questions asked, and many of the responses elicited, seem to have been devoted to making it ring in the jurors' minds that the defendants were radicals – which is, of course, precisely what they claimed – rather than to establishing that their justification for their actions upon arrest was trumped up, which was the point the prosecution ostensibly wished to prove. Whether, in permitting this line of questioning, the judge properly balanced the probative value of the answers produced, as against the potential for prejudice necessarily involved, may be seriously questioned . . . there is a substantial possibility that some prejudicial influence was imparted to the trial, and an even greater probability that the judge's hostility to the defendants influenced the exercise of his discretion, particularly in such critical matters as deciding the motions for a new trial.

2   The unsolved crime

The overwhelming fact about the South Braintree crime is that the crime itself remains unsolved. Even if for the moment it is assumed that Sacco and Vanzetti were participants, there were still several other participants; at trial nothing was offered to identify who these other bandits were, or to connect the two defendants to the rest of the gang. Similarly, it is undisputed that the robbers made off with more than $15,000, a substantial sum even now, and a relatively much greater amount in 1920. No part of this money was ever traced to the defendants, and at trial the prosecution offered no explanation whatsoever as to what had happened to it. Further, six bullets were found in the bodies of the two victims. Leaving aside for the moment, the question whether one of the bullets was successfully shown to have been fired from a gun in the possession of Sacco at the time of his arrest, no account was ever offered at trial as to the source of the other five.

3   Witnesses who cancelled each other out

Without reviewing all the details, it has been asserted that several of the witnesses did not have an adequate oppor-tunity for observation: that some had previously stated that they could not identify the men they briefly glimpsed, or, worse yet, had previously identified photos of others than the defendants as depicting the assailants; that some described details of the defendants not, in fact, true, or inconsistent with the details reported by others; and that at least one had an undisclosed motive for testifying favorably to the prosecution. The defense offered several witnesses who placed Vanzetti in Plymouth and Sacco in Boston at the time of the South Braintree affair. Thus, at the core of the trial there was a direct conflict of mutually exclusive identification testimony.

4   Consciousness of guilt

Apparently the trial judge, having said that the convictions
did not rest on the testimony of the eye witnesses, was of
the opinion that what had convicted the defendants was the
'consciousness of guilt' shown by their actions and statements on the night of their arrests. Since the arrests took
place fully 20 days after the crime, and since the defendants
were not informed of the grounds of their arrests, this is
hardly solid proof of guilt. More particularly, it was precisely
this proof concerning the motivation of their actions at the
time of arrest that had been so thoroughly tainted by the
prosecutor's cross-examination, and which most clearly
invited the jury to exercise its emotions rather than its
thoughts. The jury may well have decided on this basis, and
was indeed almost invited to do so by the heavy emphasis
placed on the arrest, rather than the crime, in the judge's
charge.

5   Bullet, gun, hat

Whether one of the bullets taken from Berardelli's body was
fired from the gun in Sacco's possession at the time of his
arrest remains one of the most hotly disputed points of this
hotly disputed case.

The prosecution also tried to prove that the gun in
Vanzetti's possession at the time of arrest was connected
with the crime, having been the gun carried by Berardelli on
the fatal day. The testimony was, at best, confused.

Finally, the prosecution attempted to show that a cap had
been found at the scene of the crime which was Sacco's cap.
Quite apart from the disputes as to when the cap had been
found, and as to whether it fit Sacco, it was developed after
the trial that what may well have been the crucial identifying
feature of the cap for the jury, a tear in its lining, had been
added by a police officer while the cap was in his custody. In
sum, the overall effect of these three pieces of evidence may
well have been to convince the jury that it had more definite
proof of guilt than in fact it had.

6   Dodging the draft

During the cross-examination of Sacco, Katzmann dwelt
upon Sacco's trip to Mexico to escape the draft, even though
the trip bore no relationship to the crime. He ridiculed and
unfairly distorted the political beliefs of Sacco in a manner
that appeared calculated to rouse any anti-foreign animosity
the jury may have had toward the defendant. This line of
cross-examination was admitted by Judge Thayer.

   The prosecutor's appeal to the jury's post-World War I
prejudice against draft dodgers and alien anarchists was
intensified by Judge Thayer's opening remarks to the jury
and by the first words of his charge . . . . 'Gentlemen, I call
upon you to render this service here that you have been
summoned to perform with the same spirit of patriotism,
courage and devotion to duty as was exhibited by our soldier
boys across the seas.'

7   Power of a single judge

Little short of proof of sheer incompetence or corruption
would have persuaded the Supreme Judicial Court to reverse
matters it considered discretionary . . . .

   It is no criticism of the Supreme Judicial Court, acting
under the procedures then lawfully in force, to point out that
at almost all other times in the history of the Commonwealth
greater protection for defendants in capital cases has been
required.

   Following upon the decisions in the *Sacco* case, sober
citizens concerned with the administration of justice in the
Commonwealth perceived the error of giving a single judge
such great power over the life of a defendant. In November
1927, the Judicial Council of the Commonwealth recommended the enactment of new review provisions in capital
cases.

Pardon or proclamation?

If this was indeed how the case looked fifty years later, should
the Governor now issue a retrospective pardon? Not so, argued

his legal counsel: 'everybody knows that the word "pardon" naturally connotes guilt as a matter of English.' And concluded 'a pardon, carrying the connotation that they were in fact guilty, and appearing as but a merciful act, with the implication that they would have, even now, welcomed it, would serve not to dignify, but rather to denigrate, their own claims to innocence.' Counsel argued not for mercy, but for justice.

The right course, it was suggested, was 'a proclamation intending to remove any stigma and disgrace from Sacco and Vanzetti, from their families and descendants, and, as a result, from the Commonwealth of Massachusetts.'

That took place at noon on Tuesday July 19, 1977. There was a speech by the Governor, avoiding the direct question of innocence or guilt, and addressing itself against 'the forces of intolerance, fear and hatred which had clouded the atmosphere of their indictment, trials and appeals.' Alexander Cella, the veteran campaigner for their innocence, spoke out, and the Proclamation was formally accepted on behalf of the Sacco family by Nicola's grandson, Spencer. Press photographs caught him brushing away tears. 'We, the family, wish to accept this Proclamation on behalf of all those who have witnessed or been victims of similar injustices.' A few days before he flew to Italy to offer a copy to Vincenzina, the only surviving sister of Bartolomeo Vanzetti, and to bring back a letter: 'I thank you not only for myself and my family but also on behalf of all who in Italy and throughout the world have worked and are still working for this cause.'

Perhaps she was wise to add that phrase 'still working', for the file is by no means closed.

Republican Senators put down a motion arguing that the Proclamation violated all legal, ethical and constitutional precedents, casting a dark shadow on the jurors, the judge, the entire Appellate Court System, the Supreme Court of the Commonwealth and the Supreme Court of the United States of America, including perhaps the most distinguished jurist in American history – Oliver Wendell Holmes. They claimed that though much thought had been given to Sacco and Vanzetti and their descendants, none had been spared for the murdered victims and their families. And so they moved that the fiftieth anniversary 'be set aside and that the citizens of this Commonwealth offer a moment of silence or of prayer for the victims, families and descendants of such a brutal murder.'

Outside the formalities of the Chamber, opposing Senators were as bitter and forthright as their predecessors who defended justice in the Commonwealth of Massachusetts half a century before. 'From his proclamation, you would have thought these men were victims of a lynch mob. He used the Senate Chambers for a Cecil B. De Mille production,' said the Republican leader, Senator Locke. The Democratic Senate President, Kevin Harrington, conspicuously did not vote, and the Democratic majority leader, William Bolger, voted against the Proclamation. Even liberals, such as Senator Sisitsky, though thinking the Governor was at least partially right, did not mince words: 'If there were a couple of thousand cannibals in Massachusetts and he thought he could get their votes, he would make some gesture.'

The columns of the *Boston Globe* revealed the same deep split and still-high passions. Though the editor, Robert Healey, wrote a measured political leader arguing that 'the Governor simply said that by today's standards Sacco and Vanzetti did not get a fair trial, which they did not', this was by no means the view or tone of some of his reporters nor of correspondence to the paper. One journalist dismissed it as a 'theatrical production' transparently and simultaneously aimed at the Italian community and at the disenchanted liberal vote. Amongst the letters received were very telling ones (which I heard wildly quoted in conversation around Boston) from the two sons of Governor Fuller, Alvin and Peter: 'Dukakis has disgraced himself, his office, the state by attempting to honor the memory of two convicted murderers.' The post bag at State House was considerable. 'One thing you could say, for sure, about the letters,' said Governor Dukakis, 'they either thought the trial was a frame-up, or Sacco and Vanzetti got what they deserved. I was surprised that even now there was no half-way house.' I spoke to scores of people in Boston at the time and their reaction was almost always black and white, a case burned in their memory even though they may not have been born when the bullets were fired or the switch pulled. By chance I ran into a lady whose father, a prison officer, had received them into Concord Prison, and she used the same phrase as the Governor. 'My father came home at teatime – I was a little girl – and said "Guess who came on our doorstep this morning. Those two little devils, Sacco and Vanzetti." I've always remembered. He saw it all, first degree, second degree, hoodlums. They shouldn't let these people say it was all wrong about those two – guess they got what they deserved.' I only met one man who had unclear views: 'Saccovanetti? Saccovanzetti? I know that name. Say, it was a long time ago, wasn't it? I think he played for the Boston Bruins.'

It was time to go back and ask the Governor. The Stars and Stripes hung furled in the ante-chamber. The portraits of all the previous Governors lined the corridor. Here was the first one, John Hancock, whose huge bold signature on the Declaration of Independence made him a word in the language ('put your john hancock to this piece of paper') and here was Governor Fuller who had met Sacco and Vanzetti in Death Row across the Charles River, and Calvin Coolidge who came in as President during their seven years' imprisonment very much as the 'law-and-order' man. On the podium in the Chamber was the plaque marking the departure to high office of John F. Kennedy. Outside the snow still fell, obliterating Boston's famous 'Freedom Trail', and encasing the North Church, where Paul Revere rang the bell, as if it were an icy wedding-cake decoration. The city is dense with revered images of revolution, liberty, tolerance. All the more eerie, and yet explicable, that it was here that Sacco and Vanzetti were arrested, tried and electrocuted.

Governor Dukakis is only the second Greek American to achieve that office anywhere in the United States. The lamentable precedent is Spiro Agnew, first a state governor and then briefly Vice-President. I doubted if the Proclamation rested on new evidence in the case, though it was clearly, grounded in a surgical analysis of faults in the prosecution and procedure. Perhaps, as importantly, it showed the long-distance stamina of protest and shifting cultural perspectives on what was justice. I asked him for his story.

'I first began to think about Sacco and Vanzetti when I was at Harvard Law School in the late fifties. Part of the course we were assigned to a practising lawyer. I did my intern with Al Cella. Al was in the Senate then and trying to put a Bill through to pardon Sacco and Vanzetti. It was my job to help work up the legal submission, so I got to know the case – yes, all the procedures anyway – pretty well inside out. It was obvious they hadn't a fair trial by present standards. But the Bill was thrown out. It wasn't party fighting, the usual. It was the McCarthy spirit still hanging over everything. Afterwards, Al lost his seat. Some said the Sacco–Vanzetti thing counted him out.

'Then later I met Sarah Ehrmann, widow of Herbert Ehrmann, who did these big studies on the case. I was working with Sarah against capital punishment. I've always testified against the death sentence, and since I've been Governor, I've vetoed every move to bring it back.

'And I suppose I got some sense from my family of what it was to be a new immigrant family in Boston round those times. My father was one of the first Greek doctors. Came from Lesbos. Eighty-two now and still hard at work.

'My mother knew what discrimination meant. She was the first Greek girl to reach High School in her part of Massachusetts. She'd come over from Greece when she was nine – a little town, you wouldn't know it, between Athens and Salonika – and she made Bates College, si, beta, kappa: which was pretty big. So she was well qualified. She tried for a teaching job at Walpole, near Dedham – that's where the Sacco–Vanzetti trial was. Hey! Now you make me think! That *was* the Sacco time. It must have been all going on, though I don't think I ever heard her say that. She just wasn't political that way. But at Walpole they told her straight: *No teaching jobs for foreigners.*'

That pieced a little more of the jigsaw together. If there ever was any element of vote-catching in this, it was doomed to fail. The case still split party ranks and loyalties and fractured what are now euphemistically called the ethnic groups: Beacon Hill Anglo-American Boston, South Side Irish Boston, and North End Italian. But it didn't fracture them externally, one interest or tradition against another. It split them on the inside. I spoke to one man who represented the Italian vote at the highest levels in American politics. He was guarded, non-committal, and then rolled out what to him was clearly a well-polished after-dinner anecdote:

'I know the undertakers who handled their ashes. It didn't happen like the books say. All the factions were fighting over what to do with them. Meanwhile they stayed on the shelf at this "place of rest". They were against the Church you see. And the undertaker guy said to me – "it was really an icy morning, slipping on your ass bringing coffins in, taking coffins out, and all that squabbling going on. So we just took it down, sprinkled 'em over the walk. That's what happened to Sacco and Vanzetti. Something useful in the end. You ask Al Cella."'

The tale, though delivered with apparent authority, is clearly apocryphal. That isn't what happened. And yet apocryphal stories have their point, carry invisible messages. It reminded me that in their time Sacco and Vanzetti had opposed the Catholic Church, the very pith of the Italian community. And they had, like Al Capone, ended up in prison. Neither the irreligious nor the Mafia image was likely to be altogether welcomed by an Italian minority struggling to find its social place in America. Little of this is reflected in the literature of the case.

So I sought out Al Cella. He teaches law at Suffolk University, some two hundred yards from State House.

'Yeah, I tried and tried hard on Sacco and Vanzetti. Hell, I wasn't born till two years after they went to the Chair. But a mouse with one eye could see it wasn't a murder case, it was a fix-up by the politicos.

'Not that the Italian vote was all that hot. I ran for Senate and this guy said to me – I was out looking for votes in the street – 'Oh you boys wanna bring up all this kind of stuff. Gangsters? Well, we don't want it. My parents Italian yeah. But I'm American. We don't want that deal."

'I know all that. Anyone with an ounce of history knows you can't understand the Sacco–Vanzetti killing (the *legal* killing, I mean) unless you know the Lowell spinning strike (and all the Italian anarchists into that) and the fear of God it put into the Boston Brahmins. That's how Beacon Hill got its money – and the anarchists have shown they might cut it off.

'I read the Holt transcript in Law School, maybe 1947. Important that this was down on record. And I got on the Senate and in the fifties raised the motion. There's this clause called "right of free petition", so I got that moving.

Wanted a pardon. "No, no they said – all the Senators – there's no *precedent* for a posthumous pardon." The hell! all that stickling about precedent. I stood up and said, "Hell, there's no precedent for *not* granting a posthumous pardon."

'I was struggling to prepare the case, when I got a call from the *Crimson*. Y'know that – the Harvard student paper. Said, they'd got a student over there ready to organize things, and ready to volunteer and help, and learn something useful . . . "Yeah", I said and over came Mike, Mike Dukakis. And it kind of fascinated him.

'Not only him. Unprecedented, we had *thirteen* hours of public hearing before the Committee. All the old warriors turned up – Dante Sacco, Arthur Schlesinger, Herbert Ehrmann, Justices from the Supreme Court of other states, the old anarchist printer who put out their original leaflets. Mike sat through it all.

'Got nowhere. Tossed out on its ass. And then I lost my seat at the election. Don't count up the Italian vote on this one. It splits. There was McCarthyism true enough – Reds, Reds everywhere. Anybody who *thought* was a Red. But it wasn't altogether that. It was a kind of idleness, *an unwillingness to admit official error*. When my pardon motion was thrown out, the *New York Times* awarded me a joke Oscar: "For the greatest waste of Legislative Time". I was amazed at the depth of hostility.

'And then Sacco and Vanzetti *were* anarchists. All their letters – great, moving: but doctored. Maybe not easy to look into that now, but the letters were trimmed, softened, all the harsh bits about the evil of the Church or the inevitability of violent revolution, all these cut out. Would have offended the Beacon Hill ladies and the liberal support.

'But Sacco and Vanzetti *were* anarchists. The Thayers and Lowells saw all that clearly, and killed them.

'Remember Jefferson: "That country is best which governs least"? Sacco and Vanzetti were taking it one threatening step further: "That country is best which governs not at all . . . ."' '

More and more the patterns changed. The governing Boston establishment drew its wealth from provincial spinning towns –

Lowell was such a tiny, benevolent, wealth-producing model city. Not so unlike Sir Titus Salt's 'Saltaire' in Yorkshire – a factory; adjacent housing well above minimum standards; control of leisure and morals. To the puzzlement of the mill-owners, the working force – drawing more and more for its deadening daily round on new migrant labour – did not see it like this. There were demands, walkouts, strikes, organized by men said to be anarchists. It began to link up even more tightly with Sacco and Vanzetti. I remembered one of the notes I had taken down: 'Because of Sacco's activities in the Hopedale foundry strike and Vanzetti's leadership in the big cordage walk-out at Plymouth, they became marked men.' Marked men indeed. So was this why they were picked up that evening on the out-of-town streetcar? How otherwise had the police been there, known them?

But as these new perspectives on the case opened, my next meeting was with Spencer Sacco, grandson of Nicola. Both the Sacco and Vanzetti families had maintained a cool silence since the midnight of August 23, 1927. What was the point of bringing up a family under the shadow of the Chair?

'I was twelve when I first knew my grandfather had gone to the electric chair. My daddy – he's passed away now – was a wise man. He kept us blissfully out of the Sacco–Vanzetti thing. Then one night he was out at a PTA meeting, and I was downstairs making a model aeroplane. We had this landlord then, and his son came back drunk, very drunk. "Your grandfather was the bastard who went to the electric chair." *He* knew. It all spilled out and I just didn't understand. But I was frightened and rang up my parents.

'They hustled back and daddy said "come upstairs" and he explained it all. He was right to keep us out of it for as long as possible, but in the end, if you are a Sacco, there is no escaping it.'

I had met Spencer Sacco on a dark winter evening in State House. Almost everyone had gone home before the falling snow halted the trains and marooned the cars. We didn't know where to sit and talk, and as we hesitated a hospitable security guard ushered us into the Chamber where so much of Sacco and

Vanzetti's fate had been debated, closed the double doors on us, and left us to our talk.

'I saw Dr Cella's hearing. Rosina was there too. And I listened to the debate about the Proclamation. I'd never heard Senators before and I didn't expect the pomposity, all those insults – "The Governor is a nut" and so on. And only a handful of them in the chamber (lovely Italian marble but lousy American paintings) until the vote comes. Then dozens and dozens come out of the woodwork.

'Later, as we were going in for the Proclamation Ceremony, we had to enter the Chamber via a little cubby hole. There was just me and the Governor there, waiting, waiting. And the guy turned and said to me "Y'know – the big deal about being Governor is that sometimes, just sometimes, you can do what you really want to do."'

Spencer is now a music teacher at a Catholic college:

'But sometimes, even now, the name Sacco comes back at you. I was buying some antiques and when I passed the cheque, she said, "Sacco? – hope you're not related to those Sacco Vanzetti bastards," I said, "I guess, lady, you don't need this cheque" – and left.

'But to get back to what happened: I took the Proclamation back to Rosina and read it aloud to her. It was a red hot day, and y'know she's small and in this loose – like a nightdress – and really bothered by the heat. She has this wet cloth over her head like the north Italians do. She never changed that way.

'At first she didn't pay all that much attention to my reading, but then she got intense, more than intense, just listening. At the end she smiled and nodded. After that, it had the stamp of Rosina. It was my duty to represent the family on that nod. We gave something up – our right to rebut. Justice can never right injustice. Injustice always remains.'

The security guard put his head round the door and warned us about the deepening snow. We rose, but paused briefly to take in the loveliness of Boston's winter lights from Beacon Hill before disappearing into our separate patches of darkness. 'I couldn't verbalize what my grandfather was saying. It was utopian. Not practical now. But it was his dream of his time. And he became the victim of his time.'

Chapter Eight

Little secrets in little boxes

All over Boston are boxes of Sacco–Vanzetti papers, some in the many universities, some in public libraries, others jealously or generously kept by individuals. Much of what could be found covers ground which is only too familiar; or it concentrates on fine legal detail. If ever there was a lawyer's case in a lawyers' city, it was this. Other brown beribboned boxes conceal memorabilia – Defense Committee leaflets, contemporary photographs, autographed letters, telegrams of support, as if everyone who lived through or close to this moment in American history felt the need to leave some footprint in the sand, or some treasure trove beneath.

Fifty years later perhaps it was worth digging over that trove again for three reasons. First, bequests or searches over the years might have brought something fresh. Second, the papers of Robert Lowell were now, for the first time, open to inspection. Third, the Watergate affair and the downfall of President Nixon were followed by demands that less and less information should be kept from the public. The ripples of the new Freedom of Information Act were lapping at the edges of the Sacco–Vanzetti affair. Could the secret police files be opened, and what could they tell us?

The case of the crooked interpreter

I began in the underground Pusey Library at Harvard, which now holds the Lowell papers and also the files of Robert Montgomery, one of the counsel. In the Montgomery boxes lies a pile of papers which (I think mistakenly) he decided not to publish. These concern the bizarre role of Joseph Ross. Joseph Ross, who was born Guiseppe Rosso, was the court interpreter. On June 2, 1927 he was accused by Mrs Vito A. Romano or Revere of unfair interpretation. An investigation by assistant Attorney General Gerald J. Callahan found no grounds for complaint. The accusation may have been one of the myriad of minor last-minute bids by supporters of the condemned men. But Montgomery's pages dig a little deeper, and at least prompt further thought.

Joseph Ross had himself been a radical, but was expelled from a socialist group in Paterson, New Jersey, and had moved strongly to the right. He had served a six-month prison sentence, and according to Montgomery's sources he had a wide reputation for extortion in the Italian community. There seems little doubt too that he probably had an emotional identification with the prosecution. During the trial he had a baby son. Katzmann, the prosecutor, stood as godfather, and the child was christened Webster Thayer Ross.

Sometime after the trial his two worlds collided. He was still both court interpreter and engaged in extortion. An Italian acquaintance of his was out on bail awaiting sentence. After the day's work in court, Ross would offer the judge a lift home in his car. Judge Bruce accepted, and Ross would casually mention that he had to call briefly at someone's house on the way. The 'someone' was someone who was coming up for trial or sentence. Leaving the judge clearly visible in the parked car at the garden gate, he would draw his acquaintance to the window, point to the intimacy of his relationship, and offer to get the sentence reduced in exchange for an immediate and hefty cash bribe. It seemed a shrewd scheme. If the sentence was indeed lighter than his friend expected, then he took the credit as well as the money. If it was heavier, then it was all the judge's double dealing, and anyway the 'friend' was safely tucked away in gaol.

Unfortunately one of his victims didn't like the sentence

pronounced on him, protested and let the cat out of the bag. Ross found himself behind bars for two years.

Pondering this fragment in the archives I doubt if it takes us further on the road that leads to conclusive guilt or certain innocence. But the case that led to Death Row is all along a *tesserae* of tiny, accumulating details – the tear in the hat, the markings on the bullet, the oversized photograph. Felix Forte (later to become a Justice of the Superior Court) was sitting with the defence lawyers: as an Italian he would surely have drawn their attention to any gross unfairness in the interpretation – though one must remember that the spoken Italian of Sacco and Vanzetti was very much the dialect of their region and not the high Italian of the educated classes. No: this detail does not suggest, as Mrs Romano alleged, that they were fixed from the beginning. Rather, it reminds one (as with the identification parade, or the keeping of the exhibits) of an element of casualness in the original trial which was later to prove deadly, despite the many years of motions, counter-motions, reviews and appeals. Rosso may have been a bizarre choice. One glimpses again the violent fissures within the migrant Italian community: the church-abiding, the revolutionary, the criminal, and those, like Felix Forte, moving into the professional echelons of American society. And one is drawn back to Sacco and Vanzetti and the ultimate power of their very personal English. It is easy to forget, and indeed I have never seen it mentioned, that during the crucial stage when they gave their basic and subsequently unalterable evidence, their English was often fragile – and they needed to turn to an interpreter. Especially when they came under attack for their political views (which they never clarified in English) it must have been extraordinarily difficult for them to make the case that they were fearful, armed but pacific anarchists caught in a dense web of misunderstandings. An unsympathetic interpreter who was clearly a countryman could hardly have been a help.

The case of the extra bullet

When they were arrested on the streetcar both Sacco and Vanzetti were armed. Sacco had a .32 Colt automatic. It had nine cartridges in the clip, and a further twenty-three were loose in his pocket. The cartridges were of mixed brands. Sixteen were Peters, seven were US, six were obsolete Winchesters and three were Remingtons. At the trial it was recorded in court that four .32 shells had been found in and around the gutter where Berardelli died during the South Braintree hold-up. Two were Peters, one was an obsolete Winchester and the last was a Remington. There was certainly a 'match' of a kind there; though it could be theoretically argued that this was the mix of bullets in current circulation. I don't know if that was so.

At the trial, both sides had produced two ballistics experts each. Two disagreed with two. In 1927, during President Lowell's final review of the case, the ballistics experts had – for the first time – the use of a comparison microscope. At that stage, the two defence experts went back on their argument and assented that a bullet found in Berardelli's body and a shell picked up on the street probably came from the Colt that Sacco had tucked in his trousers on the night of his streetcar arrest. There were further tests in 1961 which supported this – though by that time 'the gun', like other relics of Sacco and Vanzetti, had been through many hands, and I am certainly not clear whether we are talking about the same weapon that was found on him that evening the police boarded the tram.

Against this very strong testimony we should also recall the way the ballistics experts for the prosecution also changed their minds or hedged their bets. All were practitioners of a very approximate, if sometimes decisive science. And lastly we must remember that Katzmann the prosecutor quite clearly framed the questioning so that Captain Proctor, the influential witness, was unable to express his doubts and had to fall back on the prepared formula about the bullet and the pistol: 'My opinion is that it is consistent with being fired by that pistol.'

So it stood until June 1977 when an amateur historian, Lincoln A. Robbins, looked at a notebook in the Harvard Law School Library. This black-bound pad was handwritten a few months before the trial by Harold P. Williams, then the assistant Norfolk County District Attorney. He was later to become a justice of the state's highest court.

Nothing has been formally published on the significance of this pad, and apart from the book itself the only information I can here draw on is the Sacco–Vanzetti Clippings File of Professor Hugo Bedau, the Austen Professor of Philosophy at Tufts University, yet another of those treasure-trove boxes on the case in which Boston abounds.

Many statements were made to the media. 'My eyes bugged out. I must have sworn out loud in the library. I simply could not believe what I was reading,' stated Robbins. The discrepancy is this: the jury was shown four shells found at the murder, but the Williams notebook quite clearly records 'Shay picked up 3 shells where Ber. fell and gave them to Sherlock.' Shay was a Braintree policeman and Sherlock a state detective. The inference is that the fourth shell was introduced into evidence later, after having been fired from the revolver, by then in police custody. It is a highly speculative line of thinking, but stiffened a little by the details of who collected the shells and to whom they handed them. These are quite clearly different in the Williams notebook and in the trial evidence. At the trial, however, it is James Bostock, a machinist at the shoe factory, who tells the jury, 'I picked up some shells . . . about two or three feet from the shooting.' He said he gave them to Thomas Fraher, the factory superintendent. This is how four shells – including the one linked with Sacco – came to be exhibits. There is a second typewritten document which notes 'Shells found on street: Shay to Fraher to Proctor.'

Mr Robbins, through and with the media, argued that there was a distinct possibility that the prosecutor and several others involved fixed this evidence at the beginning, and after that prejudice snowballed it downhill. The suggestion is that Katzmann, the prosecutor, had a clear emotional drive to win a conviction. This arose from the undiscussed matter of his having been brought to trial and acquittal of offering to drop the case if he was paid $40,000 by the Sacco–Vanzetti Defense Committee. It is clearly important that this charge is kept in mind, but hard to see the time logic. If the Williams notebook has any place in the argument it is as a hot, scribbled record soon after the event. The conflict between Katzmann and the Defense Committee comes later.

It is also suggested that the contradictions about who handled the shells arose because Shay was unwilling to perjure himself over the fourth shell, and was replaced by Bostock. A possible motive was that Fraher's firm was in trouble with its insurers

over the robbery, and he needed a quick, clear conviction. Fraher
had a record of having previously worked closely with the police.
There are several other puzzling or supporting details.

What can we make of this? Robbins, in the *Boston Globe* has
argued that Williams was well aware of the introduction of the
fourth shell, and quotes his reaction when he was congratulated
on securing the verdict: 'For God's sake, don't rub it in. This is
the saddest thing that ever happened to me in my life.'

The reaction of some historians has been that this is the first
arguable confirmation of fraud in the District Attorney's office. If
not that, then defence knowledge of the discrepancies might
have altered the trial. Alan Derstrowitz, a Harvard law professor,
commented to the press

> 'In the trial the notes would have produced a whole new
> line of cross-examination for the defense. It could have
> destroyed the credibility of the prosecution. A case is like a
> house you build with a deck of cards. You take out one
> crucial card and the whole thing collapses. The notes could
> have pulled that card.'

Perhaps so. I report the new evidence, and some may use it as
confirmation of the old belief that the two were framed from the
beginning. Personally it doesn't seem strong enough to me to
support charges of perjury. Rather it reads like more glimpses of
the casual approach that marked the first investigations, and the
deadly muddles which were obscured by the play of passion and
prejudice throughout the case.

The Boston police files

The fall of President Richard Nixon bred new demands for less
secrecy in government records. Between Watergate and Governor
Dukakis's Proclamation there were several requests – under the
Freedom of Information Act – to the Boston police for access to
their Sacco–Vanzetti files. All were refused. The reason given in
December 1976 was that this could disclose information that
might prejudice effective law enforcement. At last the Secretary
of State, Paul Guzzi, intervened and ordered the release. The

order was personally delivered to the head of the State Police
Bureau of Records, but reasons for delay were found. The police
commander said, 'We don't even know whether we have all the
records being requested. I have ordered an inventory of the Sacco–
Vanzetti files and a memorandum describing the nature of the
information in them.' The Public Safety Secretary produced
another defence: 'The nagging question is whether persons'still
alive and originally involved in the case – or living relatives of
such persons – would be affected by the release of the information.' Later a further delay was requested because several of
the sheets were written in a shorthand never before seen by the
police staff. These tactics or dilemmas delayed the opening of the
files for nine months; but on September 12, 1977 they were
released, together with a police statement.

On November 24, 1976 an individual requested access to the
records of the Massachusetts State Police relating to the
Sacco–Vanzetti case which occurred in 1920. On December 2
I denied access to the files based on an exemption from
Chapter 4 of the general law pertaining to the potential of
prejudice of effective law enforcement.

Further I strongly believe in the right of privacy and my
sincere opinion is that this right of privacy does not cease
when an individual dies.

However on August 4 1977, the Secretary of State's Office
ruled that the information did not come within the above
exemption and ordered that the files of the so-called Sacco–
Vanzetti case be made available for police inspection, with
the exception of the identity of informants mentioned therein.

A diligent search was made of the files in various locations
of the Massachusetts State Police and numerous hours were
expended in an endeavor to assure that all records pertaining to the case were uncovered.

The only information deleted from the records are approxi-
mately seven lines out of a little more than eleven hundred
pages. The deletions related to criminal offender records
which, by law, I am not entitled to divulge.

The files as I found them are 1,080 pages sorted out into three
broad sections and kept in three brown boxes. Most of the pages
are quite useless and it is surprising that much of this trivia

survived over half a century in the police archives. It is clear that we only have here a fraction of the original material. The seven lines admittedly deleted are believed to refer to Vanzetti's previous conviction for the Bridgewater hold-up. This is a pity because it was long a belief of the defence that the jury knew all along that Vanzetti was already in prison for that unsuccessful precursor of the deadly raid at South Braintree.

Some of the remaining pages are clearly stamped 'Confidential. To be either DESTROYED or placed in SECRET FILES'. Perhaps that is what happened to the missing papers. Perhaps it should have happened to these too, had some tired secretary on a Friday evening not popped them into the filing cabinet rather than the incinerator. Sifting the surviving papers, three groups are worth considering. The first are the statements of Sacco and Vanzetti on the night of their arrest.

Original statements on the night of the arrest

First of all there are a bundle of loose undated sheets from Officer Sherlock reporting the progress of his search for the murderers. This is important because radicals supporting Sacco and Vanzetti have argued that the police set out to pin something on them. For example an undated copy of the New England Civil Liberties Committee newsletter (it seems to have been issued before the trial) states bluntly 'Because of Sacco's activities in the Hopedale foundry strike and Vanzetti's leadership in the big cordage walk-out at Plymouth, they became marked men.' If so, that is not how Officer Sherlock set about his task. The records show him first of all seeking 'an Italian stick-up called Baby Tony' only to learn that he is already in New York State Prison. He then collects photographs of known Italian criminals from the Brooklyn Police and tries those for leads. There is a later note of the police acting on a tip-off and surrounding five men camping in the woods at Douglas, Massachusetts, only to find them to be harmless weekend hunters. Next three men are arrested as they board the steamer from Providence to New York. Again they have to be released. There seems no doubt that at this stage the police were looking for professional Italian criminals rather than active radicals. However, it was precisely active migrant radicals

who were being arrested and deported in the Red raids of the
time. Nowhere in the files can we explain *why* police officers
Connolly and Vaughn boarded the trolley at Campello that May
evening and picked out Sacco and Vanzetti – other than because
of Mrs Johnson's tip-off, which is not recorded. The need to
explain this was immediately overlaid by the fact that they were
armed, and then by their statements in the police station.

This is what Vanzetti signed. Presumably he was answering
questions in English, and his replies are written down and maybe
strung together in a different sequence by someone in the station.

'My full name is Bert Vanzetti. I spell my first name B-E-R-T.
I am Bartolomeo. I call it Bert for short.

'I had firearms with me when I went to Boston. I am scared
to go with the money in my pocket like that and so I bring
my firearms, a revolver. I don't know if it is a 38, long
barrel. I hear them tell about an automatic. I also had four
shells in my pocket. I take them because Nick gave them to
me . . . . I have no permit to carry revolver.

'I have not been speaking Sundays at Labor meetings in
Plymouth. I write a notice that read: "Fellow workers –
Bartolomeo will speak. The subject will be 'The struggling for
existence for laborers'." I never spoke in public on that
subject. I wrote the notice just to see if I am good or not. I
did not have it printed. I am no member of any party. I am
not an anarchist. I don't know what I am exactly. I hear
many speakers. I like to study that matter, but I don't belong
to this one or another.

'I bought the revolver on Hanover close to where the
Italian section is. I think it was a Jew store. When I bought
the revolver I give another name but I don't remember what
name. I was scared to give my own name.

'I am sure I slept in Boston but I had a woman with me –
that is why I did not want to tell you. A woman I met in
Boston. I was not with her Monday night; I went to
Stoughton, Monday. I can't tell exactly what time. I left the
woman in Boston. I don't know where we stayed in Boston;
she took me to a place. It is a woman I met that night; a
woman who goes with everybody. I met her in Hanover
Street. She asked me to come with her. I had my dinner

Sunday in a lunch room on Hanover Street. I don't know the name of it. I had breakfast in a lunch room. The woman was not with me. I think she was an American she no speak Italian. I have been telling the truth about last night.

'I left Plymouth Sunday morning. I went to Boston to a moving picture. I don't remember if I sleep in Boston, Sunday night or if I come to sleep at his house.'

There is also a note which says Vanzetti had 60 dollars on him. And a loose note which states 'June 1906 he came to America by way of France. This is an indication, probably, of flight from the police.'

After this statement the door to the death cell was always open to Vanzetti. It could have been no accident that that trolley car was boarded. Maybe there was a tip-off (erased from the records); maybe the police, having failed with their check-out of known Italian criminals, had now turned to known Italian radicals. But the undeniable facts are that he was armed, had accepted spare ammunition from Sacco, carried a surprising amount of money, denied his political activities, and produced a startlingly unverifiable alibi – he didn't remember the shop where he bought the gun, he didn't know the name of the woman he slept with, he forgot where he had either breakfast or lunch. And he couldn't explain this inconsequential trip on the trolleycar.

Some of this could be explained as the natural behaviour of a frightened anarchist (who was well aware what had happened to Salsedo and others who had committed no crimes but political ones). But clearly it was reasonable for the police to disbelieve, and press the matter further. Oddly, in this strange and perhaps fatal first statement we can see the shadow of that Vanzetti who was to grow, publicly and agonizingly, as the seven-year act played out. Here is a little of that very personal utterance of English, that intimacy of address, and maybe that act of imagination when bereft of almost any hope of escape.

Compare Nicola Sacco's original statement. I simply give a sample:

'I speak English a little. I would like an interpreter.

'I am married; have one child, two died. I live right in back of Kelley's house. Kelley is the father of the Kelley boys who own the factory.

'My name is Nick Sacco. Nick means Nicola. I spell Sacco
– S-A-C-C-O.

'That rifle is mine. I bought that, I wanted to go gunning in
Maine, not this winter, but winter before last. I had a
revolver with me last night. I don't know what I had it for, it
seems to be a habit of Italian people.

'After we got off the car last night Vanzetti did not enquire
of anybody where his friend lived. He says no use now,
find out made mistake, might as well go back.

'When I bought it I didn't give my name, afraid that I
would get arrested – just as I had to go to Italy I thought I
would use them, go out in the woods and shoot them off.'

Sacco too is surreptitiously armed, and has a pocketful of spare
ammunition. Why he is on the tramcar is obscure. Are they going
somewhere or not? And why? And if they are lost, why don't
they ask?

Again we glimpse that man in the future. More frugal of words,
less certain in the alien element of English, cautious, enigmatic:
and tied to the world by a family.

One of the police officers, John H. Scott, has left a puzzled,
sometimes naive, but tellingly sceptical note in the files:

Sacco has always had socialist tendencies and would argue
socialism to his friends and companions, but said he could
not kill. The sight of blood made him sick, yet he had a
loaded revolver and extra ammunition in his possession
when arrested, and also a rifle in his house at the same time.

Between them, Sacco's bullets and Vanzetti's words must quite
reasonably have convinced the police that they were on to
something, whether it was robbery, or revolution, or robbery to
fund revolution. That their stories were true – Sacco planning a
harmless shoot-out in the woods, Vanzetti recovering from a
night out on the town, the two coming together on a muddled
trolleybus ride – throws us back on the happenchance patterns of
life. The two themes were now to counterpoint each other for
seven years. And each would get sharper, more logical, more
exclusive: and each would now cut out the mixedupness, the
shades and contradictions of ordinary life.

If nothing else, the secret police files drove us back to beginnings, to the accidents and unplanned words which were to prove such monstrously fertile seeds.

Police penetrating the defence

It was sometimes claimed that the police were so anxious to secure a conviction and an execution that they penetrated the defence, even to the extent of planting an agent in Death Row. No trace of this remains in the files. All that is preserved is an odd cameo of Anglo-Saxon Boston during the days of the execution and its aftermath.

In late August 1927 papers are filed daily from a lady who, whilst active in the defence, is a somewhat naive police spy. Let me quote some extracts:

> Mother Bloor doesn't accept me quite so wholeheartedly as the others do . . . . There is a big book of photographs of people connected with the case which is quite closely guarded. Mother Bloor has a lot of whispering to do and always closes the door before she says anything. She is another fanatic . . . .
>
> Message from Louis Post, former Assistant Secretary of Labor. A telegram. 'I accept invitation to join Citizens National Committee to secure American rights for Sacco and Vanzetti. Their persecution evidently originated in the Department of Justice . . . . It is also of the utmost importance to lay bare what is now conceded: namely, the operations of the Department of Justice detectives in connection with the class prejudice and with the suicide or murder of their associate Salsedo.'
>
> [Notes of those who attended a meeting in Parlour C at the Bellevue] John Dos Passos, Mary Donovan, Pastor Hapgood, Mr Musanno, Mr Spellman, Edna St Vincent Millay, Mr Rority (the poet).
>
> Mrs Glendower Evans on the night of the execution got herself appointed a special reporter and got into the Prison. Her only purpose in doing so must have been there to help in case, in an unexplained way, the mob of sympathizers overcame the guards.

They even went so far as to call the Governor and President Lowell 'fools and liars' over and over again.

It is a terrible thing to have it said that there is trouble between the Governor and Mrs Fuller. It is said here that she is going to leave him because he is so cruel. I asked tonight how the rumor got started and all the actual ground I could find for it is that Mrs Fuller doesn't believe in capital punishment.

Harvard Alumni to withdraw their contributions to the various activities of Hang Man's College, to make it so hot for President Lowell that a murderer cannot retain the chair.

Meeting of Communist Party in Central Opera House. Eugene Debs speaks: 'Murder at retail is regarded as crime by the government; murder at wholesale (meaning war) makes you a hero.'

A telegram was read from Upton Sinclair who promises to write a novel at once. He will call it *Boston* and Sacco and Vanzetti will be the two proletarian heroes who will suffer dramatically for the cause of labor.

Mrs Cadman of Beacon Street threatens to cut the Governor and President Lowell the very next time they meet.

Great disgust and concern is felt and expressed that the bodies should have been mutilated and that the brain should have been sent to Harvard.

This morning Mrs Henderson brought Rosa Sacco to breakfast with me.

I will wait till 10 o'clock in case you should wish to give me any instructions over the phone.

The urn prepared for the ashes – which never came – started a discussion and it grew into a fight about whether they should divide the ashes and let Rosa Sacco and Miss Vanzetti each have half, and the other half to be taken on a tour throughout the world, and finally ended in a free for all fight to do with money and personalities.

Then the news finally came, it was received with sadness – some bitterness and a general let-down.

Shall I come home, or shall I stay here and move down to the Village and try to get into Anarchy?

It is a black farce. Sketches for a Henry James nouvelle. Yet what can we make of this surviving file? Perhaps a suggestion that the police were indeed very ready to penetrate the defence, and only this bizarre scrap is left undestroyed? Certainly a sense that something was awry (as it had been long ago at Salem) in the New England conscience. This is all Beacon Hill talk: the weapons range from cutting the Governor to writing a novel. And an intimate glimpse of men and women, forgetting the human beings in the cells, and moulding them into something else: martyrs.

Wiretapping Felix Frankfurter

One quarter – 262 pages – of the remaining files are day-to-day records of wiretapping. None of this was previously known. There are two letters of authorization. One is to wiretap the Bellevue Hotel, where the Defense Committee had its head-quarters. It gives secret permission to 'use a dictograph or other device' and is signed by the Attorney General of Massachusetts, Arthur K. Reading. All that remains is a fragment of conversation recorded at 1.30 in the morning of August 22, 1927:

'Come in.'
   'Hello. Well it looks as if they will die tomorrow.'
   'Yes, but you know they are guilty and that we have put up one grand and glorious fight for them even though we didn't have a chance.'
   'Do you really think they are guilty?'
   'Yes, I do.'

The second letter of authorization, dated August 1, 1927, is to wiretap the home telephone of Felix Frankfurter, professor of law at Harvard, legal brain of the defence, and later Justice of the Supreme Court. A note attached says: 'I respectfully submit the following report on conversations heard by me this date over the telephone at Bay Road, Duxbury, Mass. Respectfully submitted. Margaret A. Boyle. Stenographer.'
I give extracts.

8.45 a.m. August 10. Incoming call for Prof. Frankfurter. Mrs Frankfurter answered and the other party said: 'Is Prof.

Frankfurter there, this is King.' Then I heard Mrs Frankfurter say 'just a minute' and in a low voice, evidently to Professor 'King, the reporter.' Mr Frankfurter then came on the line and said 'Yes.' King said 'Professor, this is King.' Frankfurter then said 'Oh yes, can't talk now, have to run for a train, King.'

7 p.m. August 10. 'Mrs Frankfurter.'
'Yes.'
'This is Thelma Irving. Are you going to the Jitney Players with us tonight?'

August 13. 'Extremists from New York have come on here to capture the thing.' 'Most important not to tell a soul about this conversation.'

August 21. Caller: 'It is a most awful situation when your legal system will not insure moral demands: that is what leads to revolution.'
Frankfurter: 'You don't talk to me about that because I have had to listen to my wife all day. I can shut you up but not her. All day long I have had to listen to it.'
'It is terribly important not to have the fight go over into unclean hands.'

August 22. 'Elizabeth?'
'Yes?'
'This is Felix. I just called to ask and I want you to be frank with me, whether I can stay at your house tonight.'
'Why yes, I would love to have you stay.'
(Duxbury 272 is listed in telephone book as Mr Hilbert Day of Windsor Street, Duxbury.)

August 29. Frankfurter: 'I am going to sleep for a week. I went away to work on a crime.'
'Did I understand you to say "crime"?'
'"Crime" is the word.'

September 1. 'It is very important that those of us who have a concern for the merits should not disband.'

October 3, 11.20 a.m. 'Mr Frankfurter calling Kingston 24 ring 3. This is the Storey Brooke Garage. He asks them the amount of his bill, so that he can bring over a check on his way back to the city. They tell him his bill is $9.50.'

To the very end the agony and the trivia lie side by side. That the police felt it necessary to wiretap so eminent and respectable a jurist as Frankfurter gives us little confidence that they would have hesitated to penetrate the defence much earlier. Of course the motive here may have been to guard against disorder at the time of execution. But it is chilling to glimpse the automatism of secret surveillance: recording the Professor's garage bills six weeks after the electrocutions.

Chapter Nine

'There seemed to be no doubt at all'

Abbot Lawrence Lowell: the final referee

In the archives at Harvard, I discovered a short and simple letter from Abbot Lawrence Lowell, President of the University. It is addressed to an unknown Mr Jenkins, dated September 14, 1927, and penned in his lucid, unhurried hand, some three weeks after the electrocution. It reads: 'There seemed to be no doubt at all. Any impartial person who read the whole evidence would, I think, reach the same conclusion.'

Lowell was the very apex of the Anglo-Saxon social world in Boston. His colleagues on that final committee which Governor Fuller established to review guilt or innocence were hardly less distinguished: President Samuel Stratton of the Massachusetts Institute of Technology and Judge Robert Grant, formerly of the Massachusetts Court. Many of the great Boston family titles are woven into their names. For those who gave assent to the cultured, learned and wealthy Anglo-Saxon society which still dominated the major institutions of 'the freedom state', nothing could be more respectable.

Sacco never had any hope in this 'social court' but until their unanimous verdict was announced, many on the defence side thought there was a reasonable chance. After all, they often came from the same group. Henry James's nephew, Edward Holton James, was an enthusiastic advocate, bailing out Katherine Ann Porter when she was arrested on demonstrations, and later

120

taking some care of the fatherless Dante Sacco. The press dismissed him as 'the millionaire pacifist' but he hit back in his private pamphlets:

> You had a crazy judge and jury in Plymouth. You had the same crazy judge and another crazy jury in Dedham. You had a Supreme Court of Massachusetts sitting in the Court House in Boston, saying it was all right. The whole lot of them ought to be sitting in the insane asylum.

After the decision the reaction was passionate, even as we have seen, hysterical. Harvard became 'Hang Man's College' and the rumour was widely believed that the university had claimed the dead men's brains and hearts for academic experiment. Somewhere in the police files I see they took a copy of a poem by Reginald Howard Bass of the First Presbyterian Church, Whitney Point, New York, which is addressed to 'Miss Luigia Vanzetti with deepest sympathy'. It contains the line 'showing their wounds where Harvard took their hearts and brains.' Another street pamphlet collected by the police claims 'The die is cast. Yes, cast for Lowell, Fuller, et al – their criminality is established. History cannot be blind.' That the police had some reason to be wary of violent retribution on Lowell is borne out by the later bombing of Judge Thayer's home. And the police records now reveal, though without any surviving detail, that they kept Sacco's young son, Dante, under surveillance until some date after 1932 – possibly expecting him to be encouraged to return as an anarchist avenger.

Lowell sealed his Sacco and Vanzetti papers, gave them to Harvard and asked them to remain unopened for fifty years. Some supporters of the dead pressed for an earlier disclosure, and believed that here at last clear proof of a desire to pervert justice might finally be found ('hangmen in frock coats'). It was a naive belief. It is hardly likely that the President would will to his own university documents which uncovered such guilt. I went to Harvard for the delayed opening of the papers in 1978. I was not able to comb the main ones, but on the first day alone forty-five journalists did so. I am not aware that anything material was found, and am not surprised.

Time perhaps allows us to see Lowell's review and judgment in a different perspective. The shift in our prevailing values is such that we need no conspiracy theory to understand why he felt that there was 'no doubt at all'. At the time Judge Grant was seventy-five, President Lowell seventy-one and President Stratton much the same. They had grown up in a quite different America. To put it one way, Lowell was born only eight years after Karl Marx published the *Communist Manifesto*. He was now considering an allegedly anarchist crime which happened only months after the official founding of the American Communist Party. Child of an era behind which the New England revolution had triumphed over old England, his lifetime had seen the possibility of a Red revolution – once so remote a dot – travel from Europe to America. He could look back on an age which had seen the Civil War and the emancipation of the black slaves, and the arrival of large numbers of immigrants – Jews from the East, Italians from the Mediterranean – who, whatever else they were, were not the old Anglo-Saxon stock. Standing back now from his many-sided and very distinguished career, perhaps we can spotlight three strands. Taken together, they by no means give a full, fair or rounded picture of the man. But they are possibly the ones that help us see how he might see the two men in the condemned cells.

Wealth and labour

The Lowell and Lawrence fortunes came from textile mills. The towns of Lowell and Lawrence had been largely theirs. Places like Lowell, Falls River and Lawrence presented a picture of the textile industry that was decades behind Europe so far as workers were concerned. Wages were low, hours long, children at work, unions weak. At first they had recruited labour largely from the spinning and weaving towns of northern England, but this recruitment had to some extent been replaced by Italian migration – and a simultaneous increase in official or unofficial union activity.

The Lowell family was utterly opposed both to organized labour and to this shift from Anglo-Saxon to Latin immigration into the United States. When the Massachusetts legislature in 1911 reduced the working week from 56 to 52 hours, the Lawrence mills replied by cutting wages in proportion. In the riots that followed, a young girl worker was killed, and the police arrested some of the Italian labour leaders. They were subsequently acquitted.

Lowell's personal stand against unions was most vividly illustrated during the Boston Police Strike of 1919. This vivid episode, which President Wilson called 'a crime against civilization' and on which Calvin Coolidge commented 'that way treason lies' gives some sense of how Boston, once the old-fashioned cradle of American liberty, was now for a time seen in the general imagination as a violent New England soviet. The strike was straightforwardly about pay and conditions. There had been unrest for some time, and the organizers (of what the patrolmen themselves regarded as their official union) were already suspended. Then before the usual roll call began, Patrolman George Fereira, dressed in civilian clothes, stepped forward and announced to Captain Matthew Dailey, 'Sir, the Boston police are on strike.' 'Here, wait a minute, Fereira,' shouted the Captain. 'You're *already* suspended. Get out!'

Only 24 out of 700 policemen remained on duty. Before it was broken 8 people were to die, and 21 be wounded. There was theft, looting, destruction of property.

Old Boston rallied. Francis Russell in his excellent study of the strike quotes an eye-witness account: No one 'could miss the presence of Godfrey Lowell Cabot, cousin and classmate of Harvard's president, A. Lawrence Lowell, with a brace of pistols strapped on and wearing a naval cape.' Lowell's own response was measured and implacable (not unlike that of most Oxbridge heads during Britain's General Strike): 'In accordance with the traditions of public service the University desires in time of crisis to help in any way it can to maintain order and support the laws of the Commonwealth. I therefore urge all students who can do so, to prepare themselves for such service as the government of the Commonwealth may call upon them to render.' The reaction to this of Bob Fisher, Harvard's head coach was 'To hell with football if men are needed to protect Boston.' Two hundred Harvard students volunteered and more would have done so had it not been out of term. Thousands of pistol permits were issued ('See,' said Captain Sullivan, handing out cartridges to the new recruits, 'these are what we call riot pills.') The strike was broken, though a defiant remnant fought on hopelessly for years to come.

Lowell spoke of the 'pride of the University in the men who did duty'. A police strike is perhaps an extreme example of organized labour, but we might note two points. Lowell and Boston had this experience (and saw the subsequent disorder) just before the alleged anarchistic killing and robbery at South Braintree. And, second, the Boston police who sought out, arrested and built up the evidence against Sacco and Vanzetti were all ones who had just replaced the older force. None of the striking policemen got their jobs back. All were replaced by men who were judged *not* to have radical sympathies or be likely to repeat this traumatic strike. The Commissioner's Report for 1921 ends: 'Many of the new men were unequal to their task and had to be watched with special care. The police officials felt that they were doing well if they kept the system from breaking down completely.' It was the long arm of this rickety force which, rightly or wrongly, pinioned Sacco and Vanzetti.

I quote this episode because it is little mentioned as background to the case. Indeed I cannot recall it (though I may be wrong) in the main literature at all – so court-centred is that. It also illuminates Lowell a little, and reminds us that at these moments the United States sighed with relief that Boston, the Cradle of Liberty, was not to be the transatlantic Leningrad. Calvin Coolidge was swept from State Governor on Beacon Hill to President in the White House. 'Massachusetts is American,' he announced, perhaps a little to his surprise.

We glimpse a sliver more of Lowell's way of seeing matters from his energetic lobbying for the 1921 Immigration Law. His voice – even his whisper – was then influential in the corridors of power. A year after the South Braintree murder, his direct efforts are part of that social force which results in the passing of the new law that further rings Staten Island. In S. M. Lipsett's words, it was a law 'which not only put a drastic ceiling on total immigration but imposed an even more drastic national origins quota system excluding all but a trickle of immigrants from other than the Protestant countries of northern Europe.'

I do not in any way seek to place the major responsibility for this backlash (and only briefly effective) legislation on Lowell. Others in similar positions were of the same view, and for a time they carried national opinion with them. James J. Davies, who was Secretary of Labor under both President Harding and

President Coolidge had another way of putting it: 'Immigrants to America were the beaver type that built up America, whereas the newer immigrants were rat-men trying to tear it down; and obviously rat-men could never become beavers.' Given the illusions of such rhetoric, there is surely little doubt as to which part of the animal kingdom belonged – if Italian and anarchist – 'a good shoe-maker and a poor fish pedlar'.

But I would like to take the personal out at this point. The attitude was part of that high Boston culture, even at its finest. Whilst all this was evolving, the most distinguished representative of New England culture (with its locked love and hate for Old England) was a senior London bank clerk. Henry James had died four years before, but in the year of the South Braintree murder, T. S. Eliot, Harvard graduate and descendant of an old Boston merchant family – published *Burbank with a Baedeker: Bleistein with a Cigar*:

> . . . On the Rialto once.
> The rats are underneath the piles.
> The Jew is underneath the lot.
> Money in furs. The boatman smiles.

Even the finest are not only nurtured by the culture, but pock-marked by its diseases too.

Negroes at Harvard

I take as a second bearing, Lowell's major stand on the question of black men sleeping at Harvard in buildings containing white men. He said *no*.

His purpose, and indeed his achievement, was to take a very good American college and – by grafting it on to his own admiration, dreams and fantasies of Cambridge and Oxford – to set it on that course which makes it both a myth in its own society, and, in cold reality, a world university of the utmost distinction. So far as one man did that (and of course no single being alone could do that) he was pre-eminent, if not 'onlie begetter'. No small accomplishment.

This discussion does not deny that fine, committed and often lonely success. But we can ask who was pushed aside on the uphill trail. One answer is the academic black.

Lowell saw that his essential task was to transform Harvard into a residential university. He took this informal mixing together of men from different backgrounds as the secret of Oxbridge. He wanted college men and college spirit, an education which was social as well as academic. So he was tireless in raising funds for student buildings, and in pressing his committees even harder to make 'living in', at least in the first year, a precondition for a Harvard degree.

He also accepted that Harvard should have a black entry. There lay his illuminating dilemma. Those outside Harvard first became aware of it when a former student (who was black) made public Lowell's reply when he wanted to know why his son could not be considered for the elite Exeter Academy (where residence was now compulsory). To Lowell it was obvious. He wrote back: 'I am sure you will understand why . . . we have not thought it possible to compell men of different races to reside together.' It wasn't obvious to everybody, including again Lowell's steady opponent, the young Franklin D. Roosevelt.

David Riesman elegantly summarizes the position:

> In spite of his concern for breaking down the social barriers among Harvard's white students by requiring them all to live in college residences, he saw no contradiction in imposing a ban on Negroes living in the freshman dormitories established in 1914. He stated that it would be unwise 'for a Negro to apply for a room in the dormitories . . . it has nothing to do with the education he receives; that, of course, we furnish equally to all men without distinction as to race, color or previous condition of servitude. It is a different matter from a social commingling in the freshman dormitories.' Black freshmen alone had to live in segregated quarters off campus.

It was a different – perhaps irreconcilably different – view of America to that of Vanzetti:

> That was a hard year. The poor slept out of doors, and for food fumbled in the waste barrels for a cabbage leaf or a half rotten apple. For three months I walked New York its whole length and width in search of work.

The Jewish quota

In the year in which Vanzetti arrived in America and recalls in those lines, the percentage of Jews at Harvard was 6. By the time he found himself in a Massachusetts prison it had risen to 21 per cent.

Lowell was alarmed. In June 1922 his office issued a statement to say that 'the proportion of Jews at the college . . . is in the stage of general discussion . . . . If their number should become 40 per cent of the student body, the race feeling would become intense.' He later gathered support from a Student Council Committee on Education which claimed 'no college can admit unassimilables with impunity'.

Harvard backed him – again we see him not as a caricatured villain but as a big figure blending into a sympathetic landscape – and the university voted for a formula whereby each state had a quota of students. Since the Jewish intake came largely from New York rather than Utah or Nebraska, this effectively cut it back. Under Lowell it now began its decline to 10 per cent.

Lowell's personal antagonism towards Jewish entry to the high echelons of American life went much deeper, not sparing those of quite outstanding academic distinction. Felix Frankfurter – final legal defender of Sacco and Vanzetti – was the last Jew to be appointed to the Harvard Law School until 1939. Lowell had by then gone, but not his shadow. And to be fair it was a shadow which lay across all the States and across the Italian community too.

As time's perspectives shift, and with them the value ground of our judgment, I have selected three aspects of Lowell's attitudes. More could be added: his fight against the legislation reducing child labour in the textile trade; his attempt to prevent Louis Brandeis from becoming a Justice of the Supreme Court; his resilient opposition to Franklin D. Roosevelt's move towards the New Deal.

What is now evident is that all these views are part of a coherent whole. When he began the review, Lowell told Judge Grant that he expected to discover injustice. There is little need for dark hints about an ultimate conspiracy against Sacco and Vanzetti, vindicating traces of which might be found as the Lowell archives are opened and scrutinized. Moreover Lowell was a large, crucial but by no means a single figure. His views plainly represented a substantial body of American opinion then. They also offended a considerable number. They united much, maybe most, but by no means all, of the Anglo-Saxon establishment, together with very many of those workers of originally north European stock who were threatened by black emancipation or by new generations from Slavic, Jewish and Mediterranean backgrounds.

The courts, the universities, the police, and much of the media then 'belonged' to this group. And yet, to style his attitude prejudice is to simplify too much. It was a first snarl of an older, dying America.

Looking back from our own precarious vantage point, perhaps we can accept that the appointment of the Lowell tribunal was disinterested and serious. It took immense pains over its difficult duty. And yet there was a thumb in the scales of justice. Not personal: not at all. The blind spot was there in the culture. The weaknesses in the case that inexorably led to the execution of Sacco and Vanzetti were transparent fifty years later to the committee of Governor Dukakis. To President Lowell of Harvard they were invisible.

Chapter Ten

'Have you agreed upon your verdict?'

I began this book in the clear belief that Sacco and Vanzetti were innocent. At the end I list the main part of the very considerable literature on the case. Almost without exception it assumes or argues innocence. In all that extensive bibliography I can only find four exceptions and one doubtful. One is *Sacco and Vanzetti in the Scales of Justice*, an apologia by one of the jurymen at the trial. This simply rehearses the case for the prosecution. The second is a minor, fugitive pamphlet. This is the Hon. William Renwick Riddel's *The Sacco–Vanzetti Case from a Canadian Viewpoint*. He puts aside charges that Judge Thayer ('I'll show that no long-haired anarchist from California can run this Court') was openly biased: 'in a trial lasting six or seven weeks, an occasional exhibition of irritation is to be expected. If a judge is to be condemned for an outbreak of this kind, now and then, who will escape?' Nor, writing in 1927, does the age of the Lowell Committee trouble him, saying it 'does not have any weight in the connexion in the estimation of a man who was born in 1852 and has daily converse with Canadian judges who were born in 1843, 1846 and 1847'. Apart from reminding us that judges do indeed live (and practice) to a ripe age, the essay carries more charm than conviction. It claims that 'a fair trial' took place in which 'no evidence was wrongfully excluded or admitted' and 'that the great delay in executing the sentence was due to Motions made by the condemned men and the extraordinary tenderness of the law of Massachusetts'.

The most substantial study coming out against Sacco and Vanzetti is Robert Montgomery's *The Murder and the Myth* ('the Sacco–Vanzetti Myth is the greatest lie of them all'). This moves carefully over all the major particulars of the case – the identification, the alibis, the bullet, Sacco's cap – and agrees with the jury's decision. What it lacks utterly is any sense of the politics of the case, any feel for what it was like to be an Italian anarchist in that America, how others might see you and how you might behave.

The doubtful is of a quite different calibre, and I shall return to it. There is some detail in Francis Russell's altogether striking study *Tragedy in Dedham*.

This radical consensus is not perhaps surprising. Yet it has its factual, intellectual and moral pitfalls. The prosecution had done its work. The men were dead. Now the literature was appealing over the heads of the courts to the world. The defence too attracted the sympathies of people who read and wrote, and not only is the case remarkable for the writings of the defendants, the pamphleteering at the time, and the legal books afterwards but also for the surge of creative writing that it stimulated ('A telegram was read', said the informer, 'from Upton Sinclair who promises to write a novel at once. He will call it *Boston*.')

So violent were the passions generated that you were either for Sacco and Vanzetti or against them. 'Don't you see the glory of the case?' declares one of the characters in *Boston*, 'It kills off the liberals.'

Part one of this book is based on a reading of all the published literature available in Britain. At the end of that I had no doubts as to their joint innocence. Part two took me to Boston, with the opportunity of talking to people at first hand and burrowing for new information. That worked in an odd way that I did not expect: *both* the case for innocence *and* the case for guilt seemed strengthened. In this part I would like to see if we can reassess the case now that the immediate passions are largely (though not wholly) dissipated. Were they guilty or not? What was the significance of their anarchy, and of their death?

The case for guilty

The arrest

Looking at the original statements made by Sacco and Vanzetti on the night of their arrest, we can see what immense damage they did. The police are acting on a tip-off. They board the trolley and see two men who roughly fit the descriptions of the ones they want, they are linked with a Buick which could be the getaway car, they are not only armed but considerably so, they are professed anarchists, and their statements are transparently full of evasion and fantasy. Vanzetti's affidavit is an important work of that free imagination which suffering will smelt into something more tough and tempered. Sacco is completely unable to explain why he carries a gun. ('I don't know what I had it for. It seems to be a habit of Italian people.') It is quite reasonable for the police to detain them. Indeed it would have been unreasonable to let them go. Consciousness of guilt is a fair element to weave in to the prosecuting case, and it is abundantly clear that whether or not they felt guilty about the South Braintree murder, they certainly felt fearful or guilty *about something*.

It was the 'consciousness of guilt' charge that the prosecution were most powerfully able to develop. From this basis they were the more strongly able to build their charges of draft dodging and violent anarchical attitudes. These may have been, in context, unfair or even illegitimate, but the subsequent argument about that obscures the events at the time of their arrest. The Sacco and Vanzetti on the trolley and at the police station were hardly the Sacco and Vanzetti of legend.

The guns

There is no avoiding the fact that Sacco and Vanzetti were armed. Vanzetti, who was to become the pre-eminent spokesman for peace, says he bought his revolver under a false name. He has no permit. He has bullets in his pocket which he says 'Nick gave me'. His reason for carrying a gun on public transport is that he is worried about the $60 in his pocket.

Sacco too has bought his gun under an assumed name. It is loaded and carefully concealed down his trousers. He has twenty-three loose shells in his pocket. He carries a revolver, he says, as 'a habit'. At home he has a rifle.

Two of the defence explanations at the trial, (a) that Sacco had planned to go hunting, and (b) that he sometimes worked as a nightwatchman, have worn wafer-thin with time. The third explanation – not so prominent at the trial, but developed by Sacco and Vanzetti's defenders – was that they were getting rid of the guns and bullets, just as they were dumping their anarchist literature. Yet even so, why did they possess such an armoury?

The bullet

At the trial the ballistics experts disagree. We can now see that, through a legal trick, Katzmann framed the influential question to Captain Proctor so that instead of replying 'no', he could say that the fatal bullet was 'consistent with being fired' from Sacco's pistol. But ballistics was an imperfect science, and by the time of the Lowell Committee more refined techniques were available. By then those who testified in ballistics for the defence wavered or withdrew. Last, on October 11, 1961, a test was set up conducted by Jac Weller, honorary curator of West Point Museum, and Col. Frank Jury, former head of the Firearms Laboratory of New Jersey State Police. They were able to use a modern comparison microscope which fuses the two images. Assuming gun and bullets were the original ones, they found that five bullets did not come from Sacco's gun, but that one certainly did.

Doubts

Many of those closest to Sacco and Vanzetti, and many of those who defended them most strongly in public, doubted their innocence. Katherine Anne Porter, the southern novelist, who was many times arrested during the final demonstrations, was shocked to come across Communists in the group who believed them guilty and wanted them to be executed – the purpose was only to make a political event out of the case and death. But the doubts went much deeper, sufficient for Francis Russell, the historian of the case, to change his mind about Sacco's guilt. According to Upton Sinclair, once their major public advocate, their lawyer Fred Moore believed them guilty. Moore had made a serious attempt to trace an Italian gang who may have been involved in the hold-up – and of course we know there were more than two people on the South Braintree raid. He was told to stop by the Italian anarchists on the Defense Committee. Upton Sinclair also comments, 'I had visited Sacco's family and I felt certain that there was some dark secret there. Nobody would be frank with me, and everybody was suspicious, even though I had been introduced and vouched for by Mrs Evans, a great lady of Boston.' Of course it may be that the Sacco family had good reasons for distrust and great ladies were not their concern, since great gentlemen had sent Nicola to his death. But these intimate doubts niggle on. In 1943 Max Eastman did a profile in The *New Yorker* of Carlo Tresca, the veteran anarchist. He had been closely involved in the Italian anarchist group around Sacco and Vanzetti. When he returned to see him (and Tresca had the impeccable police record of thirty-six arrests) he 'felt close enough to ask him one day, when whispers had reached me concerning Upton Sinclair's distressing experiences in Boston:

"Carlo, would you feel free to tell me the truth about Sacco and Vanzetti?"

'He answered "Sacco was guilty but Vanzetti was not". At that moment some people entered the room where we were talking and I lost the chance to ask more. I lost it permanently, for I had no opportunity to see Carlo again before he was himself shot by an assassin.' Unfortunately Eastman did not publish this until much later, and again the prompt was indirectly Upton Sinclair.

And one must remember that even Thompson, their final lawyer, who recorded his moving interview with Vanzetti just before the execution, still felt he had to ask the question and seek some final reassurance that the long and unsuccessful defence had been grounded in truth:

Vanzetti then told me quietly and calmly and with a sincerity which I could not doubt, that I need have no anxiety about this matter; that both he and Sacco were absolutely innocent of the South Braintree crime, and that he was equally innocent of the Bridgewater crime.

What is remarkable about these doubts, and indeed disbelief, is that they were so persistent, rooted amongst those most intimately involved in the defence, and yet almost utterly erased in the public stance or in the considerable literature that followed. There was a *political* case to make for Sacco and Vanzetti even if one believed they were guilty in the *criminal* case.

The case for not guilty

Fearful behaviour

Their behaviour and explanations on the night of the arrest were to help lead them to the electric chair. Certainly, looked at in the narrow terms of the case as tried, it was very damaging and combined with other evidence, damning. As their defence, under Fred Moore, grew more radical in tone, they argued that it was natural that their behaviour was fearful. Not only were the police arresting Reds in the Palmer raids, but the anarchist leader Salsedo had mysteriously died in police custody.

Robert Montgomery, a very fair and representative lawyer, dismisses this point, much as the jury did:

> The *death* of Salsedo is an event of no consequence in determining any issue in the Sacco Vanzetti case. Sacco and Vanzetti learned about it on May 4 1920 from newspaper accounts which do not suggest it was anything but a suicide. It is impossible to believe that before the evening of the next day they had decided that Salsedo had been murdered and that they were in danger of being murdered by the Department of Justice, and for that reason armed themselves, menaced a policeman, and told lies to Stewart and Katzmann.

But reflect on the sequence from their point of view, and consider the state and the police through their eyes. They are armed, they have a mass of anarchist literature. Both must feel they are known to the police. Sacco had been arrested for attending an illegal anarchist meeting in 1916. In January or February 1920, he had been told by his employer, George Kelley, that Federal Agents were asking questions about him.

On February 28 Salsedo is arrested and kept in custody. On April 15 comes the South Braintree hold-up and murder. On April 16 Coacci is arrested and deported the very next day. On April 28 Vanzetti is sent to New York by the anarchist committee to try and find out what had happened to Salsedo. As a prominent anarchist on such a mission he must assume that the police probably have eyes on him – whether they do or not.

On May 2 Sacco attends an anarchist meeting at which Vanzetti reports what he has discovered about Salsedo. At 4 a.m. on the morning of May 3 Salsedo jumps through a window on the fourteenth storey at Park Row. The papers call it suicide. The police hint that he has told all, betrayed his colleagues and then felt remorse. It is not 'impossible to believe' that they decided this was a police murder. That indeed would be the first explanation – then as now – that any radical might entertain. Suicide whilst in police custody has a well-justified place in the left's chamber of horrors. Even the subsidiary explanation, that Salsedo under pressure (these are the days of the third degree) had implicated his comrades, might be terrifying enough. How long, they might think, before they too were falling out of fourteen-storey windows? The very style of Salsedo's death, if murder, could have been meant to frighten and flush out the leaders of the remaining anarchist cells.

The very next day, May 4, Sacco returns to the Italian Consulate and seeks a passport. This episode was prominent in the trial partly because of the outsize nature of the photograph he took along. What he brings is really a large family picture, not a passport photo. Its oddity is one reason why the consulate clerk, Guiseppe Andrower, claims to remember his first calling on April 15 with it. He is disbelieved as to the date. Under ferocious questioning he admits dealing with 150 to 200 callers a day, and though he fails to remember a single one on April 16, April 17, April 19, April 21, April 24, April 29, May 2, May 3 or May 4, he says he recalls Sacco on April 15: the day of the murder. It seems highly unlikely, but it also serves to obscure the matter of the unusual photograph. Why did Sacco do this? Others didn't, and he was hardly the most ignorant of the Italian community. Was it so as to stand out, and help establish an alibi? But then the day would have been wrong. Surely it is much more likely to be the sign of a man in a hurry to get out of America? This is the effect of Salsedo's death. The next day he and Vanzetti set off to get rid of the guns and literature. And that evening they are arrested. Naturally they lie to Stewart and Katzmann, not because of South Braintree but because they are armed anarchists and now find themselves where Salsedo was.

The guns

It remains difficult to find a credible defence on this point. It can be argued that the rifle at Sacco's house has nothing to do with the case, and was – as he claimed – bought for a future hunting holiday in Maine. This remains an uncomfortable defence, though, since there is nothing in Sacco's life which suggests he had ever gone hunting before or would be in any way the kind of person to be interested in such a sport. The trip never took place.

Much more important was the gun he was carrying. The strongest part of the trial defence was that he was anxious to use up the ammunition before he left for Italy or before police raided him as a known anarchist. This certainly could account for the large amount of spare ammunition he carried. How he was likely to get rid of this on their apparently aimless trolley ride remains obscure. It would have been simpler to toss gun and bullets into the Charles River.

Why Vanzetti also was carrying a gun remains an awkward fact. Time has only sharpened its bleakness. The Lowell Committee insists he had a pistol 'resembling' the one taken by the killers from the dying Berardelli. Vanzetti's argument is that it was his own and a defence against robbery. None of this fits with the pacifist position that he maintained during his long imprisonment.

The soundest defence is perhaps the most trivial one, or one that could not be developed at the trial because of the posture that the defence had taken up. This is that gun-carrying was a not uncommon display of *machismo* in the Italian community, and that both Sacco and Vanzetti, if unlikely to shed blood, were not above playing with guns as they were not above playing with revolutionary ideas. The large amount of spare ammunition is consistent with the idea of having a final small-boy fusillade in the woods, and the reason this never happened – just as they never found Vanzetti's friend or even discovered his address – was due to plain incompetence.

The fatal bullet

Time leaves three lines of defence, all frail but all possible. First is the more rough and ready nature of ballistic identification at that time. It was a matter of eye and judgment, and the experts simply disagreed. Second is the inefficiency of the police. Even if we rule out the idea of the police deliberately planting the significant bullet (and after all this has been done before) then – to say the least of it – this damning evidence was most carelessly handled. How many bullets were there? Who took charge of them? Did anyone test fire Sacco's gun, and did *that* bullet creep into the exhibits at court? This kind of muddle was again not uncommon. Major Goddard, the decisive ballistics expert to the Lowell Committee (*against* Sacco) was later to be involved in exactly such a mix-up of bullets in a case at Cleveland.

Third comes the 1961 test. On the face of it, this conclusively points to Sacco's guilt. But there is a hole in the centre of the argument. Was this gun and these bullets the same ones as those that appeared in court forty years earlier? During those intervening decades both had passed into private hands, souvenirs of a famous case. It is not impossible that many revolvers were bought and sold as 'the gun that Sacco had'. This doesn't wholly account for the match between gun and bullet, but it is not an unlikely explanation. The 1977 Report to Governor Dukakis dismisses this evidence against Sacco, perhaps too casually, in a brief footnote: 'There was no trail of continuous custody, not any witness who could reliably establish these bullets and gun as the bullets and gun put into evidence.'

Accumulation of detail

It was not so much one item which appeared to lead to a guilty verdict. It was the sheer accumulation of detail. Much of this has been eroded by time. Sacco's cap – and the tear in it where he hung it on a nail at work – now seems a ludicrously trivial detail with which to push a man towards his death. Yet it bulked large in the drama of the trial. It is now reasonable to think that the tear anyway was added by the police, whether inadvertently or not.

Similarly the identification evidence would no longer stand up. There hangs over this part of the case both a readiness to think that one Italian looks much like another, and – in the age of Al Capone – to think they all look like gunmen. We now know a good deal more about the mistakes witnesses may make even in very well organized identification. How much more likely is error to creep in when we have Sacco crouching like a Mafia hitman and pretending to point a pistol?

Where is the money?

Lastly the case is remarkable in that none of the rest of the gang were detected nor was the money found. The police simply did not provide the depth of knowledge one would expect in a case like this; and in the courtroom the whole enquiry – by the defence as well as by the prosecution – is oddly foreshortened.

Verdicts of time

Francis Russell mentions the remark of Ferris Greenslet, the historian of this Boston period. 'In his Ingwall Lecture at Harvard, Lowes Dickinson inquired "Is immortality desirable?" I almost think it is, if only to get at the truth of the Sacco–Vanzetti case.'

As I suggested earlier, the passing of the years has, para-doxically, strengthened both the case for guilt and the case for innocence. The reader will have his own views, but several answers are open to us. The first is that they were both guilty. This rests largely on their being heavily armed, the evidence of gun and bullets, their initial behaviour and statements, and the fact that Vanzetti had already been tried and convicted by a separate jury (if the same judge) of the White Shoe Company hold-up. To this can now be added their failure to convince many of their closest supporters of their innocence. And perhaps the paradox of 'a good shoemaker and a poor fish pedlar' being armed robbers is not so strange to us as it was then. We live in a world in which men and women of high ideals – associated with the Irish Republican Army, the Palestine Liberation Front, the Black Panthers, or many of the radical groups in Europe or the Third World – use violence both to fund their movements and to disrupt the society around. The anarchist movement in the United States, as elsewhere, had a history of violence, and both the Bridgewater and South Braintree hold-ups could be explained as attempts to capture funds for the movement. The clumsiness of both (the first was a farce, the second a tragedy) points away from a professional gang.

There is a second possibility. That is that one was guilty, one innocent. Carlo Tresca the old anarchist thought at the end that Sacco was guilty, Vanzetti not. Their lawyer, Fred Moore, at one stage considered pleading guilty for Sacco in order to win an innocence verdict for Vanzetti. When he tried to raise this with Vanzetti, he was met by the opposite advice: 'Save Nick, he has the woman and child.' Francis Russell in his study of the case comes to the same split conclusion.

It is possible. But I find it very hard to believe. It means that one man carried the other to death with him, and both knew it. And yet over those seven emotional years – even in the periods of mental instability from which both suffered – neither even hinted at it to those closest to them.

In researching and writing this study, I began, as I said, with a belief in their innocence. But at many later points in the work I doubted it, changed and rechanged my mind. What we can see, I think, is that Governor Dukakis was right. By the standards of today they did not have a fair trial. A 'not proven' verdict is unavoidable, and the use of capital punishment ended whatever hope there ever was of learning more about the truth.

Personally, though I retain some scintillas of doubt, I can only conclude that the State of Massachusetts executed two innocent men. Not perhaps the men whom their supporters presented to the public. The liberals who were drawn to their defence, and the propaganda which they necessarily radiated around the world softened the image, transforming them into gentle humanists. A striking example of this was the editing of their letters from which hatred of the church and the need to fight the class war was all excised. As radical spirits Sacco and Vanzetti were in the end silenced by the prosecution, but on the way they were muffled by the defence.

Unlike their defenders and earlier writers, I now find them – imperfectly through time and record – as men who at least entertained the idea of violence as a cleansing force in a rotten society. In the social conditions and conflicting philosophies of their time, this was perhaps their most logical and most natural position. Both were sharp-edged revolutionaries who went to their deaths as uncompromising anarchists. No 'parlour socialist' could possibly have maintained the basic ethic of nihilism, or any of the main branches of anarchy, when facing the chair for seven years. Their defenders were overwhelmingly liberal humanists, quickened by a sense of individual injustice in one particular trial, in one especial state. And both Sacco and Vanzetti were gentle and caring men in their immediate and daily relationships. Yet both had that touch of iron without which no revolution would pay the price necessary for success. We know they were capable of dying for anarchy. We may debate whether they were capable of killing for anarchy.

Their trial was an intricate legal exercise by a state whose pride in its new-world law blinded it to the injustice of those narrowing procedures which placed so much power in the hands of a single judge. One recalls the wiretapper overhearing the remarks in Felix Frankfurter's apartment: 'It is a most awful situation when your legal system will not insure moral demands: that is what leads to revolution.' As a case, the evidence was much more evenly balanced, and more elusive than either side would admit. A reasonable man could have his doubts both ways, but it can hardly be maintained that guilt was proven at the time. Theirs was not an age of reason in American history. Both were guilty – and proudly so – of a cultural crime. They were foreign, working class, armed and anarchist. This clouded all judgments. In the end it was for this that the state executed them.

Chapter Eleven

Culture or anarchy

'There will have to be bloodshed. There will have to be murder. We will kill because it is necessary. There will have to be destruction. We will destroy to rid the world of tyrannical institutions.' I take these words from a piece of pink paper left fluttering outside the house of Mitchell Palmer on June 2, 1919. A. Mitchell Palmer was Attorney General of the United States. This small study began with his defiant counter-words:

> Each and every adherent of this movement is a potential murderer or a potential thief, and deserves no consideration. The Red Movement is not a righteous or honest protest against alleged defects in our present political and economic organization of society. It is a distinctly criminal and dis-honest movement in the desire to obtain possession of other people's property by violence and sabotage. All their new words, 'Bolshevism', 'Syndicalism', 'Sabotage', etc. are only new names for old theories of vice and criminality.

Maybe. Underneath the Attorney General's rhetoric, and behind that stray fragment of pink paper, lurk the classical principles of one school of anarchism. If 'Property is Theft', then only violence breaks the established order and opens the way to a free and equal society which celebrates instead of repressing the rights, liberty and creativity of the individual. Perhaps, in this essay, it is time to remind ourselves of what anarchy means and why these two men unwillingly yet unwaveringly held to that belief. We hear about the lost bullet, the missing money, the eels on Christmas Eve, the nail-tear in the flat cap. Yet in all the many commentaries on this testing case there is not a handful of pages to explain the political ideas that yet determined so much. To do that we must start with an America unwillingly drawn into its first World War, and with anarchy, a diverse theory of revolution which in those tremulous years threatened to shake the United States. Neither Sacco nor Vanzetti nor Stewart the police chief at Bridgewater, Katzmann the prosecutor, Thayer the judge, Palmer the Attorney General – nor all the jurors and jurists – were fools. I doubt if any of them were fixers. The arrest and trial of Sacco and Vanzetti was a frontier battle between culture and anarchy, as each side determined those terms. For a brief spell of American history, certainly of New England and New York history, it seemed to those involved that all could be won or all could be lost. As indeed it had, at that same moment, and surrounded by an identically indifferent population, in Petrograd. On November 7, 1917, when the Bolsheviks took over only six people were killed, and Chaliapin sang undisturbed at the Opera.

But first let us go back to the Attorney General. The pink manifesto was picked up after an attempt to bomb his home. The reason was almost certainly the Palmer raid on the radicals in which 4,000 arrests were made. Search them out, short-cut the law, short-shrift them with group trials, ship them back home to Europe.

The bomber died in his task. Like many anarchists before and after him, he blew himself up. The American police quite brilliantly traced his identity from the remaining patch of his snappy polka-dot tie and from the heel of his remaining shoe. The trail led back to the New England anarchists whose most prominent figures – though they worked in New York, Chicago and elsewhere – were Luigi Galleani who published *Cronaca Souversiva* (the *Chronicle of Subversion*), Salsedo who was to fall fourteen storeys from the police office, and Carlo Tresca, later to be assassinated by a Soviet agent. Among minor characters in the misty background were Coacci and Boda. Both left the United States in some haste soon after the South Braintree murder. Two others in that circle who did not – or did not get out in time – were Nicola Sacco and Bartolomeo Vanzetti.

Their America was a political paradox. Georgia in 1915 had

seen the refounding of the Ku Klux Klan. S. M. Lipset estimated that it was to grow so astonishingly as to include between 25 per cent and 30 per cent of adult male Protestants. July 1919 saw the formation of the American Communist Party. It was a paradox which stretched across the Atlantic. John Reed, chairman of that meeting which founded the Communist-Labor Party was a graduate of Harvard. He was also an eye-witness of the October Revolution in Petrograd and author in 1919 of *Ten Days that Shook the World*. He now lies buried under the Kremlin wall.

Trotsky was a minor refugee in New York at the same time that Vanzetti was a migrant worker there. For Trotsky it was 'a peep into the foundry in which the fate of men is to be forged.' One carried, through his words, the black flag, the other, the red. But the sense of America was overwhelming to both. Trotsky noted:

> It is a fact that the economic lot of Europe is being shattered
> to its very foundations, while American wealth is growing.
> As I look enviously at New York – I who have not ceased to
> feel like a European – I wonder anxiously: 'Will Europe be
> able to stand all this? Will it not decay and become little
> better than a graveyard? And will not the world's economic
> and cultural centres of gravity shift to America?'

On March 27, 1917 Trotsky left New York on the Norwegian steamship *Christianafjord*. Despite a farcical interception by the British naval police at Halifax, Nova Scotia, on April 3 (all foreigners being the same, he was put into a German prisoner-of-war camp, soon converted many and was sent off by inmates singing the *Internationale*), he arrived in Petrograd on 17 May. Trotsky, like Lenin in his closed train from Switzerland, carried his revolution from West to East. Attorney General Palmer might well have understood. After all he was soon to commandeer liners to despatch the anarchists, communists and socialists (249 on a single boat in December 1919) 'back home'. ('My motto for the Reds,' said Guy Emprey then, 'is ship or shoot'.) But whilst Trotsky, like the ageing Prince Kropotkin, went East, Vanzetti was still in New York, Sacco in Boston – washing dishes by day and – in what free time there was – searching for the rebellious Petrograd of the West over which the black and not the red flag might yet fly. For a moment in American history it must have seemed just possible.

Only a few Octobers later Italy, which had sent not only Sacco and Vanzetti but many thousands of radicals to the United States, was to hail the fascist march on Rome. Indeed Mussolini became one of the voices pleading with the Commonwealth of Massachusetts for their lives. The skeins which were to make the Sacco–Vanzetti case led round the world.

But there was much about their America which both helped to explain the paradox and which was yet special and sometimes unique to that country, nowhere more so than in Massachusetts. Its capital, Boston, was where Paul Revere from the North Church rang the bell that was to toll the knell of British rule. The old bridge at Concord where 'the shot was fired that rang round the world' is only thirty miles away. To come to Boston is to take the Freedom Trail. No city anywhere more densely celebrates – in its parks, statues, parlance, mythology – rebellion and revolution and individual liberty, above all in its laws – the very ones whose labyrinthine complexity ensnared Sacco and Vanzetti. Those laws had become (and remain) a wealthy industry: a new estate of the Commonwealth ('It is a most awful situation when your legal system will not ensure moral demands.') If the Massachusetts of the Great War and the frenetic 1920s was an America in miniature (though it wasn't quite that) then we could consider its culture from several sides. Back in time lay the glorious rebellion against the British, cradled here. Within the lifetime of Robert Lowell and Webster Thayer resided memories of the Civil War and the emancipation of the black slaves. Nowhere else – except perhaps in Britain – did the libertarian tradition boast such credentials. Elsewhere Sacco and Vanzetti would have disappeared like so many migrant, criminal or political prisoners 'unmarked'. The paradox of their drama lay in the setting. Boston was British. A breakaway city permeated with a pristine sense of Anglo-Saxon culture, touched – as it often is still – with a nostalgia for England. Around it a continent of such opportunity and such wealth as the European mind (cramped in its ancient and intricate patterns of survival) dare hardly comprehend. In Boston, Massachusetts, Anglo-Saxon culture was reborn, amassing vast wealth, asserting a new moral pride, breeding and spreading its values, its literature, its universities, its governance, its law. Boston – or rather *that* Boston – could always remain aloof from America. But 'salt water isolation' from

Europe was brief. Europe filled the migrant ships: the working-class English, the Irish, the Germans, the Poles, the eastern Jews, and the Italians. Their skills and labour became one of the foundations of even Boston's riches and style. And they brought with them ideas. Ideas about that skill, that labour, that distribution of wealth and the place of the person within the state. The old notions of *égalité*, *liberté*, *fraternité* were being reworked around the looms of Lowell mills.

The war of 1914–18 pulled America back into Europe. Death or honours there bonded the two. And then the new and rapid technology – wireless, cable, aeroplane – stitched the two.

Sacco and Vanzetti, whether innocent or guilty, represented an idea that the old Beacon Hill culture found hard to comprehend – precisely because it was its own past speaking with a new voice.

For what did the black flag of anarchism stand? If you read the trial manuscript or all the many books and pamphlets on this crucial case, it is astonishing how the political culture of the defendants is either ignored or passed off as a label: 'dodging the draft', 'anarchistic bastards'. Any developed sense of what anarchism meant was clearly lacking with the prosecution, the defence, the Governor, the Lowell committee, the press, and the legal and academic commentators. In those courts and all the long prison years, only Sacco and Vanzetti seemed to know what anarchism was and to what it aspired. That is part of the poignancy of their letters, letters often addressed to a quite different cultural understanding than that within which they were entrapped.

Perhaps one should review the anarchist tradition that they took with them to America, and there ('at street corners to scorning men') tried to radiate. To that Boston and New York anarchism meant bearded European emigrés throwing random bombs for incomprehensible ends. And not without reason. Though it is not mentioned anywhere in the Sacco–Vanzetti papers or commentaries, their trial, fate and pardon was prefigured in American history, and quite central to the fears, doubts and actions of any anarchist in that country at that time. The 1977 advisers who recommended a retrospective 'not proven' verdict to Governor Dukakis of Massachusetts even then saw it in the tradition of the old New England witch hunts and persecutions.

('In Massachusetts, the Legislature has resolved that "no disgrace or cause for distress" exist for Ann Pudeator, executed in 1692 for witchcraft, and her descendants. c. 145, Resolves of 1957; and Governor Dukakis on August 25, 1976, by proclamation revoked the 1637 banishment of Anne Marbury Hutchinson.') But there is a more political lineage.

On May Day 1886 there was a strike on at the McCormick Harvester Works in Chicago. Some called it a lock-out, and certainly fresh workers were taken on. They were watched by 300 armed Pinkerton detectives. As at South Braintree, the employer was protecting his property by gun-carrying private guards. The picketing, demonstration and provocation was led by the anarchists. Half of America's 6,000 membership of the movement came from the German and Czech migrants of Chicago.

On May 3 the Chicago police fired on the crowd. Several were killed, many wounded. On May 4 a huge protest meeting took place in the rain at Haymarket Square. Police moved in to break it up. Suddenly someone threw a bomb from a side-alley. Seven policemen were blown up. The rest began firing (sometimes, in the panic, at each other). Some of the demonstrators produced guns and shot back. It was all over very quickly. Some twenty of the crowd lay dead in the Square. It was a scene from nineteenth-century Russian and European history that could have been a prologue to a different American future.

There were mass arrests of anarchists. Eight were charged with murder. They included two anarchist intellectuals: August Spies, editor of the Chicago *Die Arbeiter Zeitung*, and Albert Parsons who put out *Alarm*. The case against them was drawn almost entirely from the strain of violence in anarchist literature. Seven were found guilty, and four were hanged.

Several years later Governor Altgeld set up an enquiry, much like Governor Dukakis, and found that though the hanged men were undoubtedly anarchists, and linked closely to the violence of language, nevertheless there was no evidence at all that they had been involved in the bomb-throwing – or that some of them were anywhere near the Square at the time.

Every anarchist in America knew the story, even if many lawyers had forgotten it. It rehearsed so many elements of the Sacco–Vanzetti case: the anarchist propaganda, the attempt to move in on strikes and lock-outs, the presence of the private army, guns and the police, discounted alibis, prejudice and law and retrospective pardon. Frank Harris writes about the Haymarket killing in his almost forgotten novel *The Bomb*, as Upton Sinclair was to place Sacco and Vanzetti in documentary fiction on the pages of *Boston*. On the night Sacco and Vanzetti were arrested, they had every reason, aware or unaware of the Braintree crime, to know what 'anarchist' meant to a cop, a judge, a jury, or public opinion.

The black flag of anarchism is an old banner. In the United States it drew from two strains. First was the frontier tradition, the sense of man making his own terms with the wild, the animal kingdom, and distant cities. No state had a finer tradition than Massachusetts, nor more superb writers to celebrate it. In Chapter 7 Sacco and Vanzetti ('those two little devils') are imprisoned only a couple of miles or so from where Thoreau (author of *On the Duty of Civil Disobedience*) retired from the social into the individual life in *Walden*.

The high Anglo-Saxon culture of New England could be sympathetic in retrospect to this style of life and its explorations. But there was a tendency to feel it as retreat, even as vacation or weekend living in the woods.

But Sacco and Vanzetti carried with them not only this pastoral sense but like many other migrant anarchists, an altogether more powerful, subversive and sometimes violent philosophy of anarchism from Europe. It is almost impossible to describe the anarchist tradition because it is itself so anarchic. Better accounts than mine will be found by reading modern writers such as Herbert Read and George Woodcock, or the great and successful arch-enemies Karl Marx and V. I. Lenin. All I can do in this brief space is to recall three founding figures – Pierre-Joseph Proudhon, Prince Peter Kropotkin, Michael Bakunin – and the two men who most widely spread the pacific sense of the idea – Leo Tolstoy and Mahatma Gandhi. And, to an extent, some of Martin Luther King's thinking and work could be placed in that tradition.

Pierre-Joseph Proudhon (whom Vanzetti struggled to translate during his hallucinatory spell in the Bridgewater Hospital for the Criminally Insane) published in 1840 his immensely challenging *What is Property?* His pithy answer was 'Property is theft'. The idea was realized, and a property-owning world was to expend a century hunting it down.

The Greek word *anarchos* is old enough, and has a fair lineage as a term of political abuse. Whilst Gerrard Winstanley, that mysterious figure from the age of Oliver Cromwell, was leading his Diggers, planting turnips by the Thames, as an act of positive defiance of both old King and new dictator, government press statements were denouncing 'Switzering anarchists'. But as a modern philosophy of society, it begins with Proudhon.

Pierre-Joseph Proudhon came from working-class stock: 'In my father's house, we breakfasted on maize porridge; at midday we ate potatoes; in the evening bacon soup.' His father was a cooper and then a hopeless innkeeper. He himself became an apprentice printer in Besançon. When he earned his craft credentials his depressed partner killed himself. For thirty years he had to pay the financial debts of that sudden act.

He was a self-educated man who, with astonishing energy, wrote, won prizes, and found publishers for a long line of pamphlets and books. In 1840 he wrote himself into the history of the nineteenth century when he published *Qu'est-ce que la Propriéte? ou recherche sur le principe du droit et du gouvernement.* Karl Marx in his review welcomed it as 'the first decisive, vigorous, and scientific examination' of the question of property. He was soon to learn that he and Proudhon could not be further apart.

Proudhon celebrated 'the eternal germ of life' – individual independence as the absolute basis of a new society. The communists were more and more to clarify Marx's belief that only the state – collective socialism – could ultimately redistribute or create equal life-chances for everyone. But for decades there was a foggy and sometimes bitter debate. The famous phrase that the state, under communist control, would in the end 'wither away' must, I think, have been one of the many attempts at verbal compromise with the anarchists. But black and red could never meet. In their last uneasy alliance during the Spanish Civil War they were as likely to kill each other as the fascist enemy.

But Proudhon genuinely sought a state which did indeed 'wither away'. Early on he entertained ideas of the necessity for violence. The revolution will come, he somewhat vaguely threatens in his *Advertisement aux propriétaires*, not through 'regicide, nor assassination, nor poisoning, nor arson, nor refusal to work, nor emigration, nor insurrection, nor suicide; it is something more terrible than all that, and more efficacious, something which is seen but cannot be spoken of.' But increasingly he dreamed and radiated the idea of peaceful change: a 'war of the workshops' in which society would break down into networks of nearly self-sufficient villages, guilds of local craftsmen, free and voluntary associations, and above all individual liberty. It was an idea whose facets he shared with Thoreau in New England, William Morris in old England ('And dream of London, small and white and clean'), Leo Tolstoy in Russia and M. K. Gandhi in India. It is a powerful and persuasive idea which lives today in notions or experiments in self-sufficient living, alternative technology, the breaking down of professions and bureaucracy and the release of rights to the client, the consumer, the family, the child.

During the great revolutionary year of 1848 he argued that the working class 'must emancipate itself without the help of government'. He threw himself into immediate politics, had his papers suppressed, spoke out in defence of the insurrectionists in the Constituent Assembly ('irremediably dull', reported the British Ambassador) and during years in the Sainte-Pélague prison or in frontier exile in Belgium almost inadvertently created a huge following. In Flanders he received hand-delivered messages from Michael Bakunin, then exiled in Tomsk. Tolstoy came to call on him as he was drafting *La Guerre et la paix* ('the end of militarism is the mission of the nineteenth century'). It is perhaps now forgotten that Tolstoy was to remember both title and idea, and in *War and Peace* speaks in fiction across the centuries when Proudhon in abstract argument was much more confined to the revolutionary generations between the risings of 1848 and the Paris Commune.

Like William Morris he argued for 'the world we have lost': village, craftsman, guild. 'Each citizen, each town, each industrial union will make its own laws.' Like so many later anarchists he had a sense of a United States of Europe, built up from small crafts associations and villages. He doubted if winning the vote by itself ultimately changed the lot of ordinary working people: Parliamentary democracy modulated but did not alter the distribution of power, of privilege – and most keenly for him – of liberty, freedom, independence. The French Revolution of 1789 was only half accomplished. One could argue the same about the

American revolution. Each needed a second stage. His followers lost their libertarian argument to Marx at that *First International* which was, through the stream of ideas, to change the world. Yet his appeal, which is eternal, was powerful in the small villages of France and Spain and especially Italy. At that moment it seemed that 'Italy' need not go the way that Cavour, Mazzini* and Garibaldi led it and become the nation state which Mussolini took over. It might instead become a loose, free federation of province, city, *campagna*. As it turned out many there – like Sacco and Vanzetti – had to seek an alternative future to Europe in the United States. Again the very name evoked imaginings of the federal world that they planned.

Prince Peter Kropotkin, second of the three seminal anarchist figures, was an utterly different man. Bernard Shaw was much later to describe him to George Woodcock as 'a shepherd from the Delectable Mountains' and Woodcock himself, that very fine scholar of anarchism, reached for Matthew Arnold's phrase in *Culture and Anarchy*: Kropotkin brought 'sweetness and light'. But Peter Kropotkin was born a hereditary prince in the royal house that once ruled, and never quite forgot, Smolensk. He was a page ('an actor in court ceremonies') to the Tsar, Alexander II, who in 1881 was assassinated by an anarchist. In the same year all America was to be astounded at the killing, on July 2, of the President, and whether his assassin was an anarchist or not, the very word became encrusted with layers of violence.

Kropotkin joined the Mounted Cossacks of the Amur and served in Siberia. He spent much time on glacial topography, earned a fine scientific reputation within the questions which Darwin had framed, and was offered the post of secretary of the Russian Geographical Society. It was the sight of dying political prisoners in the gold mines and the salt pits of Siberia that changed all that.

He resigned his commission after the execution of escaping Polish prisoners in his area, read Proudhon at the suggestion of the exiled poet M. L. Mikhailov, and went to western Europe. In the Jura mountains he met his first working libertarians: 'after a week's stay with the watchmakers, my views upon socialism were settled. I was an anarchist.'

From being a Prince, a royal page and an Imperial officer, he returned to Russia as the radical peasant Borodin. In the end he was arrested and immured in the Peter-and-Paul prison. He describes his spectacular escape from that notorious gaol in *Memoirs of a Revolutionist*, and published it in Boston in 1899, only a few years before Sacco and Vanzetti arrived there.

Kropotkin, like Marx, was to find long shelter in England; and, like Marx, spend hours researching and writing in the British Museum. But first he was to attract vast international attention when, to his complete surprise, he was arrested on a visit to France. There had been a number of explosions in the Massif Central and in the late autumn of 1882 the authorities reacted with mass arrests of known or suspected anarchists. Kropotkin, though quite out of touch with this French unrest, was picked up in the net. As was later recommended during the Palmer raids which preceded the arrests of Sacco and Vanzetti, the police aimed at mass arrests followed by mass trials in the hope of achieving maximum convictions. On January 3, 1883 Prince Kropotkin found himself in the dock at Lyons alongside fifty-three other anarchists. It was difficult, or rather impossible, to connect Kropotkin or any of the others with the Massif Central explosions, and the prosecution changed tack completely. They were instead accused of being members of the International – a proscribed organization – which indeed Kropotkin had been. All the defendants were very well aware that the International no longer existed. It is not clear that the prosecution or the judge knew or believed this. Like many anarchists before and after them, they turned the theatre of the courtroom into Proudhon's old weapon, 'the propaganda of the word'. Kropotkin addressed the court in scornful irony: 'scoundrels that we are, we demand bread for all; for all equally independence and justice.' He was given five years' imprisonment.

There was protest from all over liberal Europe and radical America. Victor Hugo presented a petition to the President of France whose signatories included William Morris, Swinburne, Leslie Stephen, Burne-Jones, John Morley and the major officials of the British Museum. The French Academy of Sciences offered a personal library service in his prison at Clairvaux. The *Encyclopaedia Britannica* asked him for contributions. It may have been then that he wrote for them the entry on Anarchism in which he presents his ambivalent defence of the use of violence by men of peace: 'Violence is resorted to by all parties in proportion as their open action is obstructed by repression, and exceptional laws render them outlaws.' Both Sacco and Vanzetti lived under 'exceptional laws'. First, the general law against anarchist immigrants which, erasing the promise of the Statue of Liberty, was passed under Theodore Roosevelt's presidency in 1903. This followed the building-up of public revulsion against the Haymarket bombing of 1886, the attempt in 1892 by the anarchist Alexander Berkman to murder the financier Henry Clay Frick (in revenge for the killing of strikers by private security guards during the Homestead steel strike), and ultimately the assassination in 1901 of Roosevelt's predecessor, President McKinley, by the young Polish anarchist Leon Czolgosz. Second, the draft law which compelled them to enlist for the nation state war of 1914–18 to which they were utterly hostile. The anarchist campaign against that law was largely organized (with Emma Goldman) by the same Alexander Berkman who had put three bullets into H. C. Frick. Released after fourteen years in Allegheny Penitentiary, he was by 1914 editing *Mother Earth*, in 1915 founding *Blast* in San Francisco, and appealing to anarchists to stay out and get out. This was when Nicola Sacco fled to Mexico under the alias of Mosmacotelli, an act which was to throw him open to the most deadly line of questioning at his trial. ('Is that your idea of showing your love for America?')

Kropotkin oddly was the only anarchist of any standing to take sides in the war. In his long years in Britain he mellowed, and was prepared to respect the loose coalition – craft, union, chapel, Marxist, Fabian – which was the stuff of the Labour Party. He wrote his most influential works – *Fields, Factories and Workshops* in 1889, *The Conquest of Bread* in 1906 – and in between them the anarchist book which seems to me to be as prompting and as practical today as it was for many then, the *Mutual Aid* of 1902. No other anarchist thinker so tried to sketch the blueprint of their Utopia. How exactly would a world work in which (to recall Proudhon) hunger, destitution, pauperism were annihilated, and yet man reduced his acquisitive wants so that what followed was not unrealistic abundance and wealth, but a modest, universal and independent self-sufficiency? Re-reading him now one sees how very much he is caught up in nineteenth-century arguments – now challenging Malthus, whose influential thesis that population would always tend to outstrip the supply of food dominated the early part of that century, as it still often does in the Third World today; later challenging Darwin, especially the devil-take-the-hindmost strain within that total competition (the 'gladiators' show') which was involved in the evolution of species. Leaving aside the Victorian sources of evidence to which Kropotkin turned – rocks and the Bible, spiralling population growth, competition or co-operation amongst animals – there hangs over all the sense of many, many hungry mouths and finite wealth to feed, clothe, house and help. And yet Kropotkin touches the edges of a manageable future. He probes the ideas of communes, small workshops, informal training, and queries the need not only for the state but for the military, economic, technical and bureaucratic systems that it breeds and which come to be seen as necessary struts in the world in which we live. He has a possible, rather than an apocalyptic or utopian sense of an alternative society, or, as Nicola Sacco said to Chief Stewart on the night of his arrest, 'Some things I like different.'

Kropotkin himself left for Russia after the February Revolution of 1917. Whereas Lenin negotiated his arrival perfectly for the October Revolution and Trotsky hurried from America late for a very important date, Kropotkin was too soon and misread what he saw. He was welcomed at the Finland Station in Petrograd by the *Marseillaise* and Kerensky. Kerensky and his middle-of-the-road supporters were all to lose everything within months to the Bolsheviks.

Kropotkin played no part in the decisive revolution. Many fellow anarchists did, and after its success they were amongst the first to be rounded up. 'This buries the Revolution,' said Kropotkin. He protested unsuccessfully to Lenin, and, confined to his desk, wrote his *Ethics* and his final *Letter to the Workers of the World*: a dream of anarchist Russia in which the state truly had withered away.

In December 1919 Alexander Berkman and Emma Goldman, who had organized the anti-draft campaign in which Sacco and Vanzetti had joined both left the United States for the glamour of the Russian revolution. It was the same month that the pay truck of the White Shoe Company in Dedham, Massachusetts, was incompetently held up – for which Bartolomeo Vanzetti was to receive a sentence of fifteen years in Charlestown State Penitentiary.

In Russia Alexander Berkman grew as disillusioned as Kropotkin. What he saw was new authority taking over from old. He published his disappointment in *The Bolshevik Myth* in New York in 1925. Emma Goldman had issued her own *My Disillusionment* in Russia in the same city two years earlier. On February 8, 1921, just before the death of Lenin, the flight of Trotsky and the rise of Stalin, the old Prince Kropotkin died. George Woodcock described the funeral:

> A procession five miles long followed his coffin through the streets of Moscow; it was the last great demonstration of the lovers of freedom against the Bolsheviks, and the black banners of the anarchist groups bore in scarlet letters the message, 'Where there is authority there is no freedom'. In such dramatic fashion did the last of the great anarchist theoreticians pass into history.

Michael Bakunin was quite a different personality. Third of the three central anarchist figures, he was not a theoretician at all. For him life meant 'the propaganda of the deed'. He too was a member of a Russian aristocratic family and served in the Tsar's army, but found himself stifled by military discipline, the mechanical task of being part of a regiment in occupation of Lithuania, and above all by the anti-intellectual atmosphere of the officers' mess. It was Vronsky's world in *Anna Karenina*. Like many young Russians he was fired by the idea of a passionate union of the Slavic peoples, transcending nation states. And he was conscious, despite the leaky censorship, of ideas and actions stirring in the West. In 1839 he left for Berlin in search of a 'spiritual baptism'. There his closest friend was Ivan Turgenev. Literature has always been attracted by the personal nature of anarchist protest. It was to be so with Sacco and Vanzetti. It was so now. Turgenev turned Bakunin into the startling protagonist of *Dmitri Rudin*, his first novel. Bakunin began writing in radical publications – 'a new world into which I plunged with all the ardour of a delirious thirst' – and the *Deutsche Jahrbücher* published (under a disguised name – the game was already beginning) his essay on *Reaction in Germany*. In it comes the sentence which will always be associated with his name, and which captures the ambiguity at the centre of anarchy. 'Let us put our trust in the eternal spirit which destroys and annihilates only because it is the unsearchable and eternally creative source of life. The urge to destroy is also a creative urge.' Bakunin was by no means yet an anarchist but that road was opening to him all the time. A German working man, Wilhelm Weitling, then prominent in the Communist movement, gave him the missing words: 'The perfect society has no government.' Bakunin was soon on the road to Paris to talk the nights away with Proudhon ('the master of us all' he afterwards declared).

But it was Bakunin's ideas about the mystical union of all the Slavs and the discovery of the 'real Russia' that first brought the police to his door. He spoke at a meeting of Polish refugees, and at the request of the Russian ambassador was immediately deported to Belgium. He moved to Prague and was involved in the unsuccessful rising against the Austrian army. He is often credited with having fired the first shot – from the window of the Blue Star Hotel. 1848 was the great revolutionary year, and the year of Marx and Engels's *Communist Manifesto*. Bakunin was caught up in the unrest all over Europe, and in March 1849 took part in the Dresden uprising, which was not anarchist in the slightest. Oddly it was Richard Wagner who drew him into it.

It failed. He was captured by the Saxon army, condemned to death and held in prison for a year. Then, in the intricate politics of middle and Eastern Europe, he was handed over to the Austrians. They too sentenced him to death, and held him in chains for eleven months in the dungeons of Olmütz. Next he was handed over to the Russians who put him, as they did Kropotkin, in the Peter-and-Paul prison, and kept him there for six years. Conditions were grim, but as so often with political prisoners, they steeled his beliefs. 'It has made them more ardent,' he told his sister Tatiana, 'more absolute than ever, and henceforward all that remains to me of life can be summed up in one word: liberty.' But he also wrote a *Confession* to the Tsar in the hope of securing his release. This was discovered by the Communists in the secret official files after the 1917 revolution, and naturally released in order to discredit the anarchists. I have not been able to locate the original of this *Confession* (which was published in Paris in 1932), and until one does there must always be the suspicion – in the age of the Zinoviev Letter – that it might to say the least, have been edited. However, wholly genuine or not, it did not get Bakunin out of Peter-and-Paul. In the end family influence did that, and he was exiled to Siberia where the Governor, Muraviev-Amurski, was his cousin. In Irkutz and Tomsk he found the congenial company of other political exiles, and was soon, if unsuccessfully, trying to persuade the Governor to overthrow the Tsar. His cousin was replaced, but Bakunin's luck held, and the new Governor too turned out to be a relative. It was time to escape. From the Governor he obtained a post which involved travelling round the province. From friends he obtained money. And then it was Bakunin's world – disguises, deceptions, and the luck that laughs at locksmiths – a long journey down the Amur, an American ship at Nikolayevsk and breathing freely in Japan. He carried his ideas and stimulating presence from coast to coast of America, and then made for the London of Charles Dickens and Karl Marx. This was now the Europe of reaction in which Marx was slowly forging the Communist movement of the future, but Bakunin brought back with him the immediate revolutionary spirit of 1848, preserved alive from the moment he had been thrown into a Saxony prison. He was soon engaged in a surrealistic attempt by 200 Poles to hire a British ship in Stockholm and invade Lithuania. But it was Italy where he found his natural home and where — though there were endless rifts, muddles and quarrels (usually over money) – he inspired the growth of a dynamic anarchist movement. Alongside that came his long duel with Marx (whom he personally liked). Marx argued for a series of political steps until a successful revolution was credible. Bakunin wanted immediate rebellion. Marx sought ultimately for nationalization of the main industries. Bakunin wanted workers' co-operatives. Marx aimed to take over the state and transform the distribution of wealth through central government. It was a classic conflict between the red and the black. Bakunin, distracted by uprisings here and there, chaotic in his own affairs, pamphleteering against Mazzini and his new nation state of Italy, and far outmanoeuvred by Marx, lost utterly: 'Henceforth I shall trouble no man's repose, and I ask, in my turn, to be left in peace.' Of course he did so trouble, and of course he was not left in peace. Nor did he leave others in that condition, innately incomprehensible to him. 1874 saw him escaping (disguised as a priest with a basket of eggs) from the failed anarchist uprising in Bologna.

Bakunin had tried setting up anarchist groups in Italy – *La Societa dei Legionari della Rivoluzione Sociale Italiana* – but they were shadowy structures, if structures at all. Nevertheless anarchist groups grew, and police estimates in 1874 put them at 30,000.

Of the many striking figures in Bakunin's Italian anarchist movement, which was to become the cultural background in Italy of Nicola Sacco and Bartolomeo Vanzetti, perhaps the major one was Errico Malatesta. He was a medical student from Naples University, son of a wealthy landowning family in Southern Italy. He travelled round the Mediterranean and in middle Europe, wherever there was the chance of a local uprising, and left behind him a trail of anarchist groups based on Italian migrants. Indeed this missionary quality in Italian anarchism is extraordinary, and even as it reaches across the Atlantic, not at all easy to explain. It has, I think, to do with the immense value that anarchism gives both to the individual, and to the sense in him or her that we do not know but most pioneer and make the future. There is a quite different feel to its enthusiasm than one finds in a socialist movement. Of course there is an enthusiasm there too, and perhaps a more effective one, but there is also the stress on collectivity, and often on the 'inevitability' of history (to a Marxist) or of gradualism (to a Fabian). The Italian anarchists, especially self-educated working men (and that is what they overwhelmingly were despite the flamboyant 'drop-outs' from the aristocracy who were the public figures) came to the New World on their crowded little steamships much as the Pilgrim Fathers did aboard the *Mayflower*: adamant in their belief in individualism and in Utopia, casting off existing society, eager for work and self-sufficiency, and hungry for new converts ('If it had not been for these things, I might have live out my life talking at street corners to scorning men.')

Malatesta made the Italian movement that Bakunin had inspired. He was involved in insurrections, helped vigorously and selflessly in the 1885 cholera epidemic in Naples. (The authorities sought him out to give him a medal and a prison sentence.) He fled to South America, argued and lost the case with Marx in London. By 1898 he was back in Ancona distributing anarchist literature, but soon to find himself arrested by the police on the vaguest of charges. That led first to prison, then exile on the island of Lampedusa, then escape one stormy day in a small boat, a lucky pick-up by a ship on its way to Malta, and a passage to the United States.

Behind the hunt of the Italian authorities remained the memory of the November day on which the cook Giovanni Passanante had leapt on the carriage of King Umberto and tried to murder him with a knife carefully engraved with the words 'Long live the international republic'. America seemed a quieter haven after this. But he had counted without his anarchist friends. At a meeting in Paterson, New Jersey (where Guiseppe Rosso, interpreter at the Sacco–Vanzetti trial, was once a radical) Malatesta drifted into a quarrel with the local American anarchists, and one of them shot him.

He slowly recovered, and in 1913 returned to Italy. Nicola Sacco was then on the New England picket lines, and Bartolomeo Vanzetti working on the railway at Springfield ('the Italian live and work like a beast').

I think it is worth reviewing the fragmentary history and philosophy of anarchy. Sacco and Vanzetti, seen from the perspectives of Beacon Hill, or of President Lowell's Harvard, or of Judge Thayer's court or of the many commentaries on the case, seem like two odd and sometimes bizarre workmen, caught – rightly or wrongly – in the net of legal fortune. It is not so.

If one moves away from the high Anglo-Saxon culture of Boston as it was and sees them from a European viewpoint, then their ideas, their voices, their action and their bearing, make a new sense. They belong to a tradition.

It was a tradition within which they were more than apprentices. They were part of a movement that sought the third way: not capitalism or country, not socialism or Communism, but a dissolution (by violence, argument, or example) of world society into its smallest possible co-operating units.

There is nothing naive about what Sacco and Vanzetti had to say, though some of their protagonists presented them (for example in bowdlerizing the *Letters*) not only as innocent, but as innocents. They are self-educated working men, under extreme emotional pressure, writing in an alien tongue. 'For the things of beauty and of good in this life, mother nature gave to us all, for the conquest and the joy of liberty.' Sacco is writing in classical words that would have commanded a hearing from Proudhon in France, or William Morris in England or Thoreau at Concord.

And Vanzetti, in the death cells, is richly nostalgic for that natural world against which all anarchist notions of today's liberty and tomorrow's Utopia set themselves:

> You ought to see the king wasps, big velvety, lucid ravishing forcefully on these flowers calices, and the virtuous honey-bees – the wasp, the white, the yellow, the forget-me-nots, the hedge's butterflies and the variated armies of several genuses of grass eaters, the real conconinas, the meadow gri-gri . . . . Well, I have told you something about my native place.

It is as pre-Raphaelite as a Millais painting.

I make this point, somewhat lumberingly, because it is not at all difficult to see 'culture' personally represented in Beacon Hill. Consider the Lowell Committee. Governor Fuller had instinctively pointed up the old strengths of New England: Lowell was President of America's most famous university, Samuel Stratton guided the Massachusetts Institute of Science and Technology which looked more closely to the America of tomorrow than the rural roots of Sacco and Vanzetti's prose. And Judge Grant represented the original spirit of the Commonwealth of Massachusetts: laws to release liberty from oppression. To an anarchist the very title of the state and the country carried hope. The *Commonwealth* of Massachusetts is a title going back through time to Cromwell's revolution, and within that to those who – like Gerrard Winstanley and the Diggers – took it at face value. And as I have mentioned, the *United States of America* stands in name like the federalist flag that Michael Bakunin sought to plant on the grave of the old nation states and the rise of the *United States of Europe.*

What now becomes more obvious is that Sacco and Vanzetti represented a culture too. Even at their ultimate and blackest moments there is a surge of anarchism. On the night before his execution, Sacco wrote to his son Dante about this 'horrible death-house, that should be destroyed with the hammers of real progress – that horrible house that will shame forever the future of the citizens of Massachusetts. They should destroy that house and put up a factory or school . . . .'

In this clash of cultures, New England was double checked. It was threatened by its new migrant workers who were potentially, indeed often, much more than passive labour. The First World War had bonded America to Europe with the blood and experience of that generation. Then it tried to be an island again. I suspect that the McCarthy years after the Second World War drew on a similar revulsion at, or fear of, the Old World. But the Saccos and Vanzettis carried ideas with them. As it happened, the anarchist idea lost badly in what became the century's great war: welfare capitalism against Marxist Communism, with Fascism crushed in between. Sacco and Vanzetti were the latest in the line of anarchy's great martyrs, just as the surrender of the workers' republic of Barcelona to General Franco's column seemed the last chapter in that old history of libertarian insurrection.

I doubt if this is so. Anarchism as an idea is pristine, paradisal, paradoxical and eternal. It will thrust up like the flower through the concrete drive.To some extent that may be so because man fears the complexity of modern living, seeks for experts, structures, authority. It seems difficult, even incredible, to believe that the most important skills lie within oneself or close at hand, or can be loosely organized, though it is now a hundred years since Proudhon spoke 'de la capacité politique des classes ouvrières'. The anarchism of Sacco and Vanzetti clearly looks back, in the busy streets of New York and Boston, to a peasant past and works from there 'destruam et aedifico'.

I am not an anarchist, and so, pondering this strange case, I ask the questions doubtfully. Does this mean that anarchism – in its bombs as well as its oratory – is a last, lost cry of a rural universe? Is it, paradoxically, an act of simultaneous hate and nostalgia: a refusal to accept industrialization, technology, a shrinking globe, and complex human interdependence? Or does it defy that element of 'inevitability' which Darwin and Marx embedded both in their ideas and in the propaganda of their ideas: ideas which make our world and make us? Is anarchy the underground alternative: deeds of despair, and endless, if often ephemeral, attempts to bring a world back to personal and modest living?

For their second deadly challenge to New England lay in that province's own dissident heritage. In Charlestown prison Vanzetti, reading Emerson for the first time, found him 'so exquisitely anarchist'. And what would Thoreau – the subject of

such countless student and doctoral theses at the many universities of Boston – have thought? I remember (though I have
forgotten the provenance) his rich phrase 'the institutions of the
dead unkind'. Did this busy, mercantile, migrant, academic
Boston ever treat his essay *On the Duty of Civil Disobedience* as
more than bedtime relaxation? Perhaps that was to be left for
much later years: the India of Mahatma Gandhi, the South of
Martin Luther King. I doubt if Sacco and Vanzetti's judges saw it
like this, yet here was the nerve of conscience that their anarchy
touched in New England. For them it simply led to a pyro-
technical display of legal procedures and possibilities. Long ago
liberty had become the law, and there was only ever a slight
chance that their new questions might dislodge that embedded
link.

And yet to see Sacco and Vanzetti within the culture of anarchy
is to be reminded of how close, within that tradition, lies the
paradox of violent act and pacific life. Not of course that all or
most of the violence lay under the black banner. 'The unarmed
heroism of the crowd cannot face the armed idiocy of the
barracks' was the way that Tolstoy saw it. They knew in
Charlestown prison of the Chicago hangings of innocent
anarchists after the Haymarket bomb, of the Mooney affair, the
shooting of Joe Hill ('I was a tramp, a Swede and an I.W.W.').
Salsedo had fallen to his death from a police window just before
they were arrested. Carlo Tresca was himself to be killed years
later. In prison Vanzetti had a rare visit from the old Wobbly
Ralph Chaplin (Wobbly was the nickname given to the American
radical movement Industrial Workers of the World, I.W.W.). His
first questions were about the Mexican anarchist Ramon Majon
who had played an enormous and popular part, despite the
intervention of President Theodore Roosevelt's border troops, in
the overthrow of Porfiro Diaz's dictatorship in Mexico. The wheel
of fortune turned, Majon was arrested and had died in his cell.
Vanzetti had no more doubt about what happened to Majon than
what had happened to Salsedo.

Nicola Sacco and Bartolomeo Vanzetti, picked up on a late
streetcar at Campello, entrapped in the mesh of professional law
in which Boston even today expensively excels, were a threat to
the Commonwealth of Massachusetts. In broken English they
were calling the state back to her origins, and reaching across the

Atlantic to join her with Europe: a new Europe which was as dark and southern as it was Irish or Anglo-Saxon. What Sacco and Vanzetti then said they said in their utterances and letters and in their deaths. It is never easy to explain what an anarchist is saying, because – unlike communists or socialists or fascists or capitalists or indeed any other 'ists' of which one can think – with a classical anarchist the 'propaganda of the word' and the 'propaganda of the deed' are so intimately enmeshed. Doing and being is all.

As to the shape of tomorrow, the anarchists are the only ones who seem to lack the street map of the new Jerusalem. After his many labours on Bakunin, Professor E. H. Carr concludes his lengthy biography with: 'it is hardly possible to arrive at any clear notion of his ideas.'

Nicola Sacco and Bartolomeo Vanzetti had no such trouble. Nor perhaps did most working-class anarchists. They responded to a feeling: small is beautiful. Anarchism protests against present society, creates cells of alternative life, glimpses Utopia as a desirable but ever-receding city in the sunset. The pathway up there is unknown. 'How will society be organized? We do not and we cannot know,' said Errico Malatesta.

Such prisoners were culturally a long way from Beacon Hill, Boston, even though they lay only across that slow indigo flow of the Charles River and almost next to Harvard University. They attracted the hostility of the Commonwealth and the sympathy of the liberals. Whether they attracted any political understanding in their time, I am less sure. They were the rare stuff of which martyrs are made. And by which martyrs in strange, atmospheric ways, help change the world.

Chapter Twelve

'The storming of heaven'

'When men of false doctrine are killed,' wrote John Foxe in 1581 to Queen Elizabeth, 'their error is not killed; nay, it is all the more strengthened, the more constantly they die.' He was protesting to her against the burning at the stake in Smithfield ('in great horror with roaring and crying') of anabaptists and dissident Catholics. He was later to write his *Book of Martyrs* which, along with the Bible and Bunyan's *Pilgrim's Progress*, was to become the basic reading matter and a shaper of values for two centuries throughout Britain and New England.

Foxe wove his tapestry with great care. He several times rewrote his book, each time documenting the deaths more fully. He is frank and full about his sources, honest about what he doesn't know – and very little of his account has been destroyed by the many attacks on it which lasted until Victorian times.

Foxe's book took over Europe. In England the Convocation of Canterbury ordered it to be placed in Church alongside the Bible. John Bunyan took it with him to Bedford jail, re-reading it as he wrote *Pilgrim's Progress*. Edition after edition of this very long and extraordinary hagiography appeared for over 300 years. The last real edition was in 1877, and the book died as a living voice precisely when the Catholic versus Protestant debate was drained of meaning by the challenge of Darwin, Marx, Freud and their fresh articulation of a mass non-Christian society.

Until then its long line of martyrs had always strengthened the force of the Christian church and their role within it is well recognized. But there are also martyrs of the left: men, women and children whose deaths broadly advanced the cause of liberty, equality, fraternity, whether they were Christians or not.

I began this small study of the Sacco and Vanzetti case as a chapter in a projected book of such socialist martyrs. But the riddle of the case took over as did the elusive task of seeing it freshly after the passage of fifty years and placing it in its cultural and political context. So it must remain a prologue. Nevertheless there does remain this final element: martyrdom.

Sacco and Vanzetti, as martyrs, lived in the consciousness of liberals and radicals until the Second World War. I do not know how much their effective 'memory' was then handed on. A newer generation had the execution of the Rosenbergs for alleged spying, the assassination of the Kennedy brothers, of Martin Luther King, of civil rights workers in the South, the deaths in Vietnam, or the shootings at home in Kent State University to ponder.

Martyrs seem to come at special moments, at times when the destruction of the present order is desired by some, dreaded by others – but credible to both. At such moments ordinary people may impulsively thrust themselves into the role, as did Jan Palach burning himself to death in the main square of Prague as the Russian tanks crushed their way into the city. Annually a wreath of flowers is surreptitiously laid on the spot. Just as regularly, the authorities remove it. The force of martyrdom remains, if only for a generation.

Or they may be ordinary people, caught up in crowds and ferment, who find themselves at the wrong spot when the cossacks or the hussars or the steel-helmeted riot police make their charge. Many martyrs of the left are anonymous faces in the crowd, like those who died in the Sharpeville massacre. Or take the moment that was to stiffen the radical spirit throughout Victorian England through all the decades that ultimately led to universal suffrage – the charge of the Manchester, Macclesfield and Chester Yeomanry on Monday August 16, 1819 – 'Peterloo'. Samuel Bamford, the radical poet, was slipping off for a drink with a friend and saw the unbelievable suddenness of it from a distance:

In ten minutes from the commencement of the havoc, the field was an open and almost deserted space. The sun looked down through a sultry and motionless air. The curtains and blinds of the windows within view were all closed. The hustings remained, with a few broken and hewed flag-staves erect, and a torn and gashed banner or two drooping; whilst over the whole field were strewed caps, bonnets, hats, shawls and shoes, and other parts of male and female dress; trampled, torn and bloody. The yeomanry had dismounted – some were easing their horses' girths, others adjusting their accoutrements; and some were wiping their sabres.

It could be Kent State or Sharpeville or the demonstrations against the Vietnam war during the Democratic convention in Chicago which, when the police moved in, had, in Norman Mailer's words, 'the absolute ferocity of a tropical storm', and just as sudden an end.

But if there are martyrs who impulsively seize that role (or plan it, as did Emily Davies, the suffragette who threw herself under the King's horse), and if many others are, like the Tolpuddle Martyrs, barely known – despite annual and ritual commemoration – by their individual names, there are two groups whose identity is very well known. First are the assassinated leaders: Wat Tyler in medieval England, Rosa Luxemburg at the beginning of Weimar Germany, Mahatma Gandhi in the new India, Patrice Lumumba in independent, black Africa, Martin Luther King in the civil rights campaign in the United States.

And the second are those, like Sacco and Vanzetti, put on trial by the authorities, who go through all the due processes only to find, as Foxe long ago said, that 'their error is not killed'. James Connolly, the socialist leader in the Dublin rising on Easter Monday 1916 is one of these. He was severely wounded when the rebellion was put down, tried (there was no doubt at all of his guilt), solicitously nursed back to health, and then taken from his hospital bed and shot by the firing squad. Nothing could have made the cause of Irish liberty more invincible. For previously one man's sense of the apocalyptic moment was another man's routine Monday morning. James Stephens, the poet, describes going to work in the usual way on the morning the Irish rebels seized the General Post Office, only five minutes' walk away. He hears some firing in the morning, but assumes it is recruits practising. At lunchtime he strolls through the centre of the rebellion ('I saw nothing') and only on his way home from the office is he puzzled by people silently standing and staring:

> On the spur of the moment, I addressed one of these silent gazers. 'Has there been an accident?' said I. 'Don't you know?' said he. And then he saw that I did not know. 'The Sinn Feiners have seized the city this morning.' 'Oh,' said I.

What turned this unsuccessful uprising into an irresistible movement of liberation was the power of martyrdom. And of course some martyrs realize the unexpected potency within their grasp ('had it not been for these things'), and use it – either in the theatre of the court, or in letters to friends, or in the manner of their dying. Lenin's elder brother, Alexander Ulyanov, attempted to kill the Tsar on March 1, 1887 (on the sixth anniversary – so strong are these imaginative patterns – of the assassination of Alexander II). He failed. Then the prosecution lost the key document for the summary trial setting out the radicals' aims, hopes and plan. Alexander re-wrote it in his cell, and handed it over in court. In Isaac Deutscher's words, 'he embraced his martyrdom' and 'his stand in the dock was so evocative of the heroism of the 1881 martyrs that Alexander himself was compared to Zhelyabov.' On the day he was hanged, Lenin himself was taking a six-hour mathematics exam, which he passed *summa cum laude*. His headmaster at the time was Kerensky. Nowhere in all his speeches and writings does Lenin mention Alexander. Just as his brother felt himself as a reincarnation of the 1881 martyrs, so Lenin seemed to internalize his martyrdom and transmute it into burning revolutionary energy.

In this long line of martyrs of the left, Nicola Sacco and Bartolomeo Vanzetti have many of the characteristics of their predecessors and of their successors. So has their environment: politicians warning of Red threats, newspapers full of the case of the corset salesman and his murdered mistress. They had the quality of faces coming out of the passing crowd – two men one night on a Boston streetcar (who remembers riding with them?) – and suddenly clicking into sharp focus. Like many martyrs (and revolutionary leaders) of the left, they are migrants. The poor and able may be forced to travel in search of work and opportunity and education. With them, ideas cross national frontiers (as happened with the early Christian martyrs and with the rise of Protestantism). They may admire their adopted country but, searching for their elusive ideal, find themselves its most active critics: all the more resented because they came as strangers. There is a good deal of this in the prosecution pressing the question of did Sacco love 'this United States of America in May 1917?' And if so why then did he flee to Mexico to avoid the draft? His answers seem incomprehensible to the prosecution, though they are consistently logical for an anarchist.

This raises a dilemma too if one considers martyrs of the left. They may have adopted a new country (as Marx adopted England). This arises quite frequently: James Connolly came not from Ireland, but from Scotland; Che Guevara not from Cuba but from Argentina; Rosa Luxemburg not from Germany but Poland. Their creed is international (as they hoped their revolutions would be) but they are always in danger of being placed in national pantheons, even though all they stood for was against the idea of competing nation states. This is what has happened to Connolly in the Irish myth. What he had to say is misted over in the Celtic twilight, just as Sacco and Vanzetti nearly disappear from sight as international anarchists and become almost parochial figures in a fifty-year dispute which is really about local pride in liberal American law, especially in the Commonwealth of Massachusetts.

Perhaps the radical spirit would be the stronger if, like the Christian church or the nation state, it took more trouble to keep alive the memory of its own martyrs. Even the record can be sketchy. If we simply confined ourselves to the Sacco and Vanzetti time, there is now very little memory left of others whose trial and death – the Mooneys in California, Joe Hill in Salt Lake City – were not dissimilar.

Martyrs can have an immense effect: over a moment, a generation, an epoch. There are of course martyrs of the right and martyrs of nationalism. Their influence may narrow people's vision, or pull us back to the past. Ireland is permeated with this sense. But the martyrs to whom I am relating Sacco and Vanzetti here all did, do or could pull humanity towards a more equal and libertarian future. It is a terrible and unique way of so doing. And

I say could so, because the left has never developed its hagiography in the way that new nation states or old religions often have. Perhaps the rational element in radical thinking works against it, or maybe the different strains in the left, from anarchism to Communism, look to their own sub-traditions. Nevertheless 'the storming of heaven' – which was Marx's comment on the Paris Commune of 1871 – may in part depend on the mythologies created out of martyrdom. With Sacco and Vanzetti we see that their potency – especially over a generation – as martyrs is an encrustation on, or amplification of, their actual lives; different from the question of innocence or guilt (a martyr may be perfectly guilty of the crime with which he is charged); additional to their politics (few of those who supported Sacco and Vanzetti shared their anarchist belief). At times, particularly towards the end, they knew this strange dimension into which they had entered.

'Viva l'anarchismo. Farewell my wife and child and all my friends,' said Nicola Sacco, as he entered the green chamber of death. From him the black flag still flew. Setting out to Johnson's garage at Cochesett on the late afternoon of May 5, 1920, he could never have dreamed that this would be the end of his journey, his remembered role in and after both life and death. We have looked again at a case which still troubles the conscience of America. Time has brought some new evidence, but whatever the verdict of posterity, the men are dead. Half a century also helps us see both as part of a political tradition which, pacific or violent, spasmodically erupts through the surface of modern society. At the time it may seem incomprehensible: but martyrs are people caught at rare and sometimes eerie flashpoints as ideology consciously or unconsciously clashes with ideology. They throw long shadows.

Later in April 1927, as he prepared for that final walk to the electric chair, Bartolomeo Vanzetti was seen by Philip D. Stong, a reporter for the New York *World*. A formal interview was forbidden, but Stong scribbled his words in shorthand on the margin of a newspaper:

> 'If it had not been for these thing, I might have live out my life, talking at street corners to scorning men. I might have die, unmarked, unknown, a failure. Now we are not a

failure. This is our career and our triumph. Never in our full life can we hope to do such work for tolerance, for justice, for man's understanding of man, as now we do by an accident.

'Our words – our lives – our pains – nothing. The taking of our lives – lives of a good shoemaker and a poor fish pedlar – all. That last moment belong to us – that agony is our triumph.'

Background sources

1 Proclamation of the Commonwealth of Massachusetts, Tuesday August 23, 1977

The Proclamation by the Commonwealth of Massachusetts on Tuesday August 23 about the Sacco–Vanzetti case was preceded by this submission to the Governor by his legal counsel. It is reprinted here, with permission, for the first time.

THE COMMONWEALTH OF MASSACHUSETTS
Report to the Governor in the Matter of Sacco and Vanzetti

> THE COMMONWEALTH OF MASSACHUSETTS
> EXECUTIVE DEPARTMENT
> STATE HOUSE · BOSTON 02133
MICHAEL S. DUKAKIS
GOVERNOR

Report to the Governor in the Matter of Sacco and Vanzetti

To: Governor Michael S. Dukakis

The accompanying Report has been prepared under the auspices of the Office of the Governor's Legal Counsel* in response to your questions: first, as to whether

---

* Invaluable assistance was rendered in the preparation of this Report by, among others, Alexander J. Cella, Esq., Alan M. Dershowitz, Esq., Thomas Quinn, Todd D. Rakoff, Esq., Deborah M. Smith, and Lewis H. Weinstein, Esq.

there are substantial grounds for believing – at least in light of the
criminal justice standards of today – that Sacco and Vanzetti were
unfairly convicted and executed, and, second, if so, what action can
now appropriately be taken. It is my conclusion that there are
substantial, indeed compelling, grounds for believing that the Sacco
and Vanzetti legal proceedings were permeated with unfairness, and
that a proclamation issued by you would be appropriate.

DANIEL A. TAYLOR
Chief Legal Counsel

July 13, 1977

Report to the Governor

August 23, 1977, will be the fiftieth anniversary of the execution by the
Commonwealth of Nicola Sacco and Bartolomeo Vanzetti. Controversy
has surrounded the Sacco and Vanzetti case ever since its inception. The
continuing doubts as to the legitimacy of their convictions and executions
have prompted reconsideration. Two issues are raised: (1) are there
substantial grounds for believing that Sacco and Vanzetti were convicted and executed without a fair trial demonstrating their guilt of
murder beyond a reasonable doubt and without an adequate appellate
review of that trial; and (2) if so, what action should appropriately be
taken in the present circumstances:

1. Were Sacco and Vanzetti convicted and executed after a fair trial
demonstrating their guilt of murder beyond a reasonable doubt, and
after an adequate review of that trial?

(a) *The basic chronology**
On April 15, 1920, at about three p.m., Frederick Parmenter, paymaster
of the Slater and Morrill Shoe Co., and his guard, Alexander Berardelli,
were robbed of the payroll they were carrying, some $15,000, and shot
to death, in South Braintree, Massachusetts. At least two men did the
robbing and shooting, leaving six bullets in the dead men's bodies;
having seized the money, they jumped into an approaching get-away
car, containing several other men, and sped away. The murders have
always been undisputed; the only issue is who the guilty group of men
were.

Nicola Sacco and Bartolomeo Vanzetti were arrested while travelling
on a street car on the evening of May 5, 1920. They were indicted for
murder on September 14, 1920. (Vanzetti in the meantime had been

---

* See Attachment A for full chronology.

convicted, separately, of a holdup which took place in Bridgewater; his conviction of that crime was based on identification evidence that Felix Frankfurter, then a Professor at Harvard Law School and later a Justice of the United States Supreme Court, said 'bordered on the frivolous,' and in the teeth of very substantial alibi evidence. Frankfurter, *The Case of Sacco and Vanzetti* 7 n. 1 (1962 ed.).) The trial for the South Braintree murders began on May 31, 1921, and lasted until July 14; with but a few hours of deliberation, the jurors returned a guilty verdict.

In the succeeding five years various motions for a new trial based in part on newly discovered evidence and in part on alleged improprieties of the prosecution were made. All of the motions were denied by the trial judge. On May 12, 1926, the Supreme Judicial Court overruled all of the exceptions which had been taken after the trial and after denial of the various motions. *Commonwealth* v. *Sacco,* 255 Mass. 369 (1926). Various other motions, denials, and fruitless appeals followed.* In May, 1927, Vanzetti petitioned Governor Fuller 'not for mercy but for justice'; the petition was denied on August 3, 1927, in part on the basis of Governor Fuller's own review, and in part on the basis of a report the Governor had received from a specially established Advisory Committee composed of A. Lawrence Lowell, president of Harvard, Samuel W. Stratton, president of M.I.T., and Robert Grant, a former Probate Court judge.**

Early in the morning of August 23, 1927, Sacco and Vanzetti were executed at the Charlestown State Prison in Boston.

(b) *The grounds for continuing doubt*
Despite, or, perhaps in part because of, the very considerable attention paid to the Sacco–Vanzetti case prior to the execution of the defendants, there have remained, ever since, several grounds for doubting that Sacco and Vanzetti were fairly proven guilty, beyond a reasonable doubt, of the South Braintree murders. These grounds encompass both the conduct of the trial itself, with the consequence that there is doubt whether the jury's verdict represented only its consideration of rational proof of the crime charged, and also the effect of later-discovered or later-disclosed evidence, with the consequence that even if the trial jury rightly decided the case placed before it, there remains a substantial doubt whether a jury in possession of all of the facts would have

---

* *Commonwealth* v. *Sacco,* 259 Mass. 128 (1927); *Commonwealth* v. *Sacco,* 261 Mass. 12, *cert. dismissed,* 275 U.S. 574 (1927).

** Governor Fuller's decision and the Report of the Advisory Committee are reproduced in *V The Sacco-Vanzetti Case: Transcript of the Record of the Trial of Nicola Sacco and Bartolomeo Vanzetti in the Courts of Massachusetts and Subsequent Proceedings, 1920-1927* (New York, Henry Holt & Co., Inc., 1928-29) at 5378a *et seq.*

returned a guilty verdict. As will be discussed subsequently, the refusal of the Supreme Judicial Court to overturn the verdict does not answer these doubts.

Of course, many of these bases for doubt are fully intelligible only upon a complete explication of convoluted evidence, but some of the more serious points can be briefly summarized.* A more detailed outline of the more significant instances of unfairness, together with a reference to appropriate standards currently applicable to criminal trials and appeals, is appended to this report.

(1) 'The Sacco and Vanzetti case,' wrote Samuel Eliot Morison, 'was an offshoot of the . . . whipped-up anti-red hysteria' of the period just following World War One. Morison, *The Oxford History of the American People* 884 (1965). The defendants were aliens, poor – and espoused a political ideology – anarchism – which struck fear in the hearts of many Americans; that fear was later exacerbated when various left-wing movements embraced their cause. Whether prejudice against anarchists influenced the verdict, and the denial of new trial motions, is perhaps open to debate; that a strong possibility existed for that to happen is irrefutable. It was said at the time, and has been said since, that the defense itself made political beliefs central to the trial. In the sense that the defendants' explanation for their behavior, including the various falsehoods told at the time of their arrest, was that they were afraid that they and their friends were to be persecuted for being anarchists, that is true. Whether that justified the extraordinary, indeed brutal, cross-examination of the defendants, especially of Sacco, is another matter. Many of the questions asked, and many of the responses elicited, seem to have been devoted to making it ring in the jurors' minds that the defendants were radicals – which is, of course, precisely what they claimed – rather than to establishing that their justification for their actions upon arrest was trumped up, which was the point the prosecution ostensibly wished to prove. Whether, in permitting this line of questioning, the judge properly balanced the probative value of the answers produced, as against the potential for prejudice necessarily involved, may be seriously questioned. The Supreme Judicial Court ruled only, not that the questions were proper, but that the trial judge had not abused his discretion in permitting such questions within the traditionally broad scope allowed to cross-examination. *Commonwealth v. Sacco, supra,* 255 Mass. at 439.

---

* Even beyond the specific points, the mere fact that for the last fifty years countless authors have debated the merits of the case, without a clear victory either for the proponents of innocence or for the proponents of guilt, is in itself a reason to think that a miscarriage of justice may have occurred. Extensive bibliographies are included in Russell, *Tragedy in Dedham* (1971 ed.), and Ehrmann, *The Case That Will Not Die* (1969).

Whether the trial judge was as impartial as the reliance by the Supreme Judicial Court, here and elsewhere, on his discretion would indicate, has also been seriously challenged. In the years following the jury's verdict, many claimed to have heard the trial judge make statements, which if indeed made, would indicate a fixed prejudice on his part, both during the trial and later, against the defendants. The Governor's Advisory Committee, even while not fully crediting some of these statements, concluded that the judge had been guilty of 'a grave breach of official decorum' in his discussion of the case; and further felt that his judicial qualities had been sufficiently called into question as to make it advisable for the Committee, on its own, to reconsider the merits of the discretionary new trial motions. Report at 6, 8. In themselves serious, these judgments were mild compared to the conclusions reached by other qualified commentators. Professor Frankfurter, writing at the time, described the judge's opinion denying a new trial as 'a farrago of misquotations, misrepresentations, suppressions, and mutilations.' *The Case of Sacco and Vanzetti, supra,* at 104. Professor Morgan, writing with 20 years' added perspective, described the judge as a man 'whose prejudices made him overlook misconduct of the prosecutor, made him determine every discretionary matter against the accused, and permeated the proceedings from beginning to end with its vicious influence.' Joughin and Morgan, *The Legacy of Sacco and Vanzetti* 157 (1964 ed.).

Whether the judge was prejudiced to that degree, or whether, whatever his prejudice, his biases had that great an effect on the course of the proceedings, is beyond our now knowing. Nevertheless, there is a substantial possibility that some prejudicial influence was imparted to the trial, and an even greater probability that the judge's hostility to the defendants influenced the exercise of his discretion, particularly in such critical matters as deciding the motions for a new trial. The other problems present in the proof offered against the defendants have to be considered in the light of these possibilities.*

(2) The overwhelming fact about the South Braintree crime is that the crime itself remains unsolved. Even if for the moment it is assumed that Sacco and Vanzetti were participants, there were still several other

---

* Allegations were also made that one of the jurors, prior to his selection, had indicated his firm intent to hang the defendants. The trial judge denied a new trial motion based on this information, and the Supreme Judicial Court overruled the exception thereto, stating that the judge had the discretionary power not to believe the underlying affidavit. 255 Mass. at 450-51. The Advisory Committee also rejected the contention on the basis that 'it is extremely improbable that Ripley was so different from other men that he desired the disagreeable task of serving on this jury, and he had only to reveal what he had said to be excused.' Report at 10. Whatever the truth may be, that reasoning is surely a supreme example of begging the question; if the juror wanted the men hanged, of course he would want to serve on the jury.

participants; at trial, nothing was offered to identify who these other bandits were, or to connect the two defendants to the rest of the gang. Similarly, it is undisputed that the robbers made off with more than $15,000, a substantial sum even now, and a relatively much greater amount in 1920. No part of this money was ever traced to the defendants, and at trial the prosecution offered no explanation whatsoever as to what had happened to it. Further, six bullets were found in the bodies of the two victims. Leaving aside, for the moment, the question whether one of the bullets was successfully shown to have been fired from a gun in the possession of Sacco at the time of his arrest, no account was ever offered at trial as to the source of the other five. Numerous more minor points also remain unresolved; and, of course, the Madeiros statement, which specifically exonerated Sacco and Vanzetti and served to implicate the Morelli gang of Providence, was never adequately investigated. In short, this was not a trial where the evidence adduced served to explain the entire event in such a comprehensive fashion that each detail gained persuasiveness from being a composite part of a complete whole. Rather, the jury was asked to find that, even though it could not on the evidence know all that had happened, or even most of it, the jurors still could know beyond a reasonable doubt that the two defendants were guilty. While juries must, of course, often make such judgments, the fact that the full story was not known doubtless increases the likelihood that the conduct of the trial influenced the result; that fact also serves to highlight the importance of the accuracy of each specific piece of evidence that was offered.

(3) At trial, the prosecution offered several witnesses who purported to identify one or the other of the defendants as participants in whichever aspect of the South Braintree robbery they had witnessed. Large parts of several books have been written dissecting the various identifications. Without reviewing all the details, it has been asserted that several of the witnesses did not have an adequate opportunity for observation; that some had previously stated that they could not identify the men they briefly glimpsed, or, worse yet, had previously identified photos of others than the defendants as depicting the assailants; that some described details of the defendants not, in fact, true, or inconsistent with the details reported by others; and that at least one had an undisclosed motive for testifying favorably to the prosecution. The defense offered several witnesses who placed Vanzetti in Plymouth and Sacco in Boston at the time of the South Braintree affair. Thus, at the core of trial there was a direct conflict of mutually exclusive identification testimony.

If that were all, it would be unwise to second-guess the jury's determination as to which witnesses were truthful; even then, it would still be troublesome that the trial judge passed over the bulk of the defendants' evidence in but one sentence of his extensive charge. (The material portions of the charge are set out at 255 Mass. at 388-403.) But that is not all. After the trial an additional witness, Roy Gould (who had not testified although he had spoken to the police), affirmed that he saw the bandits, and that they were not the defendants. Gould, who had had a bullet put through his lapel by the robbers, 'certainly had an unusually good position to observe the men in the car,' in the words of the Advisory Committee. Report at 9. The trial judge denied the motion for a new trial based on this evidence, stating that 'these verdicts did not rest, in my judgment, upon the testimony of the eye witnesses'; and the Supreme Judicial Court held his denial not to be an abuse of discretion. 255 Mass. at 457-59. The Advisory Committee dismissed the importance of this evidence as well, on the basis that it was 'merely cumulative' and was balanced by two new witnesses supporting the prosecution's claim. Report at 9. Neither of the prosecution's new witnesses was as impressive as Gould; but even if the point be granted, the need to weigh the testimony of one eyewitness against another confirms the need for a new trial rather than supporting its denial.

(4) Apparently the trial judge, having said that the convictions did not rest on the testimony of the eyewitnesses, was of the opinion that what had convicted the defendants was the 'consciousness of guilt' shown by their actions and statements on the night of their arrests. Since the arrests took place fully 20 days after the crime, and since the defendants were not informed of the grounds of their arrests, this is hardly solid proof of their guilt. More particularly, it was precisely this proof concerning the motivation of their actions at the time of arrest that had been so thoroughly tainted by the prosecutor's cross-examination, and which most clearly invited the jury to exercise its emotions rather than its thoughts. The jury may well have decided on this basis, and was indeed almost invited to do so by the heavy emphasis placed on the arrest, rather than the crime, in the judge's charge. If that was the sole ground of decision, the case against the defendants was certainly not proven beyond a reasonable doubt.

It seems more likely that the jury also based its decision on certain other circumstantial evidence purporting to show the defendants' participation in the crime. The trial judge's charge picked out three pieces of such evidence: the identification of one bullet; the identification of one revolver; and the identification of one hat. 255 Mass. at 391-93. In the light of the evidence discovered after the trial, the tendency of each of the three to prove the guilt of the defendants is doubtful.

Whether one of the bullets taken from Berardelli's body was fired from the gun found in Sacco's possession at the time of his arrest remains one of the most hotly disputed points of this hotly disputed case. It is beyond the competence of this memorandum to attempt to determine which of the many ballistics tests that were made, if any,* reveals the truth. It suffices to say that the jury did not have the whole story put before it, and may indeed have been misled. The prosecution's chief expert testified only that his opinion was that it was 'consistent' that the bullet had been fired from the pistol. After the trial it developed that this expert, if asked whether he had found any evidence that the bullet had passed through Sacco's pistol, would have answered in the negative, and that the prosecution knew that he would have so testified. Yet his testimony, not further developed, may well have been thought by the jury to be virtually conclusive on this issue; at least the judge appeared to think so in his charge that the testimony was that 'it was his [Sacco's] pistol that fired the bullet.'

The prosecution also tried to prove that the gun in Vanzetti's possession at the time of arrest was connected with the crime, having been the gun carried by Berardelli on the fatal day. The testimony was, at best, confused. Even the Advisory Committee, wanting forcefully to state the case against the defendants, could go no further than to state that Vanzetti had in his possession a pistol 'resembling' the pistol 'formerly possessed' by Berardelli. Report at 19.

Finally, prosecution attempted to show that a cap had been found at the scene of the crime which was Sacco's cap. Quite apart from the disputes as to when the cap had been found, and as to whether it fit Sacco, it was developed after the trial that what may well have been the crucial identifying feature of the cap for the jury, a tear in its lining, had been added to it by a police officer while the cap was in his custody.

In sum, the overall effect of these three pieces of evidence may well have been to convince the jury that it had more definite proof of guilt than in fact it had.

(5) In light of the foregoing, a serious question exists and will continue to exist whether the guilt of Sacco and Vanzetti was properly determined. The jury was invited to decide the case on the basis of appeals to

---

* The bullets and gun passed out of the custody of the Commonwealth sometime after the trial. Subsequently, in about 1960, the bullets and gun believed to have been the evidence introduced at trial were located at a personal residence in Massachusetts. There was no trail of continuous custody, nor any witness who could reliably establish these bullets and gun as the bullets and gun put into evidence. See, *Tragedy in Dedham, supra*, at 315-17.

prejudice; the eyewitness testimony was conflicting and even the judge apparently thought it to be an inadequate basis of decision; many of the facts which might have altered the jury's conclusion were not presented at trial, including further eyewitness evidence and other important pieces of evidence concerning identification; and the evidence concerning the defendants' 'consciousness of guilt' at the time of arrest was overblown, and may well have been viewed through the perspective of a cross-examination as much calculated to damn the defendants as to advance the cause of truth. While a jury's verdict in the normal case settles the facts once and for all, a verdict rendered on such a basis, and with such vital consequences, calls for much more careful scrutiny.

It is precisely for cases of this sort that procedural devices such as motions for a new trial, and especially review by a different and superior tribunal, have been fashioned. When the trial proceedings have undergone careful review, the confidence that may be placed in the verdict is much greater. Unfortunately, the system for reviewing murder cases at the time of Sacco's and Vanzetti's convictions and executions failed to provide the safeguards now present, safeguards which might well have prevented a miscarriage of justice.

To acknowledge that mistakes occur is not to challenge the importance of the criminal law in the protection of society, nor to denigrate in any fashion the criminal justice system of the Commonwealth. It is the very possibility of mistake that is one of the strongest grounds for the existence of a well-developed appellate system of justice. And it was the possibility that a mistake was committed in the executions of Sacco and Vanzetti that led to a strengthening in the system of appellate review of capital cases in this Commonwealth.

(c) *The review of the case by the Supreme Judicial Court*
It is sometimes thought that the Supreme Judicial Court, in failing to reverse Sacco's and Vanzetti's convictions, and in failing to order a new trial, endorsed in their entirety the proceedings below. This description of what the Supreme Judicial Court decided is incorrect, and deficient in crucial respects.

In its main review of the case, including the review of some but not all of the motions made for a new trial, the Supreme Judicial Court considered separately, in thirty-three numbered sections, each of the exceptions raised by the defendants; its final decision was merely to overrule those exceptions. *Commonwealth* v. *Sacco*, 255 Mass. 369 (1926). Both in this opinion, and in a later opinion considering other exceptions to the denial of further new trial motions, *Commonwealth* v. *Sacco*, 259 Mass. 128 (1927), the Court at many places grounded its decision on the basis that various matters, including the decision whether to grant a new trial because of newly discovered evidence, rested within the discretion of the trial judge. The standard of review used was that set forth in *Davis* v. *Boston Elevated Ry. Co.*, 235 Mass. 482, 502 (1920), a civil case many times cited in the *Sacco* opinions, which reads as follows:

> The question is not whether we should take a different view of the evidence or should have made an opposite decision from that made by the trial judge. To sustain these exceptions it is necessary to decide that no conscientious judge, acting intelligently, could honestly have taken the view expressed by him.

Both the language and the purpose of this standard of review indicate that little short of proof of sheer incompetence or corruption would have persuaded the Supreme Judicial Court to reverse matters it considered discretionary.

The consequence of this narrow standard of review was that on many vital issues, including especially whether a new trial was warranted on the basis of new evidence or because the prosecution had prejudiced the defendants because of their political beliefs, the lives of the defendants were completely committed to the judgment of the trial judge acting alone. This was the same judge that even the Governor's Advisory Committee described as having been 'subjected to a very severe strain' by reason of 'the criticisms made upon him,' which resulted in his being 'in a distinctly nervous condition.' Report at 8. However, even assuming the judge fully competent, it may fairly be asked whether the lives of defendants should be so fully placed in the discretion of one man, and whether one man should be asked to bear by himself such an awful burden.

It is no criticism of the Supreme Judicial Court, acting under the procedures then lawfully in force, to point out that at almost all other times in the history of the Commonwealth greater protection for defendants in capital cases has been required. For nearly one hundred years, the full bench of the Supreme Judicial Court directly heard trials for capital crimes. Not until 1872 was this practice altered, and even then the power to hear trials for murder was given to two or more Supreme Judicial Court justices. St. 1872, c. 232. In 1891, jurisdiction over capital crimes was transferred to the Superior Court, but trial was to be before three justices. St. 1891, c. 379, §§ 1 and 2. In 1894, the number was changed to two or more, St. 1894, c. 204, but it was not until 1910 that a single justice of the Superior Court was given the power to hear by himself a trial for murder. St. 1910, c. 555, § 1.

Following upon the decisions in the *Sacco* case, sober citizens concerned with the administration of justice in the Commonwealth perceived the error of giving a single judge such great power over the life of a defendant. In November, 1927, the Judicial Council of the Commonwealth recommended the enactment of new review provisions in capital cases. Commenting specifically on the proceedings in the Sacco and Vanzetti case, the Council stated (13 Mass. L.Q. No. 1, at 40-41):

> A single judge of the Superior Court now presides over murder trials and passes not only on questions of law included in the trial of the indictment, but upon mixed questions of law and fact arising on motions for a new trial. The Supreme Judicial Court on appeal passes only on questions of law. As the verdict on such an indictment involves the issue of life and death, we think the responsibility too great to be thrown upon one man. If he errs in any matter of discretion as distinguished from law, the result is irreparable. . . .
>
> It is true that the decisions of the trial judge upon matters of discretion may be reversed if there has been what is called an 'abuse' of discretion. . . . It is needless to say that such an abuse will so rarely be found by the Supreme Court to have existed that there is no real appeal from that judicial act.

Following renewed recommendations by the Judicial Council, 23 Mass. L.Q. No. 1, Prelim. Supp., at 28-30 (1937); 24 Mass. L.Q. No. 1, Prelim. Supp., at 14-16 (1938); the General Court enacted the desired legislation, St. 1939, c. 341, which, as amended, is the present M.G.L. c. 278, §33E. This statute provides that in reviewing capital cases the Supreme Judicial Court shall consider both 'the law and the evidence' and further provides that the Supreme Judicial Court may order a new trial, or direct the entry of a verdict for a lesser degree of guilt, if the verdict below 'was against the law or the weight of the evidence, or because of newly discovered evidence, or for any other reason that justice may require.'

The protection for a defendant in a capital case is thus greatly increased. Of substantial import for considering the questions raised by the Sacco and Vanzetti case, the statute now empowers the Supreme Judicial Court, not only to review the trial judge's decision on a motion for a new trial for 'abuse of discretion,' but also to exercise for itself the very powers given to a trial judge. Even more broadly, the statute requires the Supreme Judicial Court to investigate the whole case to see if there has been a miscarriage of justice. *Commonwealth* v. *Gricus*, 317 Mass. 403, 406-07 (1944); *Commonwealth* v. *Cox*, 327 Mass. 609, 614 (1951); *Commonwealth* v. *Harrison*, 342 Mass. 279, 297 (1961); *Commonwealth* v. *Baker*, 346 Mass. 107, 109 (1963). Thus, the Supreme Judicial Court now considers, in capital cases, not only the specific assignments of error, but also the record and evidence as a whole.

This change in procedure has changed results as well. For example, in *Commonwealth* v. *Cox, supra,* the Court found, in its consideration of errors of law, no error in the denial of defendant's motion for a new trial. 327 Mass. at 614. Yet, upon review of the entire case under M.G.L. c. 278, §33E, the Court concluded that 'the verdict was against the weight of the evidence, and there should be a new trial.' 327 Mass. at 615. Of like import, in *Commonwealth* v. *Baker, supra,* the Court found that there was sufficient evidence to warrant a finding of premeditation, and yet ruled that 'justice will be more nearly achieved' if that finding were not made, and thus ordered entry of a verdict of manslaughter. 346 Mass. at 119.

Had the Supreme Judicial Court of the 1920s been authorized to take this wider view of Sacco's and Vanzetti's convictions, the evidence already recounted suggests that the Court, in passing on the record as a whole, including the motions for a new trial, might well have ordered a new trial. Indeed, Professor Morgan concluded that under these later-enacted procedures 'these defendants would certainly have had another trial.' Joughin and Morgan, *The Legacy of Sacco and Vanzetti, supra,* at 177. At least, the narrow standard of review present for that short period in the Commonwealth's history has long since been abandoned. That a review process adequate to insure that the ends of justice were served by Sacco's and Vanzetti's executions was unavailable at the time should not prevent the Commonwealth from once again addressing the question whether those executions were proper.*

2. What action should appropriately be taken in the present circumstances?

(a) *The pardoning power*
The normal way in which relief is granted after conviction of a crime is by exercise of the pardoning power. This power is set out in the Constitution as follows, Amendment Article LXXIII:

> The power of pardoning offences, except such as persons may be convicted of before the senate by an impeachment of the house, shall be in the governor, by and with the advice of council, provided, that if the offence is a felony the general court shall have

---

* Little need be said about the procedural implications of the reviews conducted by the Governor and his Advisory Committee. Whatever might be said about the particular evidence relied on, or the particular arguments made, the fundamental point is that advisory review by an *ad hoc* committee is no substitute for a new trial before a jury, and was never intended so to be.

power to prescribe the terms and conditions upon which a pardon
may be granted; but no charter of pardon, granted by the governor,
with advice of the council before conviction, shall avail the party
pleading the same, notwithstanding any general or particular
expressions contained therein, descriptive of the offense or offenses
intended to be pardoned.

The statutory 'terms and conditions' upon which a pardon for a felony
may be granted are those provided in M.G.L. c. 127, §§ 152-54, see St.
1945, c. 180. Together these provisions define the pardoning power, and
such lesser powers as those of granting conditional pardons and
commutations of sentences. *Juggins* v. *Executive Council to the Governor*,
257 Mass. 386 (1926); *Opinion of the Justices*, 210 Mass. 609, 610-11 (1912).
However, while the powers so defined are suitable to usual cases, they
appear not to be applicable to the present one.

First, as a procedural matter, M.G.L. c. 127, § 152, authorizes the
Governor to grant a pardon 'with the advice and consent of the council
. . . upon the written petition of the petitioner.' This requirement of a
petition appears to be an integral part of the statutory scheme. See
M.G.L. c. 127, §§ 152-54. Assuming that by 'petitioner' the Legislature
meant to denominate the convicted person, the statute would seem to
indicate that posthumous pardons cannot be granted; or, at the least,
that the pardoning power in its ordinary course is not the appropriate
vehicle for addressing a matter such as this.

Second, in present day circumstances there are no legal consequences
to conviction for a felony that last beyond the death of the felon.
Compare 4 Blackstone, *Commentaries on the Laws of England* 402.
Accordingly, the only purposes that could be served by a pardon in
the present case are to right a wrong, by now historical, and to remove the stigma placed on Sacco and Vanzetti by their conviction and
execution. Whether a pardon would in fact accomplish these aims is
doubtful.

Judicial interpretations of the premise of the pardoning power are
mixed and conflicting. The Supreme Court has stated that 'when the
pardon is full, it releases the punishment and blots out of existence the
guilt, so that in the eye of the law the offender is as innocent as if he had
never committed the offense.' *Ex parte Garland*, 4 Wall. (71 U.S.) 333, 380
(1867). However, in a later case the same Court stated that the grant of a
pardon carries 'an imputation of guilt.' *Burdick* v. *United States*, 236 U.S.
79, 94 (1915). Whether a pardon implies guilt, or, in some circumstances
at least, implies innocence, has also been much debated among the legal
commentators. Williston, *Does a Pardon Blot Out Guilt?*, 28 Harv. L. Rev.
647 (1915); Lattin, *The Pardoning Power in Massachusetts*, 11 B.U. L. Rev.

505, 519-20 (1931); Weihofen, *The Effect of a Pardon*, 88 U. Pa. L. Rev. 177 (1939). The Supreme Judicial Court has defined the effect of a Massachusetts pardon, in at least the usual case, as removing only the consequences of the conviction per se, and not as obliterating 'the acts which constituted the crime . . . which, despite the public act of mercy and forgiveness implicit in the pardon, ordinary, prudent men will take into account in their subsequent dealings with the actor.' *Commissioner of the Metropolitan District Commission* v. *Director of Civil Service*, 348 Mass. 184, 194 (1964). Accordingly, the Court held that a pardon from this state does not restore the 'good character' of one who has been convicted of a felony.* Other courts, although not uniformly, have reached the same conclusion. Note, *Presidential Clemency and the Restoration of Civil Rights*, 61 Iowa L. Rev. 1427, 1432 (1976), and cases there cited. Whether the Supreme Judicial Court would rule differently if presented with '[a] pardon clearly granted because of the wrongful conviction of an innocent person,' 348 Mass. at 193, n. 8, it would not say; but even this phrasing of the contrary issue suggests that it might not give any different answer were the pardon granted only because of 'reasonable doubt' as opposed to clearly established innocence.

In any case, the present situation raises issues neither of the direct nor collateral legal consequences of a conviction, but rather of the more general social implications. Professor Williston has stated that '[e]verybody knows that the word "pardon" naturally connotes guilt as a matter of English,' Williston, *supra*, 28 Harv. L. Rev. at 648, and this statement was quoted with approval by the Supreme Judicial Court, 348 Mass. at 193. Assuming that the statement is correct, if not for 'everybody,' then at least for the bulk of the population, to grant Sacco and Vanzetti a 'pardon' would not only not have the desired consequences, but would in fact be taken to be the expression of a sentiment precisely contrary to that intended.

Third, because the granting of a pardon is often thought to reaffirm guilt, if not legally then at least in the eye of public opinion, it has been adjudged that a pardon is not effective unless accepted. As stated by the Supreme Court, in *Burdick* v. *United States*, *supra*, 236 U.S. at 90–91:**

Circumstances may be made to bring innocence under the penalties of the law. If so brought, escape by confession of guilt implied in

---

* Compare M.G.L. c. 276, § 100A (relating to sealing of court files).
** *Biddle* v. *Perovich*, 274 U.S. 480 (1927), did not overturn *Burdick*, but only refused to extend it to the commutation of a death sentence to life imprisonment.

> the acceptance of a pardon may be rejected, – preferring to be the victim of the law rather than its acknowledged transgressor, – preferring death even to such certain infamy.

The law of the Commonwealth appears to follow the same rule. In *Commonwealth* v. *Lockwood*, 109 Mass. 323 (1872), the Court considered the effect of a pardon granted after a verdict of guilty had been rendered, but while exceptions were pending in the Supreme Judicial Court. In addition to ruling that a pardon could be granted at that time, the Court held that the defendant had the power and the obligation to choose whether he would rely on the pardon and waive his exceptions or whether he would waive the pardon and rely on his exceptions. 109 Mass. at 339. The implication must be that the defendant had the choice of accepting his pardon or of attempting to establish the invalidity of his conviction. While the setting was of course far different from the present one, it may well be that the granting of a pardon to Sacco and Vanzetti after their deaths would be a null act, because the pardon is void without an acceptance, and no power of acceptance exists.

Fourth, in light of the foregoing it would be presumptuous for the Commonwealth to pardon these men fifty years after their execution by the Commonwealth. Sacco and Vanzetti maintained their innocence throughout their ordeal, and their protestations are a frequent reminder of the very real possibility that a grievous miscarriage of justice occurred with their deaths. A pardon, carrying the connotation that they were in fact guilty, and appearing as but a merciful act, with the implication that they would have, even now, welcomed it, would serve not to dignify, but rather to denigrate, their own claims to innocence.

In short, a pardon, or any of the forms of clemency bespeaking of a pardon, is not the proper remedy.

(b) *A proclamation*

The fact that use of the pardoning power would not be the appropriate remedy for this situation should not mean that the Commonwealth is wholly without power to take any action. It would be outrageous to decide that no power exists to give whatever redress is possible at this late date.

Since Sacco and Vanzetti suffered the supreme legal punishment, there are no lingering legal consequences of their conviction. The only thing that can be done is to attempt to remove the stigma placed on them by their conviction and execution. It is, however, of great importance that that be done, both as a simple matter of justice to them, and, equally important, as a matter of clearing the record of the Commonwealth insofar as that is possible. Even though no relief with substantial legal effect is possible, at least a statement should be made.*

The necessary statement should take the form of a proclamation issued by the Governor. The Governor is the supreme executive magistrate of the Commonwealth, Const. Pt. 2, c. 2, §1, Art. 1, and as such may take the lead in voicing the position of the Commonwealth on a matter of great public moment.

While there is no direct precedent for what is by its very nature a unique situation, Massachusetts Governors have long issued proclamations to call public attention to important matters and occasions. Furthermore, there is some legal precedent that bears directly on the matter at hand. In *People* v. *Bowen*, 43 Cal. 439, 13 Am. R. 148 (1872), a convicted felon sought to establish his competency to testify by producing a proclamation of the Governor declaring that 'whereas it is desirable for the ends of justice that he should be restored to citizenship; now, therefore, I . . . do hereby restore [him] to all the rights of citizenship possessed by him before his conviction. . . .' *Id*. at 441. After a discussion of the power provided for by the California Constitution – which is similar to that of Massachusetts – the Court concluded that while the Governor could have pardoned the individual, '. . . the executive act under review is not a pardon, nor was it intended to be such.' *Id*. at 443. While the California Court held that the disability to testify remained since 'there is [no] known relation between the competency of a witness and his "rights of citizenship",' *id*., it nevertheless recognized that the Governor's order had the effect of restoring the rights of citizenship.

Thus, a proclamation intending to remove any stigma and disgrace from Sacco and Vanzetti, from their families and descendants, and, as a result, from the Commonwealth of Massachusetts, should stand at least on the same footing as the California gubernatorial proclamation and have effect in accordance with its terms.

Appendix: Sacco and Vanzetti: trial and appeal unfairness

I. Prosecutorial abuse

A. Knowingly utilizing false evidence to mislead the jury
1. At the trial, Captain William H. Proctor, head of the State Police, testified in substance that his opinion was 'consistent with' one of the recovered bullets having been fired by Sacco's gun. Proctor, in an

---

* There is at present a healthy trend in the direction of a dignified closing of unfortunate incidents of history. The pardon of Tokyo Rose and the restoration of citizenship to Robert E. Lee and Jefferson Davis represent this trend for the Nation. In Massachusetts, the Legislature has resolved that 'no disgrace or cause for distress' exists for Ann Pudeator, executed in 1692 for witchcraft, and her descendants, c. 145, Resolves of 1957; and Governor Dukakis on August 25, 1976, by proclamation revoked the 1637 banishment of Anne Marbury Hutchinson.

affidavit (Vol. IV, 3641-3643),* subsequently stated that District Attorney Frederick G. Katzmann and Harold P. Williams were aware that Proctor could not definitively state that the bullet in question came from Sacco's gun. Proctor said he was repeatedly queried about this and repeatedly made his opinion known to the prosecutors. He also affirmed that the prosecution prearranged a question to which Proctor could say that his investigation of the bullet produced results 'consistent' with its having gone through Sacco's gun, thus creating the impression in the jury's, judge's and defense counsel's minds that Proctor's opinion was that it had done so.

(a) Katzmann's response: He did not deny his prior knowledge of Proctor's real opinion or the connivance of the trick question, but merely stated that Proctor had not repeatedly been queried on the matter (Vol. IV, 3681).

(b) This subterfuge had immense impact on the trial's outcome because the three principal bases of the state's case were the alleged identification of the fatal bullet as being fired from Sacco's gun, the alleged identification of Sacco and Vanzetti as being present in South Braintree, and their alleged consciousness of guilt. The defense counsel even characterized Proctor's testimony as stating the bullet passed through Sacco's gun (Vol. V, 5054). Judge Thayer did likewise in his charge to the jury (Vol. III, 3422). One juror later reported that the expert testimony of Proctor and Van Amburgh was the deciding factor in the case (Russell, 212).**

2. Standards violated:

(a) The government may not knowingly rely on false evidence; it may not rest its case on testimony which it believes to be incorrect. *United States* v. *McGovern*, 499 F. 2d 1140 (1st Cir. 1974).

'If "the State, although not soliciting false evidence, allows it to go uncorrected when it appears," the defendant is entitled to relief.' *Commonwealth* v. *Hurst*, 364 Mass. 604, 608 (1974).

The Fourteenth Amendment cannot tolerate a state criminal conviction obtained by the knowing use of false evidence. *Mooney* v. *Holohan*, 294 U.S. 103 (1934); *Napue* v. *Illinois*, 360 U.S. 264 (1959). In *Mooney*, the conviction was obtained by presentation of testimony known to the prosecutor to be perjured.

(b) ABA Standards Relating to the Administration of Criminal Justice (1974); The Prosecution Function:

---

* References to volume and page number refer to *The Sacco-Vanzetti Case: Transcript of the Record of the Trial of Nicola Sacco and Bartolomeo Vanzetti in the Courts of Massachusetts and Subsequent Proceedings*, 1920-27, Vols. I-V and Supplemental Volume (New York: Henry Holt 1928-29).
** Russell, *Tragedy in Dedham* (1971).

(i) '3.3 Relations with expert witnesses. A prosecutor who engages an expert for an opinion should respect the independence of the expert and should not seek to dictate the formation of the expert's opinion on the subject. . . .'

(ii) '5.6. Presentation of evidence. (a) It is unprofessional conduct for a prosecutor knowingly to offer false evidence, whether by documents, tangible evidence, or the testimony of witnesses, or fail to seek withdrawal thereof upon discovery of its falsity.'

(c) ABA Code of Professional Conduct, canons and disciplinary rules, incorporated in the Rules of the Massachusetts Supreme Judicial Court, Rule 3:22 (359 Mass. 787, 796) in 1972. The Code states that the disciplinary rules are 'mandatory in character . . . and state the minimum level of conduct below which no lawyer can fall without being subject to disciplinary action.'

(i) 'DR 7-102. Representing a client within the bounds of the law. (A) In his representation of a client, a lawyer shall not: . . . (3) Conceal or knowingly fail to disclose that which he is required by law to reveal. . . . (4) Knowingly use perjured testimony or false evidence. . . . (6) Participate in the creation or preservation of evidence when he knows or it is obvious that the evidence is false.'

(ii) 'DR 7-109. Contact with witnesses. (A) A lawyer shall not suppress any evidence that he or his client has a legal obligation to reveal or produce.'

B. Making use of unfair and misleading evidence
1. When the prosecution's eyewitnesses initially identified the defendants, no line-up was utilized and counsel was not present. Prospective witnesses observed the defendants in jail, standing by themselves (Vol. I, 248, 252, 404-06, 509-10, 606-16). The defendants were forced to assume the crouching and shooting positions of the bandits to assist eyewitnesses in their identifications (Vol. I, 473-74). The method of identification was prejudicial and leaves the validity of the eyewitness testimony in grave question.
2. Standards violated:
(a) 'The practice of showing suspects singly to persons for the purpose of identification, and not as part of a line-up, has been widely condemned.' *Stovall* v. *Denno*, 388 U.S. 293, 302 (1967). To support this statement, the Court cited several law review articles and books, including Justice Felix Frankfurter's analysis of the Sacco-Vanzetti case. See, *Foster* v. *California*, 394 U.S. 440 (1969); *Neil* v. *Biggers*, 409 U.S. 188 (1972).

C. *Withholding exculpatory evidence*

1. The name and address of an eyewitness, Ray Gould, who stood within five to ten feet of the fleeing car after the fatal Braintree shootings (Gould affidavit, Vol. IV, 3504) was in the possession of state officials throughout the trial. Indeed, Gould was interviewed by Braintree police immediately following the murder (Officer John Heaney's affidavit, Vol. IV, 3508-09), but the prosecution made no further investigation (Gould affidavit, Vol. IV, 3504). The prosecution instead relied on eyewitnesses who had less opportunity to view the assailants. Gould's identity was subsequently learned by the defense through a defense witness. Defense counsel then attempted to locate him without success (Moore affidavit, Vol. IV, 3499-3500). During this time the Commonwealth did not forward the identity and address of Gould to the defense, nor did the prosecutors secure Gould's attendance at the trial. Following the trial, the defense located Gould, who definitively stated, after observing Sacco, that Sacco was not the assailant who had been at the scene of the murders (Gould affidavit, Vol. IV, 3505).

2. District Attorney Katzmann requested that the Department of Justice determine whether the anarchist radicals in New York, some of whom were associated with Sacco and Vanzetti, had received any large sums of money following the South Braintree robbery. The Department of Justice reported that the group had not. This was revealed in a summary of the Department's files on the Sacco-Vanzetti case released August 22, 1927, to W. G. Gavin, Washington correspondent for the *Boston Traveler*. The story appeared in the *Traveler* at 3 p.m., nine hours before Sacco and Vanzetti were executed (Ehrmann, 61).* Had this information been made available to the jury, the defendants' apparent motive for the crime would have seemed improbable.

3. The prosecution utilized the minutes of the official inquest following the murder during cross-examination of defense witnesses at the trial. The minutes were not made available to defense counsel until July 21, 1927, when they were released to the Governor's Advisory Committee (Vol. V, 5251). The minutes revealed discrepancies in prosecution witnesses' testimony and contained information that corroborated the Madeiros confession. By withholding prior inconsistent statements made by prosecution witnesses the day after the murders, the prosecution denied to the defendants evidence critical to effective cross-examination.

4. Standards violated:

(a) Fair use of of evidence by the prosecutor is required 'accompanied by a duty to disclose evidence materially favorable to the defendant.' *United States* v. *DeLeo*, 422 F. 2d 487, 498 (1st Cir. 1970).

---

* Ehrmann, *The Case That Will Not Die* (1969).

. . . The Government is not forbidden to call witnesses whose reliability in one or many particulars is imperfect or even suspect. Its obligations are to make a clean breast of any evidence it has which may contradict such witnesses or undermine their credibility and not to rest its case upon testimony which it believes to be incorrect.' *United States* v. *McGovern*, 499 F. 2d 1140, 1143 (1st Cir. 1974).

(b) ABA Standards Relating to the Administration of Criminal Justice (1974); The Prosecution Function: '3.11. Disclosure of evidence by the prosecutor. (a) It is unprofessional conduct for a prosecutor to fail to make timely disclosure to the defense of the existence of evidence, known to him, supporting the innocence of the defendant. He should disclose evidence which would tend to negate the guilt of the accused or mitigate the degree of the offense or reduce the punishment at the earliest feasible opportunity. . . . (c) It is unprofessional conduct for a prosecutor intentionally to avoid pursuit of evidence because he believes it will damage the prosecution's case or aid the accused.'

(c) ABA Code of Professional Conduct adopted by the Massachusetts Supreme Judicial Court, 1972: 'DR 7-103. Performing the duty of public prosecutor or other government lawyer. . . . (b) A public prosecutor or other government lawyer in criminal litigation shall make timely disclosure to counsel for the defendant, or to the defendant if he has no counsel, of the existence of evidence, known to the prosecutor or other government lawyer, that tends to negate the guilt of the accused, mitigate the degree of the offense, or reduce the punishment.'

(d) 'It is well understood that the duty of a district attorney is not merely to secure convictions. It is his duty to secure them with due regard to the constitutional and other rights of the defendant.' *Smith* v. *Commonwealth*, 331 Mass. 585, 591 (1954); *Berger* v. *United States*, 295 U.S. 78, 88-89 (1934).

D. Failure to investigate new exculpatory evidence

1. In November, 1925, Celestino Madeiros, a convicted murderer whose appeal was pending before the Supreme Judicial Court, confessed to participation in the South Braintree robbery, and exonerated Sacco and Vanzetti. Based upon his statement (Vol. V, 4416–18) a motion for a new trial was filed May 26, 1926. Winfield M. Wilbar, then District Attorney of Norfolk County, rejected defense counsel's request that a joint investigation of the new evidence be undertaken (Vol. V, 4536-37). No independent investigation was undertaken by the District Attorney's office (Ehrmann, 409). Assistant District Attorney Dudley P. Ranney's response: 'We have been criticized for failure to investigate this matter jointly. That is the explanation. We believe we have found the truth, and in our judicial capacity – there is some to a District Attorney – having

found the truth, nothing else can matter. And that is our honest conviction. And if that is so it is a case not for investigation, and we justify our position by that alone. We will answer, but not investigate, because we know or believe that the truth has been found.' (Vol. V, 4390.)

2. Standards violated:

(a) 'Good faith and reasonable belief in the guilt of the defendant do not necessarily measure the duty of a prosecuting officer to secure a fair trial to the accused and to bring before judge and jury all that ought to be brought before them.' *Smith* v. *Commonwealth*, 331 Mass. 585, 593 (1954).

(b) ABA Standards Relating to the Administration of Criminal Justice (1974); The Prosecution Function: '3.11. Disclosure of evidence by the prosecutor. . . . (c) It is unprofessional conduct for a prosecutor intentionally to avoid pursuit of evidence because he believes it will damage the prosecution's case or aid the accused.'

E. Appeal to jury's prejudice and biases
1. During the cross-examination of Sacco, Katzmann dwelt upon Sacco's trip to Mexico to escape the draft, even though the trip bore no relationship to the crime. He ridiculed and unfairly distorted the political beliefs of Sacco in a manner that appeared calculated to rouse any anti-foreign animosity the jury may have had toward the defendant. This line of cross-examination was admitted by Judge Webster Thayer as testing the credibility of Sacco, who had earlier testified under direct examination that he 'liked a free country' (Vol. II, 1818). The following excerpts are indicative of the tone of the cross-examination:

Q. Don't you think going away from your country is a vulgar thing to do when she needs you? A. I don't believe in war.

Q. You don't believe in war? A. No, sir.

Q. Do you think it is a cowardly thing to do what you did? A. No, sir.

Q. Do you think it is a brave thing to do what you did? A. Yes, sir.

Q. Do you think it would be a brave thing to go away from your own wife? A. No.

Q. When she needed you? A. No. . . .

Q. You love free countries, don't you? A. I should say yes.

Q. Why didn't you stay down in Mexico? A. Well, first thing, I could not get my trade over there. I had to do any other job.

Q. Don't they work with a pick and shovel in Mexico? A. Yes.

Q. Haven't you worked with a pick and shovel in this country? A. I did.

Q. Why didn't you stay there, down there in that free country and work with a pick and shovel? A. I don't think I did sacrifice to learn a job to go to pick and shovel in Mexico.

Q. Is it because, – is your love for the United States of America commensurate with the amount of money you can get in this country per week? A. Better conditions, yes. (Vol. II, 1869.)

2. The prosecutor's appeal to the jury's post-World War I prejudice against draft dodgers and alien anarchists was intensified by Judge Thayer's opening remarks to the jury and by the first words of his charge. At the beginning of the trial, Judge Thayer said: 'Gentlemen, I call upon you to render this service here that you have been summoned to perform with the spirit of patriotism, courage and devotion to duty as was exhibited by our soldier boys across the seas . . .' (Vol. I, 15). In his charge to the jury, he said: '. . . The Commonwealth of Massachusetts called upon you to render a most important service. Although you knew that such service would be arduous, painful, and tiresome, yet you, like the true soldier, responded to that call in the spirit of supreme American loyalty' (Vol. II, 2239).

3. Standards violated:

(a) 'Language ought not to be permitted which is calculated by . . . appeals to prejudice, to sweep jurors beyond a fair and calm consideration of the evidence.' *Commonwealth* v. *Perry*, 254 Mass. 520, 531 (1926).

(b) ABA Standards Relating to the Administration of Criminal Justice (1974); The Prosecution Function:

(i) '5.7. Examination of witnesses. (a) The interrogation of all witnesses should be conducted fairly, objectively and with due regard for the dignity and legitimate privacy of the witness, and without seeking to intimidate or humiliate the witness unnecessarily. Proper cross-examination can be conducted without violating the rules of decorum.'

(ii) '5.8. Argument to the jury. . . . (c) The prosecutor should not use arguments calculated to inflame the passions or prejudices of the jury. (d) The prosecutor should refrain from argument which would divert the jury from its duty to decide the case on the evidence, by injecting issues broader than the guilt or innocence of the accused under the controlling law. . . .'

(c) ABA Code of Professional Conduct, adopted by the Massachusetts Supreme Judicial Court, 1972:

(i) 'DR 7-106. Trial Conduct. . . . (c) In appearing in his professional capacity before a tribunal, a lawyer shall not: (1) State or allude to any matter that he has no reasonable basis to believe is relevant to the case or that will not be supported by admissible evidence. (2) Ask any question that he has not reasonable basis to believe is relevant to the case and that is intended to degrade a witness or other person.'

II. Judicial abuses

A. Prejudicial Behavior

1. Following the earlier Plymouth trial of Vanzetti for the attempted Bridgewater robbery, at which Judge Thayer presided, he requested Chief Justice John Aiken assign him to preside at the Sacco–Vanzetti trial in Dedham (Ehrmann, 159; Russell, 127). Such a request was and is a radical departure from usual judicial decorum and indicates Thayer's intense personal interest in the outcome of the trial. It is also highly probable that after presiding at the Plymouth trial and sentencing Vanzetti to fifteen years for attempted robbery, Thayer could not claim total impartiality toward the defendants at the Dedham trial.

2. In an article appearing in the *Boston Herald*, nine days after the South Braintree murders, Judge Thayer angrily denounced a Norfolk jury for acquitting Sergis Zagroff, a self-admitted anarchist indicted for violating the Criminal Anarchy Statute (see attachment B). The evidence indicated that Zagroff had merely expressed his views but had not violated the law.

3. Judge Thayer is reported as having made numerous disparaging comments about the defendants and their counsel outside the court-room. Judge Thayer reportedly said:

(a) 'Did you see what I did with those anarchistic bastards the other day?' Judge Thayer to Professor James P. Richardson (Richardson testimony before the Governor's Advisory Committee, Vol. V, 5065).

(b) When speaking about defense counsel Fred H. Moore, Judge Thayer to several reporters, 'I'll show them that no long-haired anarchist from California can run this court!' On several occasions Judge Thayer said, 'Just wait until you hear my charge.' (Sibley affidavit, Vol. V, 4924-25.)

(c) 'Mr. [Loring] Coes said [but later disavowed saying] that Judge Thayer had referred to Sacco and Vanzetti as bolsheviki who were "trying to intimidate him", and said that "he would get them good and proper" . . . that he "would show them and would get those guys hanged."' (Benchley affidavit, Vol. V, 4928.)

(d) Judge Thayer to newspapermen: 'You wait till I give my charge to the jury. I'll show 'em!' (Beffel affidavit, Vol. V, 4929-4931.)

(e) A motion for a new trial based on Judge Thayer's prejudice was filed August 6, 1927. The motion was argued before the judge who, after he refused to withdraw, denied the motion. The Supreme Judicial Court overruled the defendants' exceptions to Judge Thayer's denial on procedural grounds (Vol. V, 5500).

(f) The Governor's Advisory Committee concluded: 'From all that has come to us we are forced to conclude that the judge was indiscreet in conversation with outsiders during the trial. He ought not to have talked about the case off the bench, and doing so was a grave breach of official decorum. . . .' (Vol. V, 5378L.)

4. The significance assigned to evidence by Judge Thayer varied dramatically, as it became necessary to deflect defense counsel's attempts to upset the guilty verdict. The judge's treatment of Proctor's testimony illustrates the judge's strong desire to prevent a new trial and uphold the verdict. During the trial, Judge Thayer instructed the jury that the fatal bullet had been shot from Sacco's gun, according to the expert witnesses for the prosecution which included Proctor (Vol. III, 3422). When faced with the Proctor affidavit stating that this was not Proctor's opinion, Judge Thayer dramatically minimized the testimony and its importance and belittled Proctor's expertise (Vol. IV, 3702). Later, when confronted with a motion for a new trial based upon the Madeiros confession, Judge Thayer once again maximized the weightiness of the expert witnesses' testimony to illustrate that a new trial was not necessary in view of the impressive evidence indicating the defendants' guilt (Vol. V, 4766).

5. Standards violated:

(a) ABA Standards Relating to the Administration of Criminal Justice (1974); Fair Trial and Free Press: '2.4. Recommendation relating to judges. It is recommended that, with respect to pending criminal cases, judges should refrain from any conduct or the making of any statements that may tend to interfere with the right of the people or of the defendant to a fair trial.'

(b) ABA Standards Relating to the Administration of Criminal Justice (1974); The Function of the Trial Judge: '3.7. Prejudicial publicity. . . . (b) The trial judge should refrain from making public comment on a pending case or any comment that may tend to interfere with the right of any party to a fair trial. . . .'

(c) ABA Code of Judicial Conduct (1972):

(i) 'Canon 2. A Judge Should Avoid Impropriety and the Appearance of Impropriety in All His Activities. A.) A judge should respect and comply with the law and should conduct himself at all times in a manner that promotes public confidence in the integrity and impartiality of the judiciary.'

(ii) 'Canon 3. A Judge Should Perform the Duties of His Office Impartially and Diligently. A.) Adjudicative Responsibilities. (1) A judge should be faithful to the law and maintain professional competence in it. He should be unswayed by partisan interests, public clamor, or fear of criticism. (2) A judge should maintain order and decorum in proceedings before him. . . . (6) A judge should abstain from public comment about a pending or impending proceeding in any court, and should require similar abstention on the part of court personnel subject to his direction and control. This subsection does not prohibit judges from making public statements in the course of their official duties or from explaining for public information the procedures of the court. . . . C.) Disqualification. (1) A judge should disqualify himself in a proceeding in which his impartiality might reasonably be questioned, including but not limited to instances where . . . he has a personal bias or prejudice concerning a party. . . .'

Attachment A: Sacco and Vanzetti chronology

April 15, 1920	Murders of Berardelli and Parmenter at South Braintree.
April 17, 1920	Inquest at Quincy with regard to South Braintree murders.
May 5, 1920	Arrest of Sacco and Vanzetti.
May 6, 1920	Interview of Sacco and Vanzetti by District Attorney Katzmann.
September 11, 1920	Indictment of Sacco and Vanzetti for South Braintree murders.
May 31–July 14, 1921	Trial of Sacco and Vanzetti at Dedham before Judge Webster Thayer.
November 5, 1921	Motion for new trial as against the weight of the evidence argued before Judge Thayer.
November 8, 1921	First supplementary motion for new trial filed.
December 24, 1921	Motion for new trial as against the weight of evidence denied.
May 4, 1922	Second supplementary motion filed.
July 22, 1922	Third supplementary motion filed.
September 11, 1922	Fourth supplementary motion filed.
April 30, 1923	Fifth supplementary motion filed.
October 1, 1923	Supplement to first motion filed.
October 1-3, 1923 November 1, 2, 8, 1923	All five supplementary motions argued before Judge Thayer.
November 5, 1923	Motion relating to Proctor affidavit filed.

October 1, 1924	Decisions by Judge Thayer denying all motions.
November 18, 1925	Madeiros confesses to South Braintree murders and exonerates Sacco and Vanzetti.
January 11-13, 1926	Argument of appeal of Sacco and Vanzetti from conviction and from denial of first, second and fifth supplementary motions.
May 12, 1926	Conviction of Sacco and Vanzetti affirmed by Supreme Judicial Court.
May 26, 1926	Motion for new trial based on Madeiros statement filed.
September 13-17, 1926	Madeiros motion argued before Judge Thayer.
October 23, 1926	Decision by Judge Thayer denying Madeiros motion.
January 27-28, 1927	Appeal from denial of Madeiros motion argued before Supreme Judicial Court.
April 5, 1927	Denial of Madeiros motion affirmed by Supreme Judicial Court.
April 9, 1927	Sentence of death imposed by Judge Thayer on Sacco and Vanzetti.
May 3, 1927	Petition for clemency addressed to Governor Fuller.
June 1, 1927	Advisory Lowell Committee appointed by Governor Fuller.
July 11-21, 1927	Hearings held before Advisory Committee.
August 3, 1927	Decision by Governor Fuller denying clemency.
August 10, 1927	Petition for writ of habeas corpus denied by Justice Holmes of the United States Supreme Court, and by Judge Anderson of the United States District Court.
August 19, 1927	Exceptions overruled by Supreme Judicial Court.
August 20, 1927	Petition for writ of habeas corpus denied by Judge Morton of the United States Circuit Court of Appeals.
August 20, 1927	Petition for stay and extension of time in which to apply to the United States Supreme Court for writ of certiorari denied by Justice Holmes of the United States Supreme Court.
August 22, 1927	Similar petition denied by Justice Stone of the United States Supreme Court.

August 23, 1927   Sacco and Vanzetti and Madeiros executed in
                         Charlestown prison.

Attachment B

Boston Herald
April 24, 1920, p. 1

Judge Scores Jurymen For Freeing 'Red'. Prosecutor Refuses to Try
Any Further Cases in Norfolk Court. Zakoff Acquitted On Anarchy
Charge.

A verdict of not guilty, returned by a jury in the Norfolk county
superior court yesterday afternoon in the case of Sergis Zakoff, charged
with advocating anarchy, brought forth a severe arraignment of the jury
by Judge Webster Thayer, who was presiding, and a refusal on the part
of Asst. Dist.-Atty. William Kane, who was prosecuting the case, to try
any further cases.

'Gentlemen, how did you arrive at such a verdict?' asked the court.
'Did you consider the information that the defendant gave to the police
officers when he admitted, according to the three police officers, that he
was a Bolshevist and that there should be a revolution in this country?
Upon his own testimony he said to the officers, in the conversation they
had with him, that he believed in bolshevism and that our government
should be overthrown. Didn't you consider the testimony given by the
police officers when you were deliberating, before you agreed upon a
verdict?'

Thought Actual Violence Meant
    In reply to the court's questions, the foreman said: 'The jury came to
the decision of not guilty after they had interpreted the meaning of
advocating anarchy, as explained by the court, as that of one who
actually used violence and not a person who expressed his opinion and
talked of overthrowing the government.'
    Zakoff was one of the alleged 'Reds' rounded up last January by the
department of justice officers and allowed to go later. Chief Harry Swift
and Officers William Barrett and Peter Curran testified that Zakoff said
to them that the government in this country was no good and that the
only true form of government was the soviet government established in
Russia. He also asserted, they testified, that the best thing for this
country would be to have a revolution, and he advised Officer Barrett to
become a Bolshevist himself.

2 Other sources

1 Documentation

I gathered material from many individuals. Principal amongst them were Spencer Sacco, grandson of Nicola Sacco; Governor Michael Dukakis of Massachusetts; Robert Healey, executive editor of the *Boston Globe*; Al Cella, professor of law at Suffolk University; Hugo Bedeau, professor of philosophy at Tufts University. But there were many others, and I hope I have mentioned them in the Acknowledgments. I am conscious though of debts to old Italian anarchists and veterans or bystanders of the case to whom I spoke in Massachusetts.

Amongst the many libraries I used, I drew principally on the archives at the Harvard Pusey Library, the Harvard Law Library, Boston Public Library and Boston Athaneum Library. I am also grateful for material and help at the Charles Weidener Library at Harvard and in England at the university libraries of Cambridge and Bristol. For contemporary background, I also drew on the clippings libraries of the *Sunday Times* in London and of the *Boston Globe*, and on some private collections in New England.

The account of the trial is based on the official transcript *The Sacco-Vanzetti Case: Transcript of the Record of the Trial of Nicola Sacco and Bartolomeo Vanzetti in the Courts of Massachusetts and Subsequent Proceedings* (Holt, New York, 1928–9). The publication of this 5,000-page record was sponsored by a group of businessmen, including John D. Rockefeller Jnr. Copies are difficult to obtain and I used the ones in the possession of Cambridge University and of Harvard University. To these volumes a *Supplementary* was added in 1929 and published by Henry Holt in New York. This includes the Bridgewater Case and some extra material. I have quoted from *The Letters of Sacco and Vanzetti* as edited by Marion Denman Frankfurter and Gardner Jackson (Viking, New York, 1928) but, as mentioned in the text, I have come to discover that this includes some deletions, made presumably in an attempt to make Sacco and Vanzetti more sympathetic. I have also used from the Harvard archives Vanzetti's own prison writings *The Story of a Proletarian Life* and *The Background of the Plymouth Trial*, and the *Financial Report of the Sacco-Vanzetti Defense Committee from the Date of Organization May 5 1920 to July 31 1925*, treasurer Aldino Felicani, Boston 1925. Finally I have consulted the hitherto confidential records of the Massachusetts State Police, some material prepared by the Governor's legal counsel for his 1977 review of the case, the proceedings of the Massachusetts State Legislature, and such copies as have survived of the *Official Bulletin of the Sacco-Vanzetti Defense Committee*.

Perhaps I should also note that Vanzetti's statement to Philip D. Stong ('If it had not been for these thing'), is, I think, printed for the first time in its authentic form. It was taken down in shorthand, and when first published in the New York *World* on May 13, 1927, the printers followed his stenographic instructions exactly, so as to catch the Italian accent ('joustice' for justice, or 'man's onderstanding of man'). However; as he pointed out in the *Saturday Review*, May 11, 1929, he added exclamation marks in the last paragraph. ('Vanzetti caught some expression, and he said what I have written very quietly, simply.') The statement, which remains an abiding grace to the language, has, I believe, previously only been published in anglicized, grammatically corrected versions, with redundant punctuation added. It speaks for itself in its raw form.

2 Books and papers on the case

There are several excellent bibliographies on the case, principally in *The Legacy of Sacco and Vanzetti* by G. Louis Joughin and Edmund M. Morgan (Harcourt Brace, New York, 1948) and *Tragedy at Dedham* by Francis Russell (McGraw Hall, New York, 1962). There is a good bibliography on anarchism in general in *Anarchism* by George Woodcock (World Publishing Company, New York, 1962; Penguin, London, 1963). I list here only those books and articles which I found most important, and used as sources for this study.

BEFEL, JOHN N., 'Eels and the Electric Chair', *New Republic* (December 29, 1920).

BROUN, H., *Collected edition of Heywood Broun* (Harcourt, New York, 1941).

BULLARD, F. LAURISTON, 'We Submit', *Boston Herald*, October 26, 1926.

COLP, RALPH, JR, 'Sacco's Struggle for Sanity', *Nation*, August 16, 1958.

COLP, RALPH, JR, 'Bitter Christmas: a Biographical Inquiry into the Life of Bartolomeo Vanzetti', *Nation*, December 27, 1958.

DEVER, JOHN F., 'Memoirs of the Sacco Vanzetti case', unpublished.

Dictionary of American Biography (Scribner's, New York, 1935).

DOS PASSOS, JOHN, *Facing the Chair: Story of the Americanization of Two Foreign-Born Workers* (Sacco–Vanzetti Defense Committee, 1927).

EASTMAN, MAX, 'Is this the Truth about Sacco and Vanzetti?' *National Review*, vol. XI, no. 16, October 21, 1961.

EHRMANN, HERBERT B. *The Untried Case: The Sacco–Vanzetti Case and the Morelli Gang* (Vanguard, New York, 1933).

EHRMANN, HERBERT B., 'The Magnetic Point and the Morelli Evidence', *Harvard Law Review*, vol. 79, no. 3, January 1966.

FEURLICHT, ROBERT STRAUSS, *Justice Crucified: The Story of Sacco and Vanzetti* (McGraw Hill, New York, 1977).

FELIX, D. *Protest: Sacco–Vanzetti and the Intellectuals* (Indiana University Press, 1965).

FRAENKEL, OSMOND K., *The Sacco–Vanzetti Case* (Knopf, New York, 1933).

FRANKFURTER, FELIX, *The Case of Sacco and Vanzetti: A Critical Analysis for Lawyers and Laymen* (Little, Brown, Boston, 1927).

FRANKFURTER, FELIX, 'Case of Sacco and Vanzetti', *Atlantic Monthly* (March 1927).

GRABILL, ETHELBERT V., *Sacco and Vanzetti in the Scales of Justice* (Fort Hill Press, Boston, 1927).

JOUGHIN, G. LOUIS and MORGAN, EDMUND M., *The Legacy of Sacco and Vanzetti* (Harcourt, Brace, New York, 1948).

LYONS, EUGENE, 'The Sacco–Vanzetti Verdict and Americans-to-be', *Unity*, September 1921.

LYONS, EUGENE, *Assignment in Utopia* (Harcourt, Brace, New York, 1937).

MASSACHUSETTS STATE POLICE, Press Release (September 12, 1977).

MILLAY, EDNA ST VINCENT, 'Fear', *Outlook*, November 9, 1927.

MONTGOMERY, R., *The Murder and the Myth* (Devin-Adair, New York, 1960).

MUSMANNO, MICHAEL A., *After Twelve Years* (Knopf, New York, 1939).

PORTER, KATHERINE ANNE, *The Case that Will Not Die* (Jonathan Cape, London, 1979).

RIDELL, HON. WILLIAM RENWICK, 'The Sacco–Vanzetti Case from a Canadian Viewpoint', *American Bar Association Journal*, December 1927.

RUSSELL, FRANCIS, *Tragedy at Dedham* (McGraw Hill, New York, 1962).

SACCO, NICOLA and VANZETTI, BARTOLOMEO, *The Letters of Sacco and Vanzetti*, ed. Frankfurter, Marion Denman and Jackson, Gardner (Viking, New York, 1928).

SCHACHTMAN, MAX, 'Sacco and Vanzetti, Labor's Martyrs', International Labor Defense, New York, 1927.

SINCLAIR, UPTON, 'The Fish Pedlar and the Shoemaker', *Institute of Social Studies Bulletin*, New York, vol. 2, no. 2, Summer 1953.

Standard-Times of Bedford, Mass., interviews with the surviving jurors of the Sacco–Vanzetti case, November 12, 1950.

STONG, PHILIP D., 'Sacco and Vanzetti', New York *World* (May 3, 1927).

THOMPSON, WILLIAM G., 'Vanzetti's Last Statement', *Atlantic Monthly* (February, 1928).

WARNER, ARTHUR, 'The Sacco–Vanzetti Case: A Reasonable Doubt', *Nation*, September 28, 1921.
WEEKS, ROBERT P., *Commonwealth versus Sacco and Vanzetti* (Prentice Hall, New Jersey, 1958).

3 Books on the social background

Again the list would fill whole libraries. I only list those directly used or quoted, and which could be of special use to students of the subject.

ADLER, S., *The Isolationist Impulse* (Collier, New York, 1961).
BURTON, ANTHONY, *Revolutionary Violence* (Cooper, London, 1977).
CAUTE, DAVID, *The Great Fear – the Anti-Communist Purge under Truman and Eisenhower* (Secker & Warburg, London, 1978).
CHAPLIN, RALPH, *Wobbly* (University of Chicago, 1948).
COOLIDGE, CALVIN, 'Whose Country is This?', *Good Housekeeping*, February 1921.
CUMMINGS, HOMER and MCFARLAND, C., *Federal Justice* (Macmillan, New York, 1937).
DEUTSCHER, ISAAC, *The Prophet Armed: Trotsky 1879–1921* (Oxford University Press, London, 1954).
DEUTSCHER, ISAAC, *The Young Lenin* (Oxford University Press, London, 1970).
EARNEST, E., *Academic Procession* (Bobbs-Merrill, Indianopolis, 1953).
FANON, F., *The Wretched of the Earth* (Penguin, Harmondsworth, 1967).
HANDLIN, OSCAR, *Boston's Immigrants* (Oxford University Press, London, 1959).
HOWE, MARK DEWOLFE (ed.), *The Holmes-Laski Letters* (Foreword Felix Frankfurter; Harvard University Press, Cambridge, Mass., 1953).
LIPSETT, S. M. and RAAB, E., *The Politics of Unreason: Right Wing Extremism in America 1790–1970* (Heinemann, London, 1971).
MORISON, S. E., *Three Centuries of Harvard: 1636–1936* (Harvard University Press, Cambridge, Mass., 1936).
POST, LOUIS F., *The Deportation Delirium of 1920* (Kerr, Chicago, 1923).
PRESTON, WILLIAM, *Aliens and Dissenters: Federal Suppression of Radicals 1903–1933* (Oxford University Press, London, 1963).
REED, JOHN, *Ten Days that Shook the World* (Communist Party of Great Britain, London, 1926).
RIESMAN, D. and LIPSETT, S. M., *Education and Politics at Harvard* (McGraw Hill, New York, 1975).
RUSSELL, FRANCIS, *A City in Terror: 1919 – The Boston Police Strike* (Viking Press, New York, 1975).

SCHLESINGER, ARTHUR M., *The Age of Roosevelt: The Crisis of the Old Order 1919–1933* (Heinemann, London, 1957).
SOREL, G., *Reflections on Violence* (Collier-Macmillan, London, 1950).
YEOMANS, HENRY AARON, *Abbott Lawrence Lowell* (Harvard University Press, Cambridge, Mass., 1948).

4 Other references cited

BAMFORD, SAMUEL, *Passages in the Life of a Radical* (1844, new edition MacGibbon & Kee, 1967).
STEPHENS, JAMES, *The Insurrection in Dublin* (Mansell, Dublin 1916).
THOREAU, HENRY DAVID, *Civil Disobedience* (reprinted Revell, New Jersey, 1964).

5 Literature on anarchy

AURICH, PAUL, *The Russian Anarchists* (Princeton University Press, 1967).
AURICH, PAUL (ed.), *The Anarchists in the Russian Revolution* (Thames & Hudson, London, 1973).
BAKUNIN, M., *The Political Philosophy of Bakunin* (ed. G. P. Maximoff, Collier-Macmillan, London, 1953).
BERKMAN, A., *The Bolshevik Myth* (no publisher named, New York, 1925).
BERKMAN, A., *The ABC of Anarchism* (first titled *What is Communist Anarchism?*) (Vanguard, New York, 1929).
BERKMAN, A., *Prison Memoirs of an Anarchist* (1912, reprinted Schocken, New York, 1970).
COLE, G. D. H., *Socialist Thought: Marxism and Anarchism 1850–1890* (Macmillan, London, 1964).
DAVID, HENRY, *The History of the Haymarket Affair* (Russell & Russell, New York, 1936).
GOLDMAN, EMMA, *Living My Life* (Garden City, New York, 1934).
GOLDMAN, EMMA, *My Disillusionment in Russia* (Apollo reprint, New York, 1970).
GUERIN, DANIEL, *Anarchism: From Theory to Practice* (Monthly Review Press, New York, 1970).
HART, JOHN M., *Anarchism and the Mexican Working Class* (Austin, University of Texas Press, 1978).
HOROWITZ, IRVING L., *The Anarchists* (Dell, New York, 1964).
JOLL, JAMES, *The Second International* (London, 1955).

JOLL, JAMES, *The Anarchists* (Grosset, New York, 1964).

KROPOTKIN, P., *Fields, Factories and Workshops* (Hutchinson, London, 1899).

KROPOTKIN, P., *The Conquest of Bread* (Chapman & Hall, London, 1906).

KROPOTKIN, P., *Memoirs of a Revolutionist* (Houghton, Mifflin, Boston, 1930).

KROPOTKIN, P., *Mutual Aid: A Factor of Evolution* (Horizon, Boston, repub. 1955).

NOMAD, MAX, *Rebels and Renegades* (Macmillan, New York, 1932).

NOMAD, MAX, *Apostles of the Revolution* (Little, Brown, Boston, 1939).

ORWELL, GEORGE, *Homage to Catalonia* (London, 1938).

PROUDHON, PIERRE-JOSEPH, *La Guerre et la paix* (Paris, 1861).

PROUDHON, P. J., *What is Property?* (Fertig, New York, repub. 1966).

READ, HERBERT, *Poetry and Anarchism* (London, 1938).

WOODCOCK, GEORGE, *Anarchism* (World Publishing Company, New York, 1962).

6   Some drama, novels and poems on the case

ANDERSON, MAXWELL, *Gods of the Lightning* (Longman, London, 1928).

ANDERSON, MAXWELL, *Winterset* (Longman, London, 1935).

HARRIS, FRANK, *The Bomb* (definitive American edition, New York, 1936).

MILLAY, EDNA ST VINCENT, 'Justice Denied in Massachusetts', *Collected Lyrics* (Harper, New York, 1943).

PASSOS, JOHN DOS, *USA – a Trilogy* (Harcourt, New York, 1937).

SINCLAIR, UPTON, *Boston* (Boni, New York, 1928).

THURBER, JAMES and JUGENT, ELLIOTT, *The Male Animal* (French, New York, 1941).

VOTO, BERNARD DE, *We Accept with Pleasure* (Little, Brown, Boston, 1934).

WELLS, HERBERT G., *Mr Blettsworthy on Rampole Island* (Doubleday, New York, 1928).

One should also add here Ben Shahn's beautiful series of paintings (1931–2) *The Passion of Sacco and Vanzetti* (Whitney Museum of American Art, New York).

Index of names

The three principal persons – Nicola Sacco, Webster Thayer and Bartolomeo Vanzetti, are omitted from this key Index of names, only because they are omnipresent.

The Index is itself a sepia snap of a time slipping just behind us into that blind spot of history. It mixes the grand and the nondescript; the lasting and the accidental players in this tragic and abiding collision of culture and of idea and of happenchance.